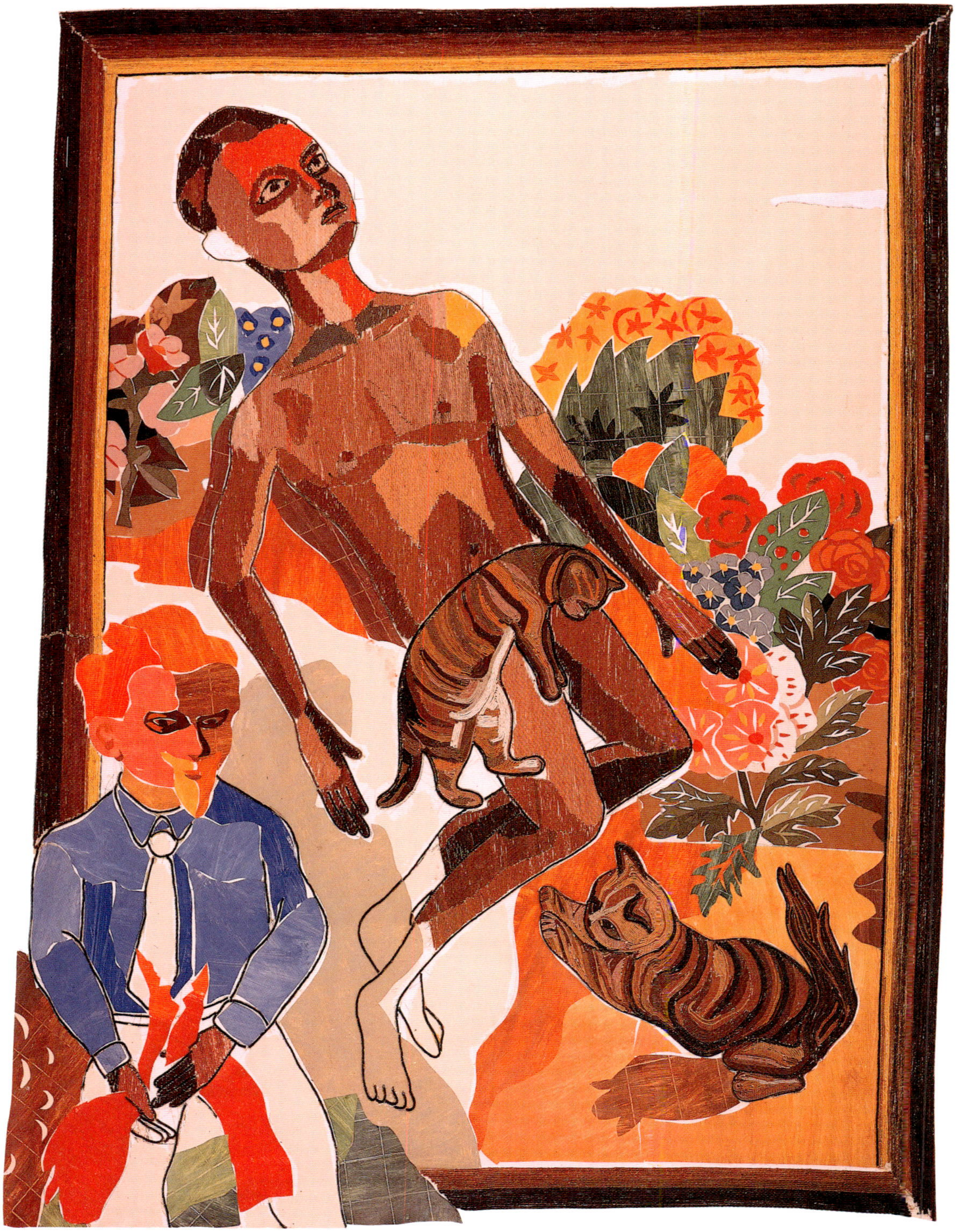

Me in the Studio, collage on canvas, 198.3 × 122 cm, 1993

The Paintings of STEVEN CAMPBELL

THE STORY SO FAR by DUNCAN MACMILLAN

MAINSTREAM PUBLISHING

EDINBURGH AND LONDON

This book is published with the help of Marlborough Fine Art and in conjunction with the exhibition of Steven Campbell's recent work at the Talbot Rice Gallery, the University of Edinburgh, 16 August to 11 September 1993, and then, from 17 September to 29 October, jointly at Marlborough Fine Art, London, and the South London Art Centre

Photography:
Frontispiece by Joe Rock
Back flap of jacket by Roger Spencer-Jones
Recent works (as listed in the catalogue) by
Prudence Cumming Associates

First published in Great Britain in 1993 by
MAINSTREAM PUBLISHING COMPANY (EDINBURGH) LTD
7 Albany Street
Edinburgh EH1 3UG

ISBN 1 85158 546 X (cloth)
ISBN 1 85158 545 1 (paper)

A catalogue record for this book is available from the British Library

Typeset in Garamond Stempel by Litho Link Ltd, Welshpool, Wales
Printed in Singapore by Toppan

CONTENTS

ACKNOWLEDGMENTS

I would like to thank the artist and his wife Carol for their friendly helpfulness while I have been working on this project. I am also much indebted to Marlborough Fine Art and in particular to John Erle-Drax for their support of this publication. Sandy Moffat has also been very helpful with advice and the loan of transparencies of some of the artist's student work.

As there is no record of the whereabouts of all of Steven Campbell's works, acknowledgment of ownership has only been possible in the case of pictures in public collections, where this is known.

Duncan Macmillan

THE PAINTINGS OF STEVEN CAMPBELL
THE STORY SO FAR

So there must be . . . some equivalent expression for the trouble and wrath of life, for its sorrow and mystery

John Ruskin, *The Seven Lamps of Architecture*[1]

In the exhibition in New York in 1983 which launched his international career, Steven Campbell had a painting called *Hiker's Ballet with Yawning Child (Pl.1)*. In it, two young men look on as a third struggles with a broken sign-post. Apparently at the moment of falling, it points drunkenly and diagonally across the picture, indicating meaninglessly 'Oxford' and 'Salisbury'. This sign-post is a recurrent feature in Campbell's work of the time and it reappears as a real object in a self-portrait installation, *Portrait of the Artist with his Daughter, Lauren (Pl.2)*, made in 1984, in which the artist and his baby daughter are posed together with it in the foreground. He appears as a traveller like Courbet in *Bonjour M. Courbet*. Like Courbet too, he has a staff in one hand, but he also has his baby in the other and he is tramping through a landscape inhabited by various stuffed animals and stocked with greenery.

This image of the artist as traveller suggests that art is a process, that the artist has to keep moving, and this has certainly been true of Campbell himself. He has never stopped, as many artists have done, to say complacently, 'This is my art, take it or leave it!'. In the fifteen years since he entered Glasgow School of Art at the age of twenty-five, his art has developed constantly though it is also its underlying consistency which has given it strength.

The background of this installation is one of his paintings of 1984, *God's in his Heaven, All's Well with the World*. Its title is from Browning's 'Pippa Passes', a poem in which a little girl also passes through a landscape. In the poem, the landscape is alive with the beauties of nature. Although in the painting these are visible in the flowers, the trees, the birds, and even the beetles, just as Pippa sees them in the poem, virtually nothing else is 'well with the world'. Everything is tipped off the vertical or the horizontal in an unstable way. In the foreground a murder seems to be taking place and a corpse is laid out behind. The 'Oxford to Salisbury' sign-post is in the foreground of the installation, between us and the painter and his baby. It is broken and pointing nowhere. Its uselessness and its contribution to a wider confusion are emphasised by a torn-up map lying in front of it.

The presence of the artist's baby daughter is an indication of how Campbell's art is very much rooted in life close at hand, even though this may not always be apparent, and this kind of image of confusion is something felt emotionally, not constructed for the purpose of painting. Art, he says, is about vulnerability, about life as it is lived, with all its knocks, all its ups and downs and with the perpetual gap between innocence and experience. This, too, is the significance of

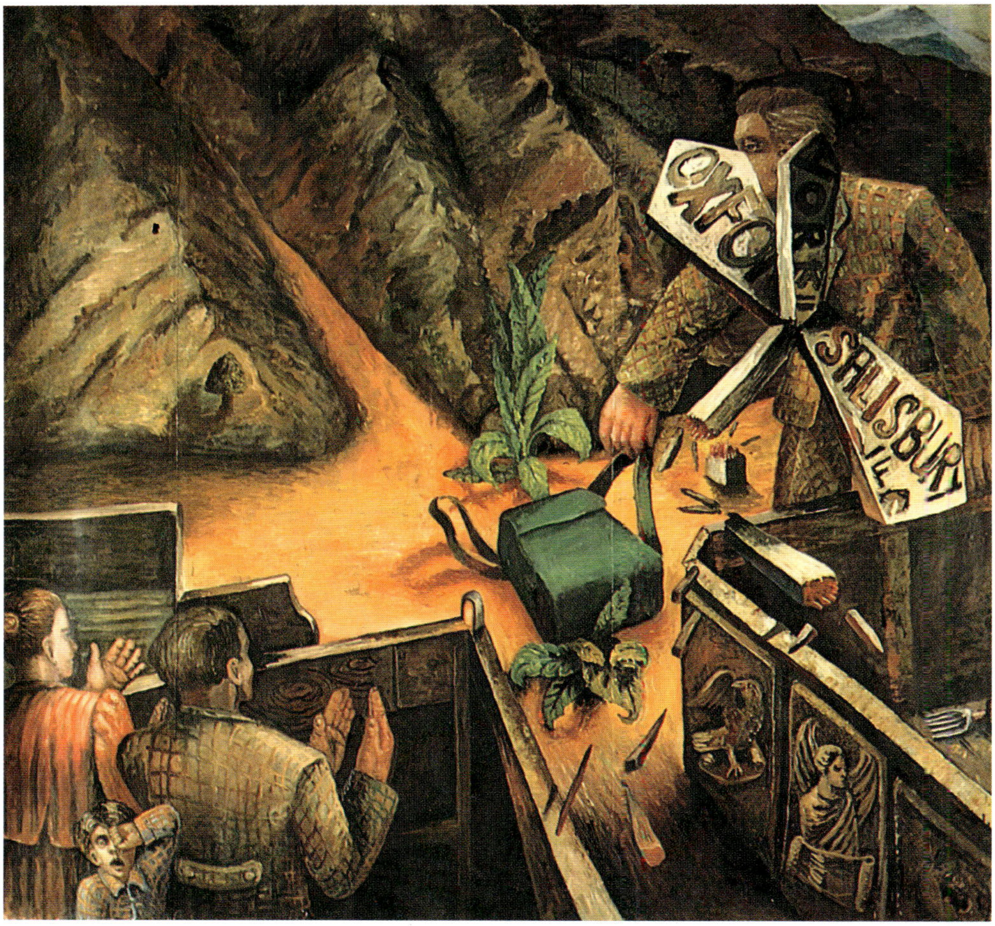

(PLATE 1) *Hiker's Ballet with Yawning Child*, oil on canvas, 289.6 × 289.6 cm, 1983

the journey. This self-portrait therefore encapsulates many of his continuing concerns as a painter. At this stage in the discussion, it is perhaps the sign-post which provides the key, however. A sign-post that points nowhere serves as a suitable introduction to an art that hinges on the paradox of signs, signs which never point to a simple 'meaning' in the classic sense. His life is a journey of exploration in which the directions are never certain, but his art is expressive, not cerebral. It is about life as it is lived and if at times the artist seems to swap ideas with the likes of Foucault and Derrida, it is because that is what things look like from the inside.

A sign is only meaningful in a context. In the middle of Salisbury Plain and in working order, this 'Oxford to Salisbury' sign-post would have a simple function as an indicator of place and direction. In a narrative painting, even a comic one say with a subject on the lines of *John Gilpin's Ride* or Rowlandson's *Dr Syntax*, such a sign, though broken as here, could also make good sense and serve a purpose, not as an indicator of direction in real space certainly, but within the space and direction of the narrative. As Campbell uses it though, it does not even serve this kind of purpose. It is a symbol of confusion. It mystifies even as it points, for whenever he uses it, the narrative, if it is a narrative, does not tell us anything about place or direction. In fact, in the first example cited above, *Hiker's Ballet with Yawning Child*, the sign-post's broken status indicates its specific inability to function *as* a sign, even though it so patently *is* a sign.

Perhaps life itself has lost its sign-posts. Certainly it is when it deals with the signs by which we attempt to make sense of the world we live in that art fulfils its function. It is not surprising therefore that it was within the discourse of moral philosophy that the proposition was put forward for the first time that in painting the sign and the signified are two quite different things. It was in the eighteenth century that Thomas Reid argued that what the artist puts down on his canvas is not a version of the real world, but a set of signs which may signify aspects of it, but which can never represent it.[2] The actual form of these signs bears no relationship to the forms of the three-dimensional reality that we inhabit and so, even though we can read an account of it from them, the account the artist gives of his experience is actually autonomous. It is a fiction independent of the rules that appear to govern the world. This meant the demise of certainty and it is in the confused, unmapped territory between sign and signified that art really functions.

Although this idea had a profound influence on painting in the nineteenth century and itself dates from the century before, it was not until the beginning of the present century, with Picasso, Matisse, Kandinsky and Malevich, that artists first explicitly accepted the creative challenge entailed in the radical autonomy that it gave to painting. It was Picasso, above all, who saw that it meant that the artist was in complete control of a world in which the signs that he chose could signify whatever he wanted them to and he could grant us access to this or not at will.

This view of painting has had a far-reaching influence on twentieth-century art and much of the history of Modernism is the story of artists imitating Picasso to play petty gods. Few of them have appreciated the irony of this position as lucidly as Picasso himself, however. It made him a joker in the pack of art. After him, Duchamp based his art on this perception, but there was also a more tragic irony. Although the painter may appear to be lord of all, he is really lord of nothing. This impotence, identified with the sexual impotence of old age, is surely the theme of the erotic pictures that are such a feature of Picasso's late work.

The painter's world, therefore, is a flat one of confused illusion and it is this world, warts and all, that Campbell consciously inhabits in his painting. Irony and humour have been important in his art, but he is not just an intellectual game player. Although it is not obvious on the surface, his art is charged with feeling. In a way it is always autobiographical and irony and visual clowning are a way either of disguising feeling, or of converting it into a currency in which it is easier to

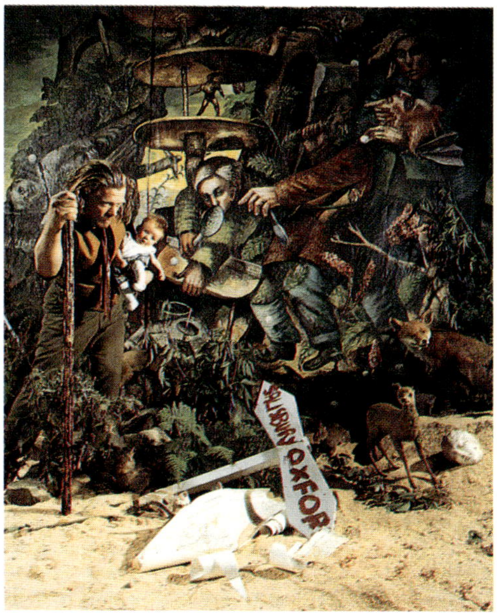

(PLATE 2) *Portrait of the Artist with his Daughter, Lauren,* photograph of installation, 289.6 × 386.1 cm, 1984

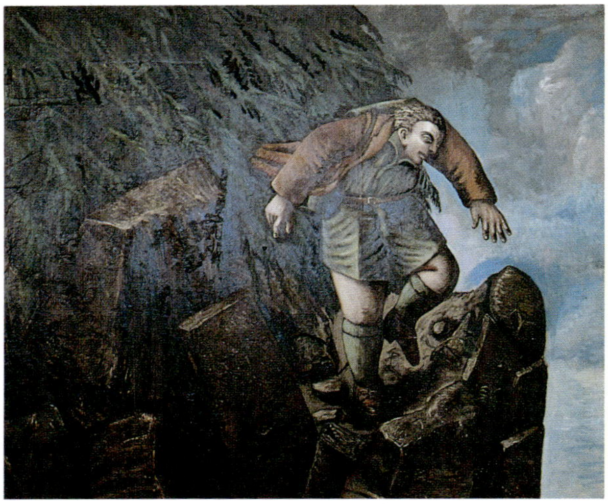

(PLATE 3) *Man Amazed at the Height He is Up*, oil on canvas, 248 × 291.5 cm, 1983

trade. In his first exhibition in 1983, there was a painting called *Man Amazed at the Height He is Up (Pl.3)*. In it, a young man looks out from a mountain and over a cliff. His face and attitude express both amazement and insecurity, not to say instability. He appears to be starting back from the cliff edge and yet also to be tempted to throw himself over it. In another picture in the series, *The Happy Camper,* he has actually fallen off the mountain. Here, with characteristic self-irony, the artist seems to contemplate the perilous exaltation of his own success; an unknown Glaswegian boy makes it in New York.

When Campbell had this success in New York, he was only a year out of art school, but it would be a mistake to see him as an inexperienced youth, a fulfilment of the persistently elusive myth of the boy genius. Born in Glasgow in 1953, he was by then already thirty. Between 1970 and 1977, he had worked as a steel fitter and he only entered Glasgow School of Art in 1978. Working in a steel works might not be seen as contributing directly to his education as an artist, but when he entered the art school, he had already read widely and, indeed, he had thought first of becoming a writer. Above all, he had had time to forge the mature determination that still drives his art and though the student work of most artists is usually only of academic interest, by the time he left the art school he had achieved some remarkable work. The outlines of his art were clearly established, as was his seriousness and his sense of both the strengths and the weaknesses of painting as a way of reaching some kind of emotional truth. There are therefore important indicators in his student output of the interests that have shaped his subsequent painting and in his later work he often reverts to themes that he first explored at that time.

At Glasgow, where Jack Knox was Head of Painting, Campbell was one of four artists in the same year who have all become well known. The other three are Ken Currie, Peter Howson and Adrian Wiszniewski. These four are sometimes presented as a group, as the *New Glasgow Boys*, but most of what united them was rivalry, a healthy stimulus in an art school class. Campbell himself said of it later:

> I didn't go to art school to be a teacher. I went to art school to learn to be a professional artist. That was my intention, and a lot of people learnt that stance.[3]

The members of this group have certainly developed very differently, though they do have in common a commitment to the use of the figure in painting. Currie and Howson have gone down the road of social realism and political comment, drawing on the inspiration of artists like Diego Rivera and the Mexican muralists, the American 'Ashcan' school and German art, both contemporary and from the inter-war years.

Campbell and Wiszniewski on the other hand, though they too learnt from con-

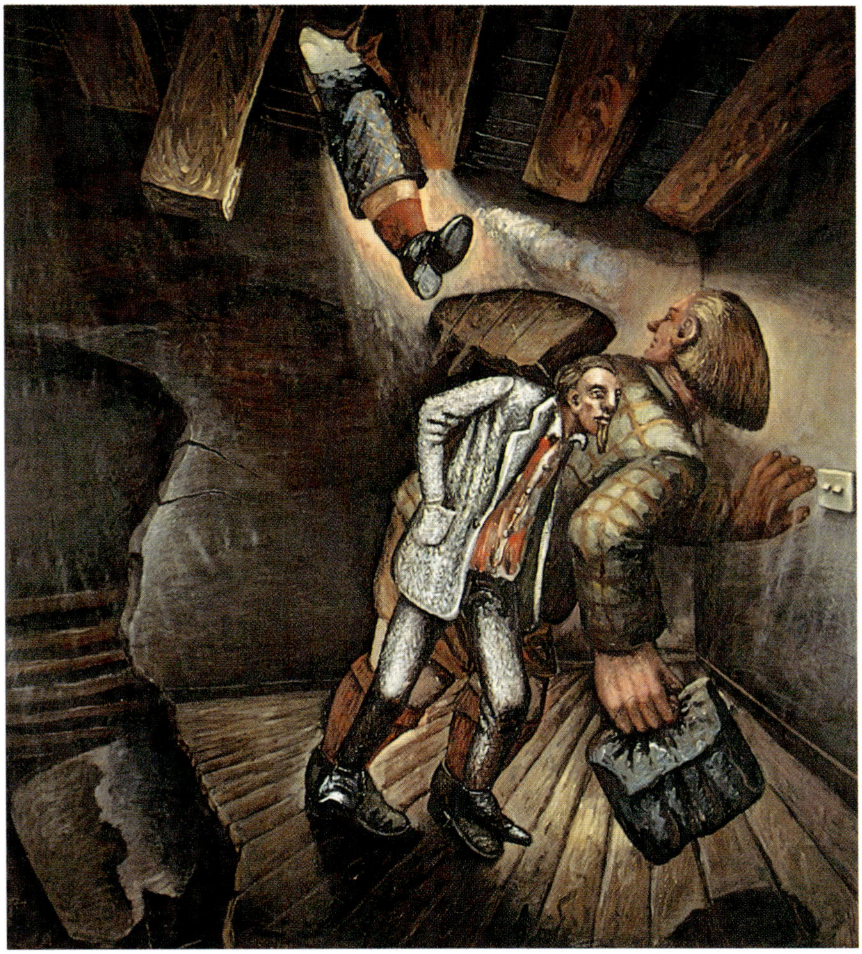

(PLATE 4) *Wee Nook Cottage*, oil on canvas, 281.9 × 281.9 cm, 1983

temporary German painters, looked to a longer tradition of figure painting. This was important. When contemporary art fails this is often because of the way it is only rooted in the thin top-soil of the present and immediate past. It is especially true of Campbell that his art is rooted in his wide knowledge and understanding of the deeper soil of art over a much longer history.

Sandy Moffat was one of the teachers closest to this group at the art school and as he put it in conversation, 'Campbell put himself through a crash course in the history of twentieth-century art'. This is perhaps not an unusual enterprise for a student, but Campbell seems to have tackled it with uncommon determination and, as I have suggested, his interests were not limited to the twentieth century. His determination reflects the project that he had set himself then and which is still essential to understanding what it is that drives his painting. It is truly 'post-modern' in that it represents an attempt to re-establish the continuities of art apparently broken by Modernism, knowing that it is impossible either simply to return to the *status quo ante*, or to compromise with it, but instead incorporating a late twentieth-century world view into this longer perspective. The problem was how to do this without merely being derivative or pretentious.

The tradition of monumental figure painting does not perhaps spring immediately to mind when looking at the tweedy characters who inhabit Campbell's paintings of the early eighties and the indignities they suffer, getting into various scrapes, or tangled in a mixture between dialectic and the confusion of nature, as in *Wee Nook Cottage (Pl.4)* of 1983, for instance, or in *Two Naturalist Philosophers Debating in a Garden* of the following year, but there can be no doubt that this has always been close to the centre of his concern.

He spent a good deal of time during his first three years at Glasgow working with Roger Hoare in the mixed media of performance and installation. His approach to figurative painting seems initially to have been through performance and by his third year, the outlines of his main project were beginning to become apparent. The most ambitious of these performances and the one for which the best evidence survives was done in 1981 and was called *Poised Murder (Pl.5)*. It was set in an artificial, stylised world like that of Dick Tracy, or some other fictional detective of the thirties or forties. It captured the remote and stylised glamour of Hollywood at the time (though the men's costumes were inspired closer to home by Napoleon Solo in the television series *The Man from U.N.C.L.E.*). This is how Campbell himself described the performance:

> There were four paintings of Violette Nozière as part of the set, standing with different murder weapons . . . In front of these paintings was a Vorticist zig-zag floor and a little bridge on which the murder took place. The men wore black trousers, black polo necks, medallions and Brylcreem. The women were in silver skirts, black tops, fishnet tights, high heels and floozied-out hair. There was a detective who crawled around on all fours and the actors adopted murderous poses to the music, which was a record by Robert Ashley It lasted fifteen minutes and we used real knives and razors.[4]

Violette Nozière was a murderess celebrated by the Surrealists. In the four different portraits she had four different murder weapons and each time the music stopped, four different murders were performed.

The tension between 'poise' and 'murder' in this is clear. It illuminates the distance between the confusion of real life – or death – which has no poise and the 'poised' imitation of it in art. Later Campbell remarked how much more 'comfortable' theatre is than real life. His own art here is as much cinematic as theatrical, however, for the distance that he stresses is even more explicit in the cinema than it can ever be in the theatre.

This idea of distance as a way of controlling feeling, even while maintaining the essential relationship between art and reality, has remained a feature of Campbell's art and it was the subject of a major installation done at this time, *The View from the Bridge*. It included a stepladder and a balcony. One detail was a red telephone, high up on the wall, indicating the difficulty and distance inherent in any communication.

Performances like *Poised Murder* clearly suggest the importance to Campbell not just of contemporary performance artists like Robert Wilson, Gilbert and George and Bruce McLean, all artists who used performance in an ironic and satirical way, and who Campbell acknowledged were part of his inspiration, but of the whole debate about the forms of art focused in performance. The formality of Gilbert and George's performances and their depersonalisation, for instance, were an ironic reflection on form in art. This was clearly echoed in Campbell's performances, but it is already apparent that his own interests were distinct. With Gilbert and George and Bruce McLean, even if they expressed it ironically, their performances were essentially narcissistic and the belief was implicit in them that the artist is his own ultimate art work.

With Campbell though, even though he did participate in his own performances, the costume and the presence of the detective take the performance away from the precious and self-conscious kind of art which flirts with the real world, to an art that is explicitly fiction. 'Only fiction from the inside has the authority to tell the outward truth,' wrote a recent commentator on Mrs Gaskell's realistic novels reflecting on their limitations compared to the novels of her contemporary, Tolstoy.[5] It is an important perception that helps to explain Campbell's consistent determination to get inside the fictional structures of art. Here he approaches them through the stylised world of crime fiction. It gives no clue to reality, as the detective crawls pointlessly round and round a running track, searching for clues and finding nothing, while the murders are committed round about him. The narrative cannot be explicit. The art *is* the mystery, not a vehicle that contains it.

This particular performance was also rather sexy in the way that the cinema can be because of its extraordinary power to unite action and abstraction. Campbell talks about his admiration for Bertolucci's *Last Tango in Paris* in the context of these performances, and a photograph of its star, Marlon Brando, appeared in the background of *Poised Murder*. *Last Tango in Paris* was certainly one of the sexiest films of the time, but it was also one which explored the nature of fiction in a most subtle way. In the film, one world is enclosed within another. The real action takes place in a flat that effectively belongs to no one and within its confines neither

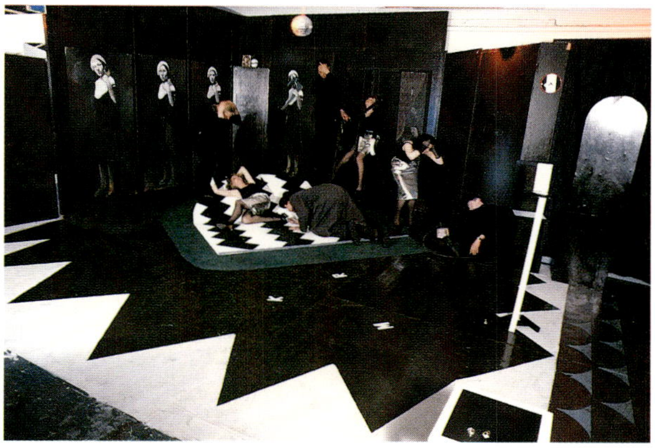

(PLATE 5) *Poised Murder*, 1981

character has a name. It is an abstract world, yet when they move outside, the heroine is herself the star of a piece of cinéma vérité. The 'real' world too is a fiction therefore and it turns out to be even more bizarre and to echo the codes of fiction more closely than the supposedly fictional world as the plot becomes melodrama with the bloody suicide of the wife of the character played by Brando and his own operatic death. The way that this film plays off one level of reality against another to suggest that in the end there is no definitive reality has a close parallel in Campbell's later painting.

The detective in *Poised Murder* perhaps is recognisable in Campbell's Van Helsing, the investigator in Bram Stoker's *Dracula* who became one of the stock characters in his later painting. There was also a character called 'Hunt' who played an important part in the artist's final year work. He then developed into one of the most important of these stock characters, the 'Lost Hiker', the traveller who has lost his way. Campbell described Hunt as inspired by a forties-style murder magazine, picked up on a Paris bookstall:

> I called him Hunt . . . I had these nineteen-forties murder magazines. I looked down and saw the headline; 'Is it Hunt, or is it . . . ?' He is athletic, wears a raincoat, walks around a

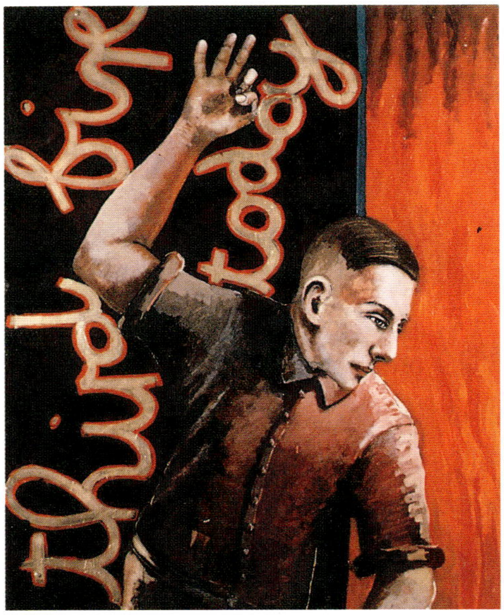

(PLATE 6) *Third Fire Today*, oil on paper, 124.5 × 114.3 cm, 1981/82

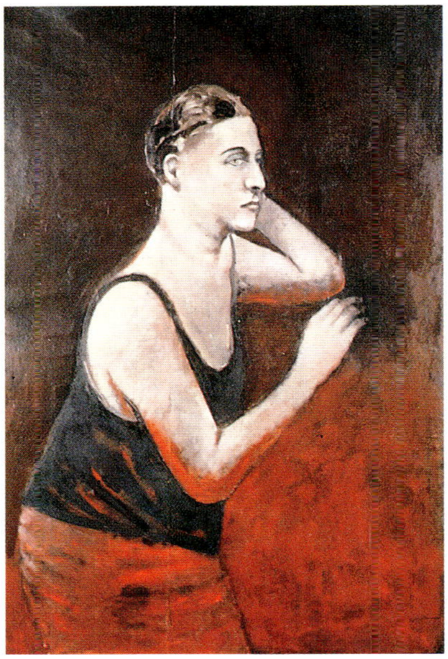

(PLATE 7) *Hunt as Hermaphrodite*, oil on paper, 152.4 × 106.7 cm, 1981/82

> lot and falls from great heights . . . He was a definite character and the entire sequence (of paintings) was called *Hunt's Fall*. He continued when I went to New York on the Fulbright and turned into the 'Lost Hiker' which became the title for many of the pictures.[6]

Campbell still talks of Hunt as a very definite personality and he was obviously more than just a fictional character. He was certainly not a self-portrait, though. He was more a kind of *doppelganger*, a personification of the hidden dark side that exists in all of us. He was a bit of a Fascist and appears in several paintings in Nazi guise and style. In one painting, for instance, he appeared against a background of pattern-painting like a field of Iron Crosses and with the unambiguous legend, 'Ich bin Hunt'. On another occasion, he appeared with a sickle like a Nazi image of Labour – 'Arbeit'. He always has red flags. They are 'for danger' but they are also vaguely Nazi in feeling. Hunt also appeared as a Brown Shirt at the edge of looting and violence, in *Third Fire Today*, but he was not a simple villain *(Pl.6)*.

Hunt seems to represent the temptation of evil. Campbell talks about the fascination of the Nazi image, about the disparity between the uniform and imagery and the horror that it concealed. It is the same gap between what is presented and the style in which it is presented that informed *Poised Murder*. It is a gap which represents a moral ambivalence in all of us and Hunt is very human. He began as a question – Is it Hunt, or is it someone else? It stresses his ordinariness. He was a bit naïve, a spectator and opportunist rather than purely evil. He joins in, but he has an uneasy conscience. The question mark also suggests a certain ambiguity and he always remains ambiguous. His indeterminate character was expressed in a pair of pictures in which he appeared naked. In one he is young and virile; in the other, a dirty old man. In another picture *(Pl.7)* he appeared in feminine guise as a hermaphrodite with a rose in one corner as an ironic symbol of femininity (a double entendre on Duchamp's equally ironic *Rose Selavy*).

There were several versions of the image of *Hunt Falling (Pl.8)*. The most elaborate of them was a compound composition of ten canvasses of various sizes, hung together in the shape of a mountain with a cut-out figure of Hunt falling off the top. Falling is an in-between state. Like art or inspiration, it may lead you to imagine as you fall that you are free, but really, though you are neither up nor down, you are on the way to a nasty knock and that is reflected in Campbell's alternative view of Hunt's falling. His Nazi sympathies arose because he was a misguided romantic and his fall was moral despair at the realisation of his mistake. Like the artist, Hunt was vulnerable and his vulnerability to life's confusion establishes the moral dimension that underlies all Campbell's art.

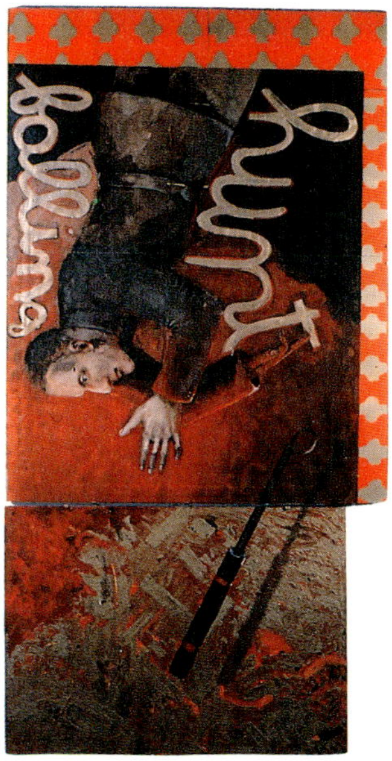

(PLATE 8) *Hunt Falling*, oil on paper, 198.1 × 76.2 cm, 1981/82

Hunt's ambivalence was too much for the external examiner at Campbell's final examination and one painting which showed him copulating with an enormous lady, part Courbet, part Rembrandt, had to be removed. It was years before Campbell painted a woman again. By his own account, however, Hunt continued as the Lost Hiker who has appeared so often in his paintings. His neatly pressed, boy-scout shorts and the knapsack of the Hitler Youth give a bizarre touch to his apparent innocence. In fact, Hunt is a constant in Campbell's work. He is recognisable in the figure of Pinocchio who has appeared in the recent works and his ambiguous status gives a clue to the artist's preoccupations, not just with the dubious credentials of style and the consequent tension between style and meaning, but with the confusion of feeling out of which, like Pinocchio, we have to distinguish truth and falsehood and therefore right and wrong.

The moral dimension was represented in one group of 'Hunt' paintings by a red, electric light. The colour of the light was reflected both actually by its fall on the surface of the picture and fictively in the colour in the painting. One of them, for example, was a half-length figure of a man, one arm raised above his head so that head and arm make a compact form in the manner of a figure in a Cézanne. He was wearing a red vest and the light along the side of his face and his arm was also painted an intense red. The frame was painted the same colour. The effect was like the intense light of a fire and one of the best of these pictures suggests that this fire is the fire of Hell. It shows a man between an accidental baptism as a jar of water spills over him and the red light of the Inferno *(Pl.9)*. This is Hunt's dilemma and there is a picture of that name done in the artist's fourth year, where he is suspended between two different painted worlds. One is red, sinful and intense. The other a rather decorative, and decorous, painterly blue. It is a moral dilemma. Like the artist, he must make a choice, but how?

The same sinister, red lighting used in the 'red' paintings was used in *Poised*

Murder and in a detective-story performance called *It's Just Violence at the Bar*, set in the same Dick Tracy world. In it, the red light cast a lurid glow on the figure of a girl lying on the floor of a flashy bar. She had apparently been knocked down, or even murdered and so the light had a clear dramatic meaning. A couple of years later, in 1984, Campbell offered an oblique comment on this theme in the painting, *Is Anaemia in Nature Caused by Disease or Lighting?*

Hunt continues, too, in the figure of the hunter, a variation on the Lost Hiker and changed, though only marginally, from Hunt to hunter. He is a man with a gun and a game bag who plays a variety of roles, but is still essentially the same individual as he strays through the painted world, somewhat at a loss, naïve, vulnerable, not completely harmless, but searching for some kind of truth. In a recent picture, for instance, *Hunter Looking for his Glasses (Pl.43)* of 1990, it is his spectacles that he has lost and he cannot see without them.

Van Helsing first appeared soon after this *Hunt's Fall* sequence. *Hope*, for instance, painted in 1983, showed Van Helsing lying in a crypt, the crypt of Dracula's castle perhaps, with a beautifully painted stained-glass window above him. *Flapping Like an Aspin (Pl.10)* also shows him in a gothic crypt with stained glass behind him. As an investigator, he was a more positive figure than Hunt though he sometimes doubles up as Hunt's successor, the Lost Hiker as in *The Poisoning and Subsequent Paralysis of Abraham van Helsing*. He was engaged in the pursuit of the bizarre, seeking to pin it down with a stake through its heart, like the artist pursuing the elusive and mysterious goals of his painting. Indeed there is something of Van Helsing's quest in the programme Campbell had set himself, confronting the 'undead', the meretricious clichés of the history of painting that rise up to haunt an unwary painter, to seduce him, to sap his strength and eventually to hold him in thrall.

Certainly, when he appears in these pictures, the Van Helsing character has something of Campbell's own appearance. A goatee beard is his distinguishing feature and Campbell still wears such a beard. When Glasgow School of Art presented him with the Bram Stoker Prize, called after Van Helsing's inventor, it is not entirely clear that it was not created to suit its recipient.

The idea expressed in *Hunt's Fall*, that falling was somehow a kind of in-between state, a moment when we do not have control and which is in this respect like art, was the germ of the inspiration of an elaborate installation called *Zoo Opera*, which began with the image of Ajax falling on his sword and evolved around the construction of a kind of tripping device made of lead and fixed to the floor. This is how the artist described it in 1984:

> I'd begun making some drawings of a Greek sculpture I like of Ajax falling on to his sword. It looked as if he was tripping up. I made a trip sculpture with a sandal to put your foot in and a lead base and a little medallion. There's a story that he was tricked by the goddess Athena and instead of killing the enemy he has been killing sheep. When he finds out he kills himself. Instead of feeling remorse because he has killed a thousand men, he is ashamed because he has killed a thousand sheep. Gradually this idea turned into a whole opera with the set and the actors and an audience of two who watched through little eye things, so when they caught what was going on, it had a fuzzy edge.[7]

This does actually seem to have been realised as an installation, though not as a full-scale performance and, though not always in an obvious way, its central ideas have often recurred in his subsequent work. Falling, Campbell said on another occasion, is like desire, between anticipation and realisation. In a connected idea, he says that poetry, too, happens when things are dislocated. In *Zoo Opera*, there were fragments of disconnected prose on the walls and the little holes that the spectators looked through were labelled punningly 'The Hole of My Art'. The whole of his art is, of course, just what they were not as through them it was only possible to see a dislocated fragment of what was presented. For Campbell, art is the process, the stage between. It too is dislocated in this way. He always talks about how, for him, his art is essentially the struggle in the studio. What comes out may be a failure, or is simply a matter of indifference compared to the experience of making it.

The link between performance and the role of the figure in narrative painting was explicit in Campbell's performances where painting also played an integral part. Sandy Moffat remembers how interesting these paintings were, even when they were there only as the backdrop. It was as though the characters on the stage were the inhabitants of the painted world taking the opportunity of a little exercise. There was a similar interchange between the real and the painted worlds in some of the installations that Campbell did at this time in which he used paintings which incorporated light. One picture, *Flag*, was a collage of painted book covers, an ironic approach to the literary in painting, each one a distinct rectangular picture, but grouped together into a single, larger rectangle in a form that he has often used since. This painting was then lit from behind so that it appeared to float in front of the wall.

It seems that Campbell did not treat the arts of installation and performance as an escape route from the problems of painting as some of his contemporaries did. On the contrary, they provided him with a way back into painting, but from a fresh angle. In a way, figurative art is implicit in performance and the revival of figurative painting in the late seventies was linked to the vogue for performance. In fact, performance was a kind of deconstruction of figurative art. Artists like Gilbert and George and Jorge Immendorf who had specialised in performance, tended to turn to figurative art and as they did so, showed no radical break in the continuity of their art. As they made this change, however, the most serious artists recognised how the uncertainty and the relativism, the conditions that had made figurative painting so difficult, still prevailed. As he too shifted from performance to figura-

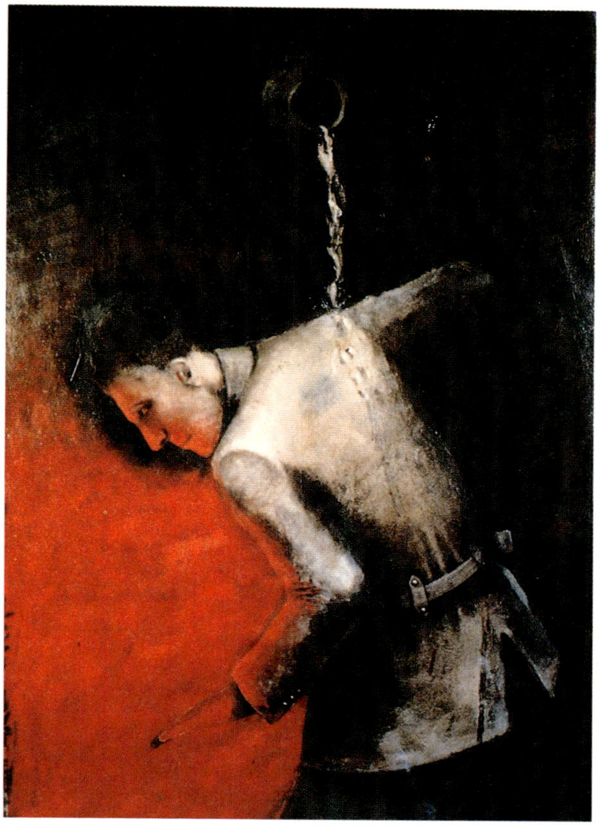

(PLATE 9) *Accidental Baptism*, oil on paper, 121.9 × 96.5 cm, 1981

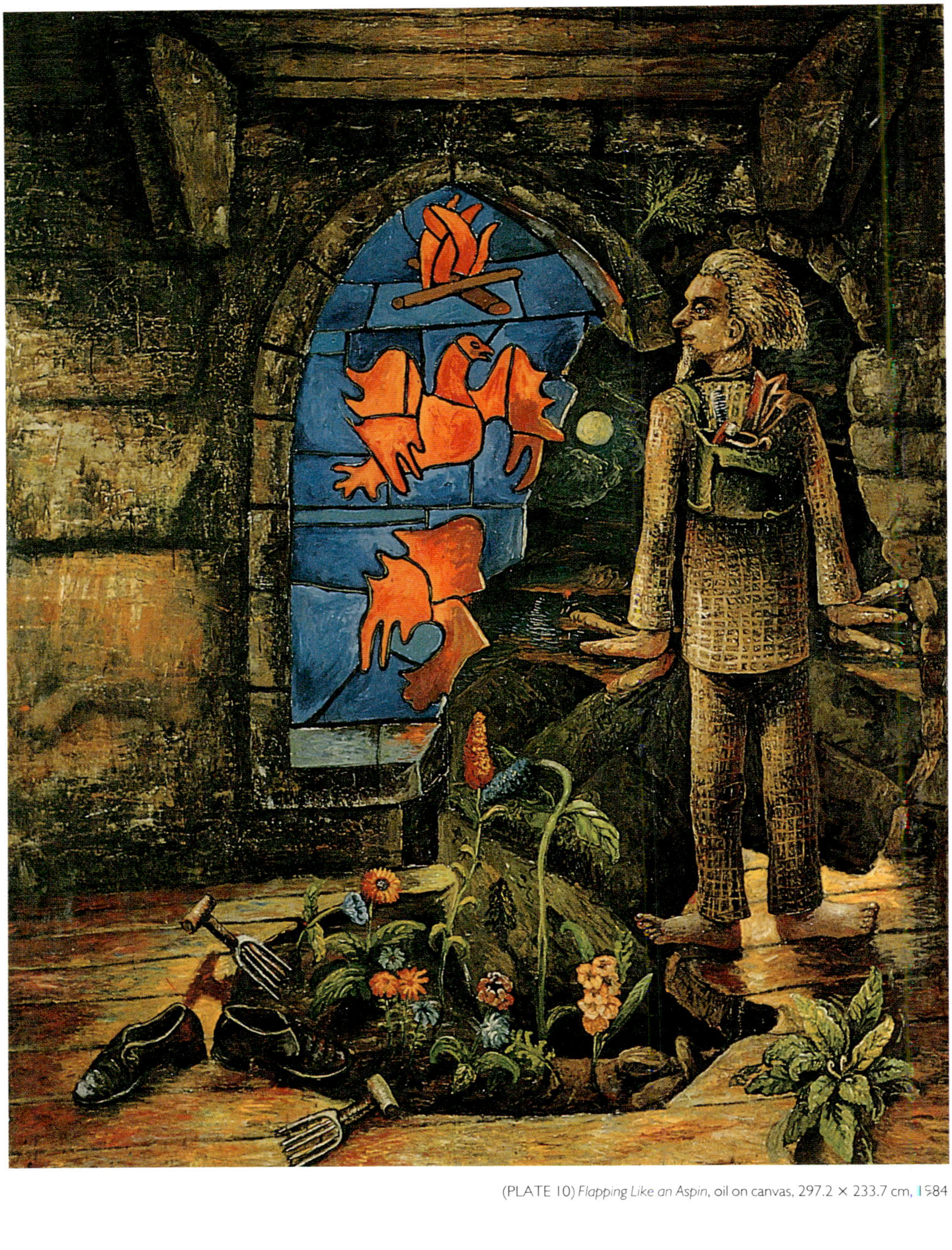

(PLATE 10) *Flapping Like an Aspin*, oil on canvas, 297.2 × 233.7 cm, 1984

tive painting, Campbell preserved this position by the way that in his pictures, he never allows us to rest with a certainty. Every apparent assertion is qualified in a way that almost contradicts it.

The conceptual and minimal art of the late sixties and seventies were also an important part of Campbell's inspiration. From one point of view, they had undermined the position of painting, but they had also cleared the ground. In a way these art forms had reopened the possibility of subject matter, but they had also reopened a more fundamental area of debate. The simple relationship between seeing and knowing, of mimesis, entailed in the idea that art depended on the representation of a 'real' world, has always been a chimera, but its blanket rejection left a serious problem of justification. Without this, at what level of 'reality' did art operate?

Many approaches to resolving this dilemma have been tried throughout the twentieth century. They have mostly depended on a simple exclusion: whatever it is that may be the object of art, it is not the prosaic reality of common experience. Minimal art argued a return to first principles, while conceptual art helped to refocus the debate and to reopen the field of art to ordinary experience, but it also made it clear that this could no longer be subjected to a simplistic view of the dependence of art on reality. Instead it was shown how art was inevitably surrounded by and must somehow take account of all the complexities and ambiguities that are part and parcel of the epistemology of the late twentieth century, but this kind of epistemology is not 'up there'. It *is* part of the prosaic reality of life as it is lived and it is Campbell's strength as an artist to reflect this in an art which is not realistic in the sense that it represents life, but is realistic in the way that it presents a truth about it.

Campbell's interest in conceptual art during his time at art school is clear. In an interview with James Collins in 1987, he said:

> Right from art school, I was more bound up with the seventies' British conceptual stuff, McLean, Gilbert and George, those people . . .[8]

His subsequent paintings bear little apparent relationship to the austerities of conceptualism. For all their topsy-turvy view of things, however – precisely because of their topsy-turvy view of things in fact – these paintings do reflect the ways in which we know, as they express the artist's own feelings about the confusion and uncertainties that beset him as they beset us all.

The other important feature of Campbell's art school work before his final degree show was his dissertation. His original proposal had been to write on the performance artist, Robert Wilson, but he settled for Picasso's neo-classical figure paintings of the years immediately after the First World War. It was an interesting choice which evidently reflected his current interests and whose influence was certainly reflected in his later work. In the late seventies and early eighties, the return to the figure in painting was seen as a bold experiment. Figure painting became fashionable as a consequence and there was, for instance, a big exhibition devoted to contemporary narrative painting in Edinburgh in 1979.[9] Contemporary heroes were painters like the American Philip Guston and the Italians, Clemente and Sandro Chia. Guston had a major show at the Whitechapel in London in 1982. His bold, semi-figurative painting hovers between the comic book and the Surreal, a bit like Campbell's. Chia's work was certainly reflected in some of Campbell's art school paintings. Writing about

Campbell's first one-man show in New York in 1983, however, Barry Yourgrau reflected on the Chia connection and made a sharp distinction:

> Chia is a red-herring – but actually an instructive one, his art being one of wit, of a worldly, playful ironist's conceits on painting history, on painting itself. Chia's giants roam Brush Stroke country. But Campbell's humor always packs a certain earnestness, like a great clown's, part sharp wildness, part sharp naïvety.[10]

Nobody now would accuse Campbell of lacking wit or irony, and he is deeply concerned with picture-making, but, though style is important, stylishness has never been part of the equation that makes up his pictures. Barry Yourgrau's identification of the clown-like character of his work is important too, for there is a depth of pathos in some of his work in which, as in clowning, the vulnerability of the human condition may be transmuted into wit and humour, but is only partly concealed by them.

Whoever one was to take as its leading representative, no doubt the current vogue for figure painting played a part in Campbell's inspiration, but there was also a native tradition to which he had access. In Scotland in the early sixties, Sandy Moffat and John Bellany had led a return to monumental figurative painting as a vehicle for the expression of present needs. In 1971, there was a Scottish Arts Council exhibition called *Scottish Realism* which toured all over Scotland and included these two, together with Ian McLeod, Bill Gillon and Bob Crozier. They showed together again under the 'Realist' banner in *Four Scottish Realists* at the Fruitmarket Gallery in Edinburgh in 1975. Their approach from the beginning had included a willingness to take direct and open inspiration from the great art of the past in a way which was unfashionable at the time, but which also suggests an analogy, not only with Campbell's interest in Picasso, but also with his lively interest in the historic tradition of figurative painting, an interest shared by all the painters in this group to a greater or lesser extent.

In the early years of the Second World War in Glasgow too, when J. D. Fergusson and Joseph Herman had revolutionised the art scene in the city, there had been an interesting flowering of figurative painting. The best known painter to emerge from this circle was Joan Eardley, but painters like Bet Low, George Hannah and Millie Frood had produced some remarkable paintings of life in the streets of the city. It was of course also in Glasgow in the war years that Stanley Spencer produced his shipbuilding series.

The approach of these artists was perhaps closer to that of Currie and Howson than of Campbell, but the analogy does illustrate how this tradition in Glasgow had never completely died. Alasdair Gray, a generation older than Campbell and now better known as a novelist than a painter, was one of a group of Glasgow artists who shared convictions of this kind. In *Lanark*, Gray includes a vivid, fictional account of the lifestyle and ambitions of just such a painter, Duncan Thaw, though he reveals a certain debt to Joyce Cary's master of confusion, Gulley Jimson, a fictional character who has been a model to more than one Glasgow artist.

Especially in *Lanark*, the awareness Gray shows of the tension between modes of representation and the thing that they represent has a significant affinity with one of the underlying themes of Campbell's paintings. Indeed, Brian Aldiss is quoted on the back cover of *Lanark* describing it as 'a saga of a city where reality is about as reliable as a Salvador Dali watch'. There is not much of Dali in Campbell, although Surrealism has played a part in his inspiration, but there is nevertheless the constant theme of the wanton unreliability of the represented world which, as it *is* a matter of representation, also mirrors the bruising unreliability of the real world.

In turning to Picasso for his dissertation, Campbell may have been guided unconsciously by some of this tradition, but he also showed that he was not prepared to take contemporary chatter at face value and that, as is his habit, he wanted to see for himself. Picasso's neo-classical figure paintings are traditionally said to have been sparked off by a visit to Rome, Naples and Pompeii in 1917, though they mostly date from the early twenties. Perhaps they reflect a reaction to the Russian Revolution and the aftermath of the First World War. They do certainly seem to have represented an attempt to recover the monumentality of the classical tradition of figure painting at a time when some reassertion of human dignity was needed and was perhaps proffered by the prospect of revolutionary change.

In these paintings, Picasso returned to the inspiration of Puvis de Chavannes and his vision of an ideal, classical world of Elysian peace. Unlike the attenuated inhabitants of Puvis's world, however, Picasso's figures are characterised by their massive bulk and their huge hands and feet. They are painted with a roughness of finish that is not at all showy, but which accentuates their mass. It is in the lightness and calm of the world they inhabit that the debt to Puvis is most apparent, but it is seen, too, in the passiveness and the innocent tranquillity, not to say the blankness, of the expressions on the faces of these figures. Campbell himself called them 'dumb eyed'[11] and this same face with its expression of blank innocence, reappears constantly in his own later work.

Although Picasso himself had abandoned this style by 1924, it found an important echo in the art of Léger. With Léger, too, its ideological implications were more explicit and he became something of a hero to Moffat and Bellany. Aspects of this style did reappear from time to time in Picasso's own work, however. For instance his version of the tranquillity of the classical face is a striking feature of the *Vollard Suite* of etchings from the thirties. It is a series which includes some of his most memorably poetic images and some of them present a very similar approach to the making of a picture to that adopted by Campbell later in his career.

In 1981, Campbell showed for the first time. It was in a group show at the New 57 Gallery in Edinburgh. The following year, his degree show was at the centre of a triumphant exhibition for Glasgow School of Art. It was followed during the Edinburgh Festival by an exhibition called *Expressive Images*, organised by Sandy Moffat and Jim Birrell, again at the New 57 Gallery. Campbell was the representative from Glasgow in a show selected from all four Scottish colleges. In 1982, he also showed in a group show at the Compass Gallery in Glasgow. The New 57 Gallery was the upper level of the Fruitmarket where the concurrent exhibition was a group show called *Scottish Art Now*. Because of Campbell's work, the two shows made an interesting contrast. His paintings were meant to be taken from his degree show, but between June, when that show closed, and early August, when the Edinburgh show opened, he had painted a completely new set of pictures. They were obviously rapidly painted and the energy and excitement were visible in them.

The work in the degree show had an appropriate level of finish and decorum, but this new work looked improvised. The painting was bold and the massive figures powerfully handled in a way that was reminiscent of Courbet. In fact, the whole show suggested Courbet was a role model: the hero of 'Realism' who challenged the Paris Universal Exhibition in 1855 with his one-man Pavilion du Realisme, much as Campbell challenged the Edinburgh Festival.

In this show big figures dominated the canvases, but the paintings were not obviously narrative and the figures did not seem to have an explicit dramatic function. *Ding-Dong*, for instance, showed a three-quarter length figure of a girl, her body and arms described in blunt, cylindrical shapes. She was more like a figure by Léger than by Picasso and she was holding out her arms with what appeared to be a bell on a chain attached to each wrist. In *The Admiral (Pl.11)*, a big, stony figure in an old-fashioned uniform, like Nelson off his column, or the Commendatore from *Don Giovanni*, holds an arm out over the shoulder of a smaller naked youth, his modesty preserved by a convenient tree trunk. They were roughly brushed, but without bravura and their simple forms and impassive faces were strongly reminiscent of Picasso. Their blankness meant that the sense of drama depended on the way they were painted, but also on gesture, much as it does in Poussin and this too has remained a feature of Campbell's later work.[12]

Beside some of the work in the lower gallery, these pictures seemed crude and vigorous, but they were so uncompromisingly *there* as painting that they made an immediate impression. Compared to much of his other work, they are unguarded and for a moment they display a fierce intensity that reveals the emotional drive of all his painting. It is expressed solely through the painted image and though it may have been sublimated in his later work, it always underlies it. Indeed it has resurfaced very strongly in his most recent work.

Among the artists in *Scottish Art Now*, Graham Durward's painting was in the same general frame of reference as Campbell's. It consisted of big, expressionistic, figurative images. Durward, too, drew on the inspiration of Picasso, especially his use of distortion, though he also drew on the work of later expressionists like Karel Appel and de Kooning. In spite of the shared inspiration in Picasso, however, Durward's work seemed almost academic beside Campbell's and even though it exploited the violence implicit in this expressionist imagery, Durward's vision seemed constrained by a notion of correct-

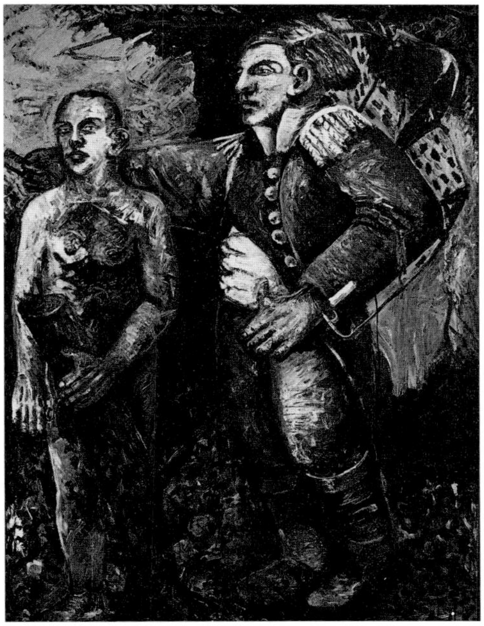

(PLATE 11) *The Admiral*, oil on paper, 218.4 × 152.4 cm, 1982

ness while by contrast Campbell's at the time seemed anarchic.

It was difficult to see then how the energy in Campbell's pictures was not just expressionistic but also came from his passionate engagement with the mainline figurative tradition, and yet for instance, even as he was exploring Picasso's monumental figure style, he was also emulating Courbet and he painted a picture *(Pl.12)* inspired by Titian's *Diana and Actaeon*. He subsequently destroyed it, but this was a variation on the theme of what are two of Titian's greatest pictures, *Diana and Actaeon* in the National Gallery of Scotland and *The Death of Actaeon* in the National Gallery in London; the former especially is a picture which lies at the root of the modern figurative tradition and is the direct ancestor of Cézanne's *Bathers*. It was the picture in which Titian seems to have given his considered response to Michelangelo's *Last Judgment* which he had seen in Rome in 1545. In it, he shows us how nature has no place for innocence, as Diana, pure and merciless, condemns Actaeon for his innocent transgression as he stumbles upon her bathing with her nymphs. She strikes at him across an illogical space, jagged with tension.[13]

Ideas such as guilt and innocence are part of the feeble sense of order that mankind has constructed as a defence against the constant pressure of imminent disorder. Titian expresses this heroically here. Campbell, too, has often returned to this kind of theme, recently in *The Croatian Blouse*, *Murder Running Through the Woods*, or *Dead Man's Cocktail Party (Pls.65, 66, 68)*, for instance. He also does so compositionally in key paintings like *Two Humeans Preaching Causality to Nature (Pl.16)* of 1984, where, as in Titian's painting, the tension between order and disorder is vividly expressed. As in the Hunt pictures, this tension is ultimately moral and thematically it underlies much of his painting in which either a provisional order barely keeps disorder at bay, or the structures of order are themselves held up to question. It seems to have been here, too, with his version of the story of Actaeon, that Campbell introduced the hunter who was to become a recurrent theme in his work acting out this search for a clue to some kind of order.

It is in the light of this kind of reflection that, like Cézanne, Campbell continues to nurse the ambition to paint the great, multi-figured composition in the Old Master tradition, not as an academic exercise, but as a way of making painting match the elementary grandeur of this theme. The recent *Dream of St Sebastian (Pl.76)* is a superb example of this, but it is surely also important that he should find inspiration so early in such a key image as Titian's picture. His own painting of this subject showed two figures in a dark landscape. They were naked and seemed to be both male, so Diana was absent, but behind the central figure, the horns of Actaeon could be clearly seen. In the picture, Campbell combined the inspiration of Titian, Cézanne and Courbet, for though the subject and some elements of the composition were reminiscent of Titian, the bulk of the central figure was clearly inspired by the figure of one of Cézanne's *Bathers*, while the one on the left, right arm outstretched, has the figure and pose of Courbet's massive *Baigneuse* of 1853. (She is the one who was called a Percheron cart-horse by the Empress when she visited the Salon.)

Campbell still declares his profound admiration for both Titian and Cézanne and indeed he still demonstrates it in his painting. It is a significant choice of heroes, for it is in the work of these two above all that we see that the relationship of the human figure to the landscape in painting is not just that of an actor to the backdrop. The compression of image that is unique to painting encapsulates dramatically the fundamental moral tension of human life, between man's perception of himself as human, and therefore apart from nature, and yet at the same time as natural and so, like the rest of creation, nature's child and helplessly subject to her whims. This is the subject of Titian's extraordinary painting of *Diana and Actaeon* as it is the theme of Ovid's *Metamorphoses* which inspired it. It is a classical picture by any definition, yet everything in it is profoundly unstable.

Campbell's *Diana and Actaeon* with its echoes of Titian and Cézanne, and the place of Courbet in his inspiration too, are all indicators of how, while he was still at art school, Campbell had formulated his ambition to take on the great tradition, even though it may have seemed at first only possible to do this ironically, to deconstruct the work of these painters, even while emulating them, and to disguise ambition with clowning. It is important too, looking at the way Campbell's art has developed, to remember from the evidence of Cézanne's early painting how it too was driven by passion so intense that it was originally almost anarchic, whatever cerebral constructions may subsequently have been put upon it.

Campbell may not have reached such a level of profundity in 1982, but, unlike so many of his contemporaries, and not only in Scotland, he had at least turned his art back into a track that could lead in that direction. Certainly it is his awareness of these complexities, of the way that they reflect reality as we know it and his ability to give this expression made urgent by feeling which makes his art continually interesting. For him, the return to the figure in painting meant a return, as hiker or hunter, to a creative environment where art itself was no longer the only subject for a painter, but conversely, his return was not achieved by mortgaging any of his art's hard-won autonomy.

When Campbell finished at Glasgow School of Art, he chose to go to New York:

> I went to America because I saw art only in magazines. Living in Glasgow, I didn't see a damn thing! And the only way, if you're ambitious, is to have a go. It wasn't because I loved American art. It's because New York was – and is – the centre.[14]

He was awarded a Fulbright Scholarship to spend a year studying at the Pratt Institute. In the end he stayed in the States for almost five years, only returning finally to settle in Glasgow again in 1986, though he spent part of 1984 in Scotland as artist-in-residence at Glasgow School of Art and he had an important one-man show in London and Edinburgh in the winter of 1984–5. New York was an obvious choice. There he could carry on the programme that he had set himself at Glasgow and study at first hand the paintings from the heroic age of Modernism in the Museum of Modern Art and the Guggenheim.

Though his success in Scotland was already significant, in New York his real breakthrough into public notice and the beginning of his international reputation came with the exhibition of just two paintings at the Barbara Toll Gallery in June 1983. The pictures were *Man Amazed at the Height He is Up* and *Poachers of the North Sea Surprised*.

The critic John Russell was sharp-eyed enough to spot them and to devote most of a short review in the *New York Times* to Campbell. He wrote:

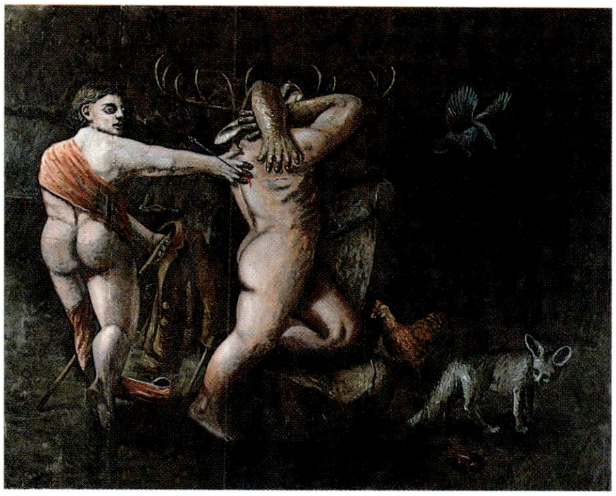

(PLATE 12) *Diana and Actaeon*, oil on canvas, 1982 (destroyed)

> At the Barbara Toll Gallery, there is a painter named Steven Campbell, whose work is really very curious. The paintings are large and they look like illustrations to Victorian novels that have been mated with the news of today in a small local newspaper . . . Of his two paintings, *Man Amazed at the Height He is Up*, shows an overweight young walker rounding a scary corner near the top of a small mountain. The rocks stand up like tombstones. The huge turbulent sky suggests that the wind may suddenly pick the young man up by his ample behind and throw him over the edge. In terms of balance, foothold and equipment, it is clear that he would never make it up (or down) K2. He won't have to of course. We don't believe that he is really very high up.[15]

What Russell did not know was that the scene, although it may have been autobiographical in a symbolic way, was also actually based on a real event, when the artist and a friend on a picnic, running through a wood, suddenly found themselves confronted by a cliff top hidden by the trees. Grounded in reality, the picture was therefore not simply a piece of game-playing and it has remained one of the artist's favourites.

Though Russell's comments are not unusually profound, he got the essence of Campbell's work across very clearly and so made it easier for others to follow. In December 1983, Barbara Toll followed

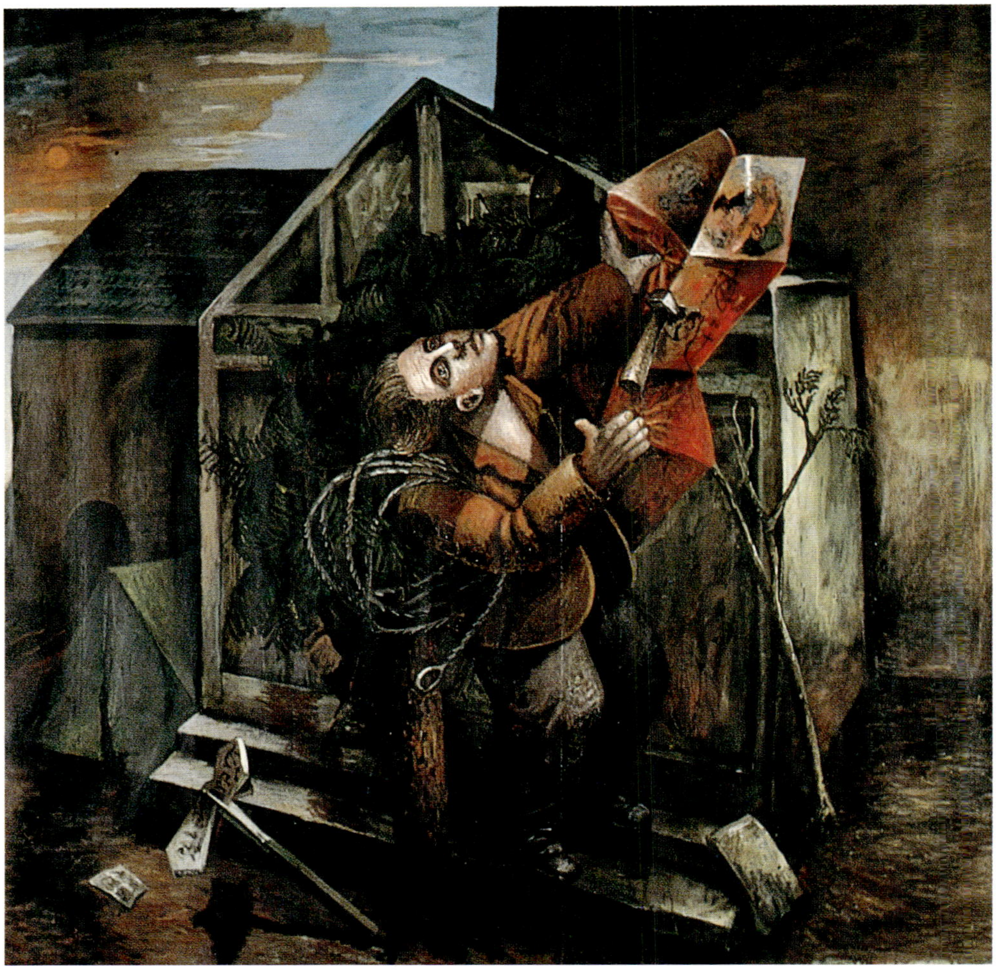

(PLATE 13) *The Man who Climbs Maps*, oil on canvas, 281.9 × 281.9 cm. 1983

this success by giving Campbell his first one-man show which included almost twenty paintings as well as drawings. The drawings were mostly full-sized, subsequent variations on the compositions of the paintings. The exhibition was widely and favourably reviewed. To the chagrin of the Pratt Institute, however, this public success coincided with Campbell's failure of their course:

> I told them I was just going there to paint. I didn't want to take print-making, geography, all that. And they got very upset. They said to themselves, 'How can a guy not take this course and get good reviews? There's definitely something wrong here.'[16]

The hikers with their tents, rocks and mountains are recurrent features of the paintings that formed this one-man show. During his first year in New York, Campbell had at first continued to paint the rather static, single, or two-figure compositions in which the memory of Picasso was still apparent, but these now had a constant, underlying theme of present, or threatening disorder reflecting the artist's own sense of insecurity perhaps. *Hiker in a Landscape Turned into a Marsh Overnight* and *The Man who Climbs Maps (Pl.13)*, for instance, are both single-figure compositions like *Man Amazed at the Height He is Up*, and like it they suggest emblematic self-portraits. In all three, there is a sense of disquiet. The heroes have lost their way. In the first, a man puts his hand to his brow in consternation. His foot is on the edge of the newly created marsh as in it, the 'Oxford to Salisbury' sign-post sinks out of sight. Though he has a climbing-rope, the young man with the maps is in the same position as the young man who is too high up on the mountain, but the two together make a play on the interlocking of three kinds of space, real, painted and narrative. This young man has stayed on the ground, but as both are representations in two dimensions, to climb a map is the same as to climb a painted mountain and so he is just as flummoxed. He too has the sign-post on the ground behind him.

In these pictures, there is a new, clown-like quality and for the first time the artist used the kind of conundrum titles that he has used ever since. The humour is overt and it comes from the apparent clumsiness of the characters in the painting as they blunder through the painted world, their innocence perpetually confounded by experience. It is a quality that marks his painting for several years from this time forward. Like all great clowning, it is a way of being serious. It sublimates feeling and it represented a shift from his previous work. The contemporary painting, *After the Hunt (Pl.14)*, for instance, does not have this quality. Instead it follows on directly from the destroyed *Diana and Actaeon*. It is the next stage in the action. Two figures stand against a mountain landscape. One is the hiker with massive legs, woolly socks, shorts, stick and knapsack. He is the same young man who appears in *Man Amazed at the Height He is Up*. The other, not dressed for hunting or the country, but in a brown overcoat, is more like the detective from a forties' comic, though without a slouch hat. They are both looking in the same direction out of the picture and their attitudes suggest vague disquiet, if not actual anxiety. In the foreground are various signs of slaughter and a dead stag is lying at their feet, but their faces are expressionless and they have the stable, architectural forms of Cézanne's *Bathers*. They buttress each other in the same way and so they have the same static monumentality as Campbell's paintings in the Fruitmarket show the previous year, though the handling is much quieter.

In some of the other paintings of this date, however, such as *Disguised as a Tennis Player, etc.*, Campbell is also beginning to pursue his new objectives by using a more complex and expressive kind of structure that reflects his first-hand acquaintance with some of the great early Modernist paintings that can be seen in New York, especially the Cubists. The most important of these new pictures was *Wee Nook Cottage (Pl.4)*. It is a picture that the artist still looks back to with pride.

The picture is clearly and strongly composed and muted in colour. It shows the inside of a derelict room, constructed with a kind of Cubist space, but no dramatic dislocation. As the artist himself pointed out in conversation, the interior is reminiscent of Immendorf's paintings, particularly his *Café Deutschland* series of 1978. The room has bare boards and rafters with chunks of plaster out of the wall. There is only one figure in the composition, but it is a composite figure made up of a tweedy hiker at the front with a diminutive Van Helsing attached to his back. The hiker is pressing a light switch, although Van Helsing's arm dis-

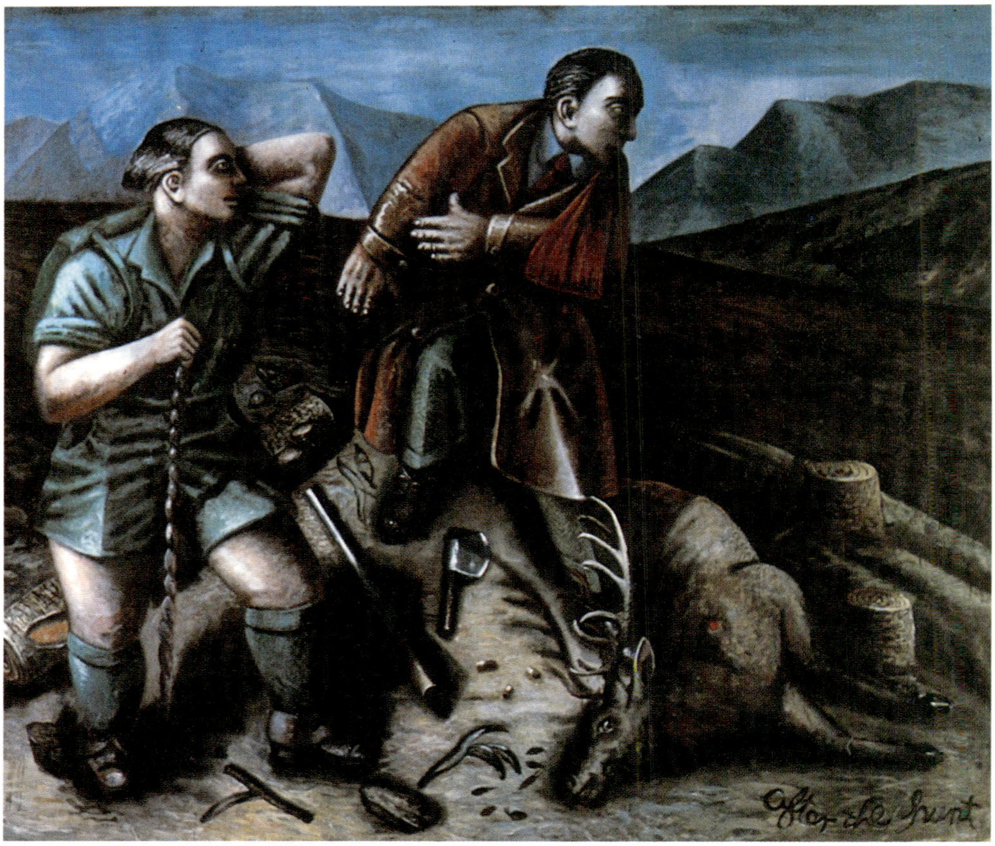

(PLATE 14) *After the Hunt*, oil on canvas, 284.5 × 299.7 cm, 1983

appears into his back in a way that implies that it could actually be he who is animating him, as the artist is doing, as though he were a puppet.

As the switch is pressed, the consequences are quite unexpected and a hefty, booted leg breaks through the ceiling. This leg is in the position that the light would be in. It descends into the room like a pendant bulb and as it does so it brings light with it. The leg is the light and, like the light, it has been switched on. The Van Helsing-Hiker has started the action and perhaps the whole picture with dramatic results. If he presses the switch again, will it all disappear? The theme seems to be life's uncertainty and the unpredictable consequences of any action, or intellectual or artistic inquiry. This is like Frankenstein and the image parallels the analogy between electricity and the creative imagination suggested by Mary Shelley. *The Enigma of Static Electricity*, painted the following year, seems to follow on these reflections as a group of hikers camping in the mountains terrify themselves by projecting a Frankenstein's monster on to the mist.

In *After the Hunt*, Campbell also took up again the theme of hunting. The dead stag in the picture is a memory, not only of Titian, but also of Landseer's unquestioning vision of the bloodthirsty Victorian attitude to animate nature as existing primarily – and especially in Scotland – to be murdered; an attitude that is still preserved among the wealthy.[17] It was epitomised long ago by Oscar Wilde in a reference to fox-hunting that will stand for this whole idea of 'sport' as 'the unspeakable in pursuit of the uneatable', an epigram that provided the title for another of the paintings in Campbell's December show, *Pursuing the Uneatable*, though the quarry there was an eagle and the lure a bloody sheep's fleece. Similar hunting imagery appears in paintings like *Landscape with Suicidal Ferns* of 1983 and *A New Hunting Rifle* of 1985.

Absurd though the convention of 'huntin', shootin' and fishin'' may be, the same theme is sublime in Titian's *Diana and Actaeon*, where the stag's antlers are a reminder of the brutality of the natural world, a brutality which we must share as we too belong to that world. Campbell's invocation of this sporting ethos typically partakes of both the absurd and the sublime, as he explores the pictorial language of the grand manner of figure painting, but neutralises its pretensions by using it to describe the kind of absurd catastrophes found in a novel by P.G. Wodehouse.

The fresh-faced, galumphing young men in tweeds, the solemn clowns who so frequently inhabit his paintings from this time forward are indeed like characters from Wodehouse. In fact *Wee Nook Cottage* took its title from the author who made such memorable art from the doings of the idle, rich and brainless in an imaginary golden age between the wars. Wodehouse's world is an enclosed one with all the conventions of dramatic narrative, but in which normality is the absurd and that of course is its particular truth.

The analogy between Campbell and Wodehouse that he himself invites reflects this in rather the same way as the analogy with Alasdair Gray suggested above, but even with Wodehouse, crazy though it is, like Sterne's *Tristram Shandy*, this fiction does partake of some kind of reality; its present reality is as perceived fiction and its implied reality is as a reflection of the world outside to which, however, it also inevitably belongs. This is like the reflection of a mirror in a mirror. The two realities bounce off each other in a diminishing recession until both disappear, one inside the other. Naturally, though he starts with an idea, Campbell improvises all the time as a painting grows, and so he finds a kind of provisional reality in this mirror fiction.

From the perspective of a Glasgow steelworker, Wodehouse's characters might as well have been inhabitants of the moon and later Campbell himself said of the kind of tweedy, male world that they lived in that it fascinated him:

> Just because it was alien. In appearance it wasn't related to me at all. And it was fantastic.[18]

It was, and is, as remote as Arcadia, an enclosed world of perpetual innocence, and indeed Wodehouse's world is Arcadian, an Arcadia of the absurd. His nymphs and shepherds pursue each other in a pastoral world where no real harm can come to them. They are an epitome of a certain classical vision. Death does not stalk their landscape, and yet Wodehouse himself was more than a little like Campbell's character, Hunt. Naïvely, he got himself ensnared by the Nazis, just as Hunt might have done, and so his Arcadian world is compromised by moral doubt, just as he himself was compromised. Though it is more benign, there is the same gap between the attraction of Wodehouse's stylised world and the muddled morality of the reality it conceals, between the polished surface and the confusion of feeling beneath it, as there is between the image of Hunt and the ambiguity of the world he inhabits.

If he too sees the absurdity of life, Campbell's vision is nevertheless more like Poussin's in *Et in Arcadia Ego*. It is a less comforting view of the innocence of Arcady. The darkness of such an underlying theme is a reminder that humour and irony are a way of transmuting feeling. The fact that the world is falling down around the ears of his Arcadians is comic, but the comedy only thinly veils a serious truth which is present implicitly in the strength and drama of the composition. In *T'was Once an Architect's Office in Wee Nook* (1984, *Pl.15*), the placidity of two young men is shattered as their office is demolished by an angry and aggressive Cubism. Nature herself strikes a blow too, as a menacing, animated branch reaches in through a hole in the roof. This animated branch appears in different forms, but usually as a kind of hostile, even carnivorous fern. In *Fall of the House of Nook with Tree Blight* from the same date, nature's counter-attack is even more advanced. Something very like the rock and seascape of Etretat as they were painted by Monet and Courbet is developing into a deluge, while trees and cacti attack the young men.

This joke confrontation is therefore also a serious one and there are often implicit, classical references in Campbell's work which reflect this. They are also seen in his commitment to large-scale, narrative figure painting as his chosen medium and in his visible admiration for Titian, Cézanne, and later for Matisse. He constantly talks of 'failure' in his paintings and of course, in one way in the classical and academic traditions, failure is a necessary and permanent condition of painting, which can aspire to, but which can never reach the ideal in the Platonic sense. On the other hand though, to succeed could be failure, if success in the same terms as his great models crossed the invisible frontier into pretentiousness. His position is rather like Hogarth's. Hogarth too wanted to succeed in terms of the great tradition, but he was only really successful when his irony negated his own pretensions and allowed some sterner kind of truth to shine through. In his consequent battle with the connoisseurs, he summed it up in a grumpy aside to posterity: '*They* think I hate Raphael and Titian! Let them!'

Campbell's interest in the figurative art of the past and in ideas that could loosely be identified with classicism was not unique at the time. In architecture an interest in 'classicism' was one of the features that superficially unified the post-modernists. In Italy, there was a whole movement of artists like Pistoletto exploring the same kind of imagery in painting and among them some, like Salvo for instance, were taking inspiration from de Chirico's work from the Fascist period. In England, there were artists like Christopher le Brun. In France painters like Garouste were working in a similar vein and sculptors like the Poiriers were making installations of a deconstructed classicism. These were all artists whose work was topical in the early eighties. Indeed, the main exhibition at the Venice Biennale in 1984, *Arte allo Specchio*, was devoted to this kind of classical revivalism and an attempt to focus a similar theme was made in Edinburgh three years later in the exhibition *Edinburgh International*.

Already in the sixties, however, Moffat and Bellany had pioneered a reassessment of the German painters of the inter-war years, especially Max Beckman and Otto Dix. This interest was made more widely topical by the *Neue-Sachlichkeit* exhibition devoted to German art of this period at the Hayward Gallery in London in 1978 It was, however, among contemporary German artists that the closest parallels could be found to the way in which in his painting Campbell at the same time both accepted and dislocated the figurative tradition. In fact the Germans, with their large-scale, dramatic and iconoclastic

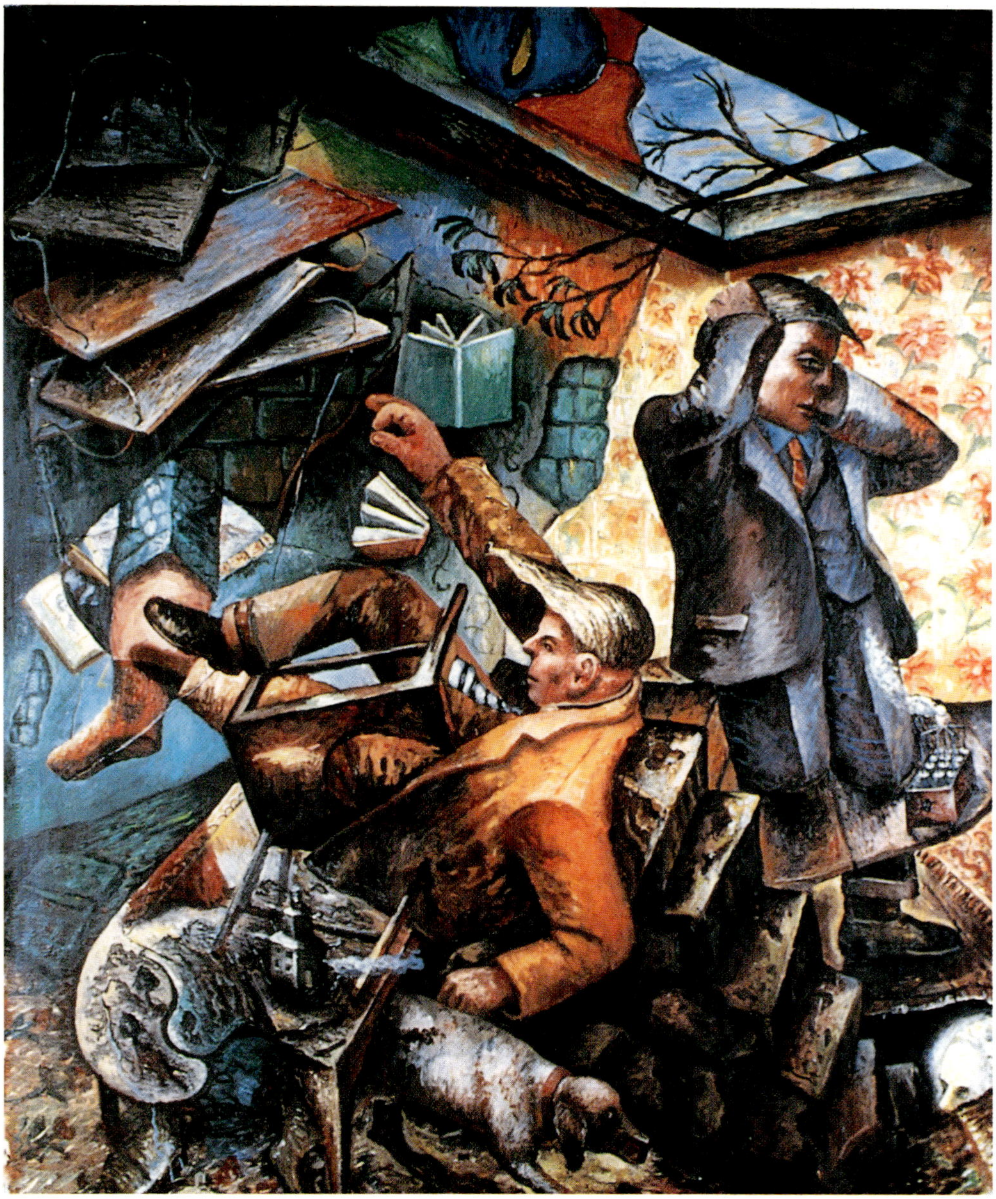

(PLATE 15) *T'was Once an Architect's Office in Wee Nook*, oil on canvas, 292.1 × 243.8 cm, 1984

painting with its strong emotional appeal, were and have remained a primary inspiration for his generation. Baselitz, for instance, sought literally to overturn the expectations which shape a spectator's response, while in the work of younger painters like Immendorf, Peter Chevalier and Hermann Albat, it is possible to see a similar tendency to force the conventions of figurative art, sometimes with distinctly neo-classical overtones, into new expressive channels.

Campbell was distinguished from most of his contemporaries, however, by the passion that drove his painting and its location in a moral context, but this also

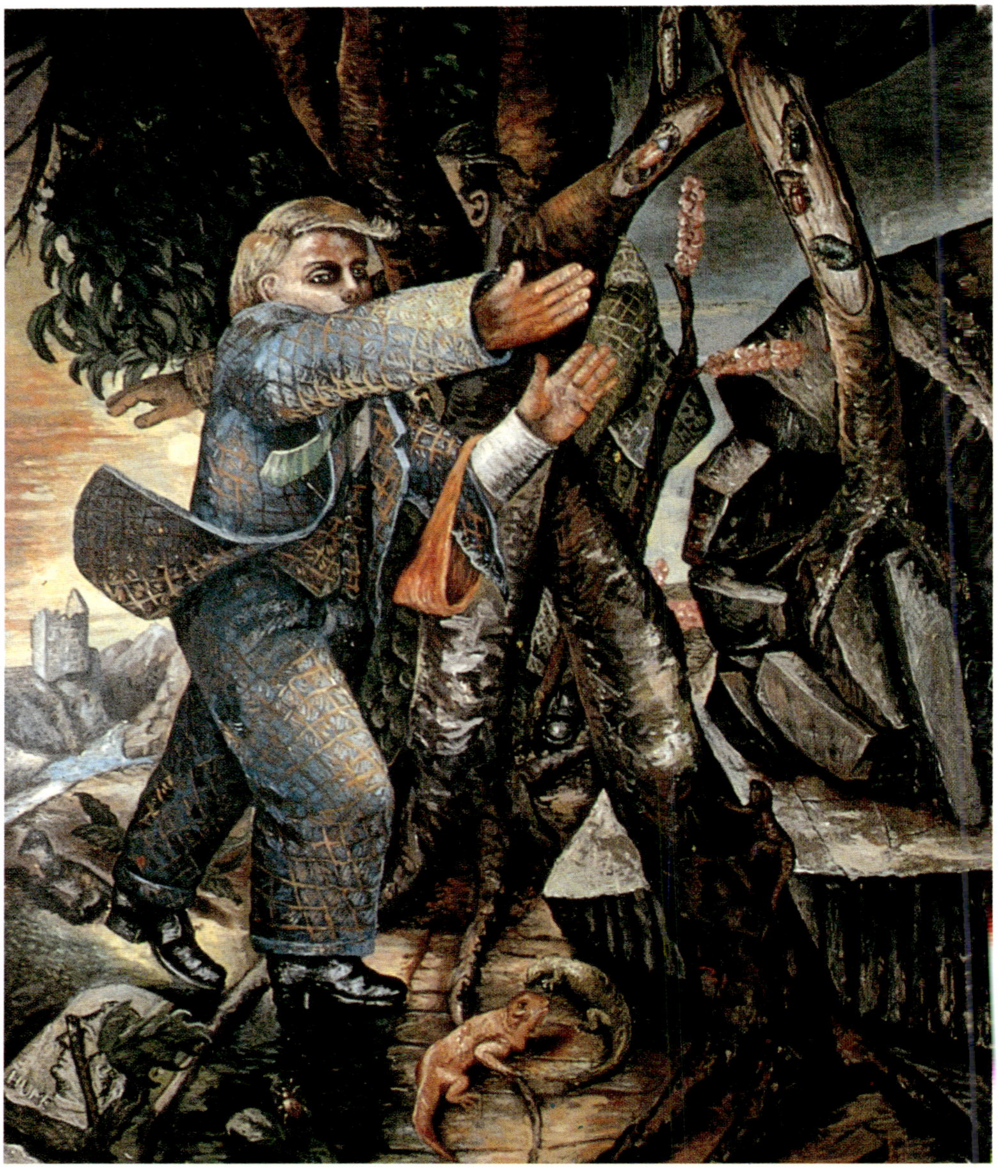

(PLATE 16) *Two Humeans Preaching Causality to Nature*, oil on canvas, 292.1 × 238.8 cm, 1984

meant that because his art was so rooted in his own experience, for the time being at least he needed to keep the distance secured by irony and humour. Through these, there is a constantly renewed awareness of the remoteness of his Arcadia, of the tragic gap between reality as it is lived and the classical ideal. Curiously though he is such a different artist in every other way, this is something that he has in common with Ian Hamilton Finlay, a champion of neo-classicism.

Campbell himself brought this debate back to Scotland with his exhibitions in London and Edinburgh in the winter of 1984. *Two Humeans Preaching Causality to Nature (Pl.16)* was one of the most memorable paintings that he showed then.

As we have seen, it picks up on the deeper theme of nature's indifference to man's insecurity in Titian's *Diana and Actaeon*. It also specifically locates the debate of painting in the wider context of philosophical thought. It is a dramatic and forceful composition, fitting its theme, but its power is deliberately softened by humour. In the picture, one figure dominates, a man in a magnificent, blue-checked tweed suit declaims, or perhaps defends himself with both hands raised. The second figure, also tweeded, is half concealed behind two trees. The two trees and the two figures interlock in a powerful knot of intersecting form and space. Lower left, a bust of Hume is half hidden by a leaf of nature, though, and throughout, it is nature that seems to have the upper hand.

In the background, a Scottish landscape with a ruined tower against the sunset invokes the appeal of the romantic view of nature, while on the right, the roots of a tree grapple with and split the stones of what might once have been a classical temple. Hume reappears in *Two Naturalist Philosophers Debating in a Garden*. Each philosopher is represented by a book with his portrait on the cover. The books are in conflict rather as the paintings are in Hogarth's *Battle of the Pictures*. Van Helsing peers suspiciously out of the undergrowth, but it is the luxuriant and disorderly vegetation that surrounds them, nature, which again has the upper hand.

Causality is the basis of Hume's account of the rational order of the universe. Hume himself, however, was also notable for his awareness of the limits of this rational explanation of the world, but here and elsewhere in Campbell's work, as his marble bust implies, he seems to stand for the classical ideal of an ordered universe, much as Newton represented rationalism for Blake. Campbell's Hume is seen in opposition to the irrationality of the actual, of nature's ability to disregard and overwhelm the fragile forms of order that man constructs for himself and which are represented metaphorically in art. The extension of this opposition into the language of art is hinted at in the way that romantic and classic are given opposite corners and they appear in this same opposition elsewhere in his work.

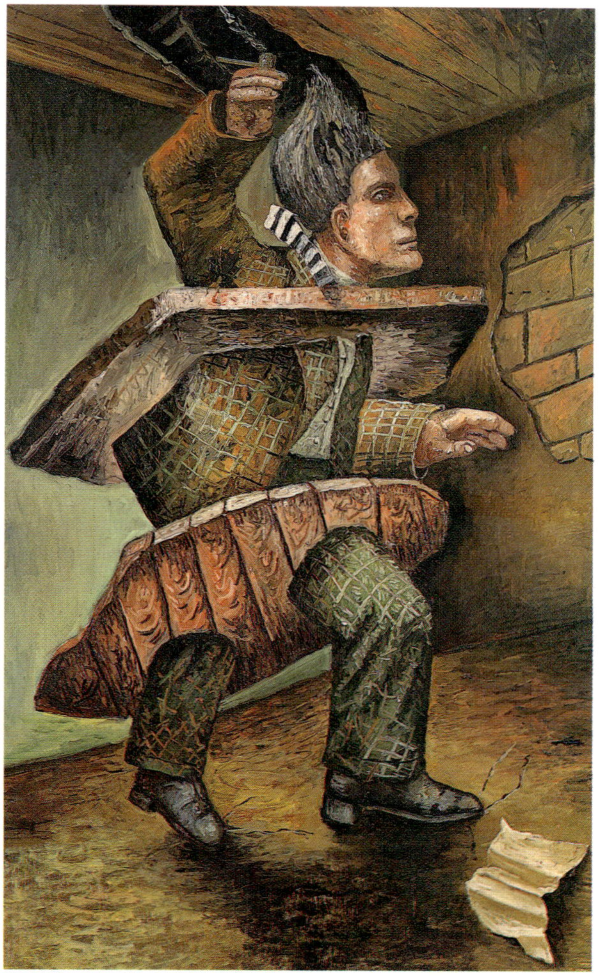

(PLATE 17) *Through the Ceiling, Through the Floor*, oil on canvas, 281.9 × 165.1 cm, 1984

Hume appears quite frequently as one of the characters in Campbell's painting and although at the time he disclaimed all knowledge of his work,[19] his presence is not a simple piece of facetiousness. Campbell has always been very serious about painting, but it is a tempered seriousness, tempered by his sense of the fragility of order, the difficulty of conveying feeling and the pretentiousness that inevitably goes with the adoption of any of the available forms of the pictorial illusion of certainty. As Stuart Morgan wrote in 1984:

> The spirit (of his art) is one of serious burlesque, treating the history of art synchronically by condensing it into a single, complex ideal which exceeds his power to attain. Ineptitude is the cutting edge of his art; protected by a kind of romantic irony which permits him to distance his own feelings from the act of painting and point to the comic pretensions of his own seriousness.[20]

Hume therefore does represent a character in an intellectual drama, but this intellectual drama is visually realised and not given a simple resolution. On the contrary these pictures seem to be informed more and more by a very personal sense of anarchy. As a result they often have such an emotional charge that one sometimes feels that Campbell's own life and personality are only screened from us by the thinnest of veils.

Campbell could never become a literary painter therefore, even though the references in his paintings at times assume a literary character. As we have seen, in 1984 in paintings like *T'was Once an Architect's Office in Wee Nook*, the relatively simple space of his earlier work begins to become more complex, even confused as the artist's exploration of these ideas progresses and his sense of the underlying confusion of things asserts itself. In *Through the Ceiling, Through the Floor* of the same date *(Pl.17)*, this aggressive, anarchic Cubism has actually taken one of the young men prisoner. He has been captured by and is breaking free from chunks of floor and ceiling, visibly reminiscent of those passages of fictive surface in the Synthetic Cubism of Picasso and Braque. The struggle is internal first of all, therefore. It is man against art and in another memorable painting of the same year, *Building Accusing its Architect of Bad Design (Pl.18)*, the work of art is actually answering back. The building is an extraordinary, Albert Memorial compound of the history of art. The unreliability of any such structure is represented by the way that the architect is perched precariously on one of its gargoyles, while his companion seems to take a dive out of the tree that has been supporting him.

In paintings like *Two Naturalist Philosophers Debating in a Garden*, or *Young Camper Discovering a Grotto in the Ground (Pl.19)*, this spatial precariousness has become a highly emotive, real spatial confusion. Along with this new freedom, during 1983-4, his painting became much richer in texture and colour. In *Napoleonic Garden (Pl.20)*, of 1983, for instance, the foreground is filled with brilliant, richly painted vegetables and flowers.

Although there are explicit references to Cubism in these pictures and in mood they are sometimes surreal, the kind of intercutting and displacement that they use is more like Chagall's poetic exploitation of the formal liberation of Cubism. It is also very much about the mechanics and dynamics of picture-making as an expressive vehicle in a way that is distinct from the concerns of the Surrealists, and the artist's own feelings are never far beneath the surface. In *The Fern's Revenge* and the related compositions, the drawing *(Pl.21)* and the painting *The Fern's Revenge–Pool* of 1984, there is a figure very like one of the floating inhabitants of Chagall's dream world, but Campbell does not allow himself to be seduced as Chagall was by the new spatial liberation of Cubism. It would be too far from the real nature of

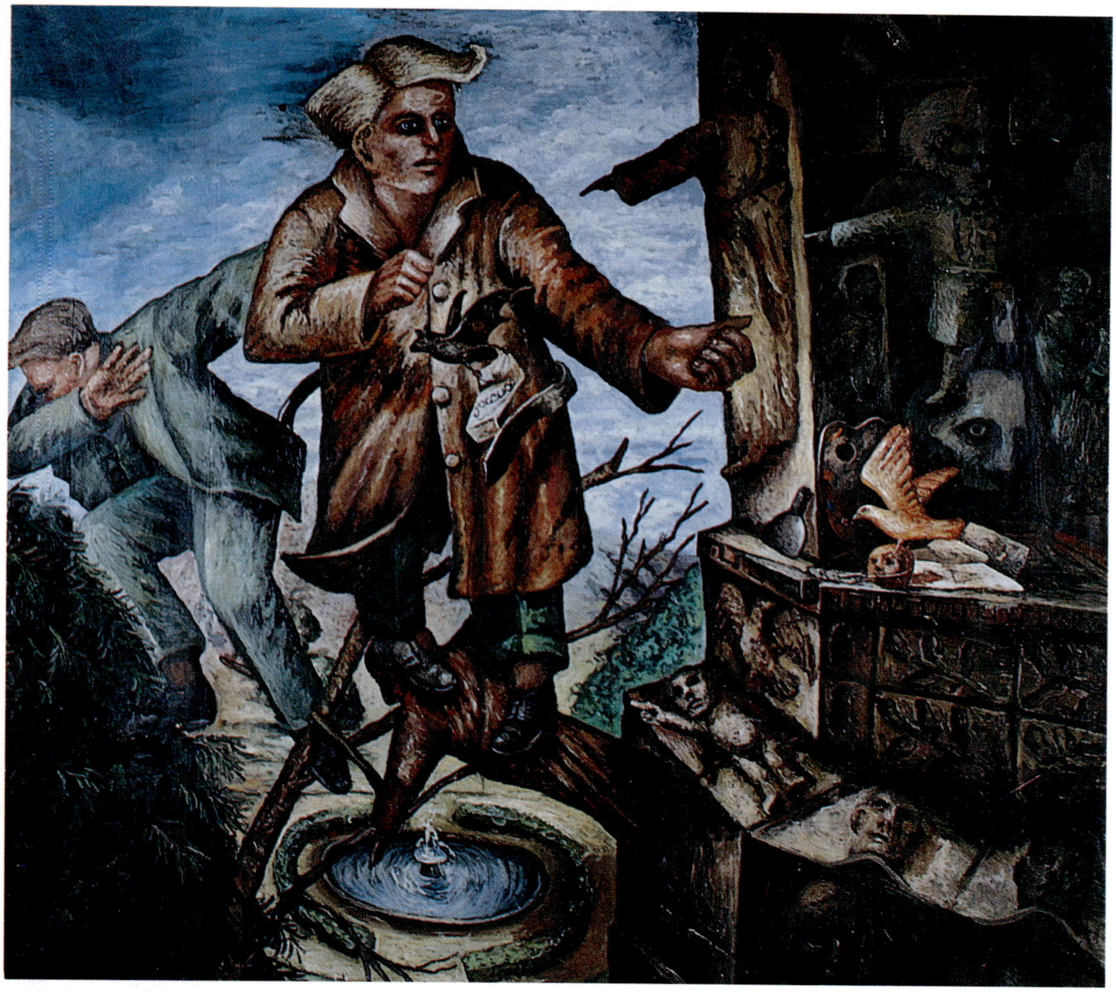

(PLATE 18) *Building Accusing its Architect of Bad Design*, oil on canvas, 289.6 × 289.6 cm, 1984
(The Laing Art Gallery, Newcastle upon Tyne)

things. The latter image contradicts the very freedom it invokes as the young man crashes to earth on his head, like *Hunt Falling* in the artist's degree show. It is the same image of desire, ambition, or inspiration and their inevitable, painful collision with reality. The young man's fate is like that of Icarus. The same figure reappeared in a drawing that Campbell did for the cover of *Artscribe (Pl.22)*, in 1984. There he is a tweedy hiker. He is still airborne and his tent is visible below him. His hair is standing on end and this led one commentator to suggest poetically that, like Icarus, he has flown too close to the sun and his hair has caught fire, but according to the artist, it is just the result of the exhilaration of being airborne.[21] Another such flying figure appeared on the cover of Barry Yourgrau's book, *A Man Jumped out of an Airplane*.

Discussing this question of the new freedoms created by Cubism, in a thoughtful essay on Juan Gris, Andrew Graham-Dixon wrote about the artist's consciousness of the limits of the possibilities still open to painting:

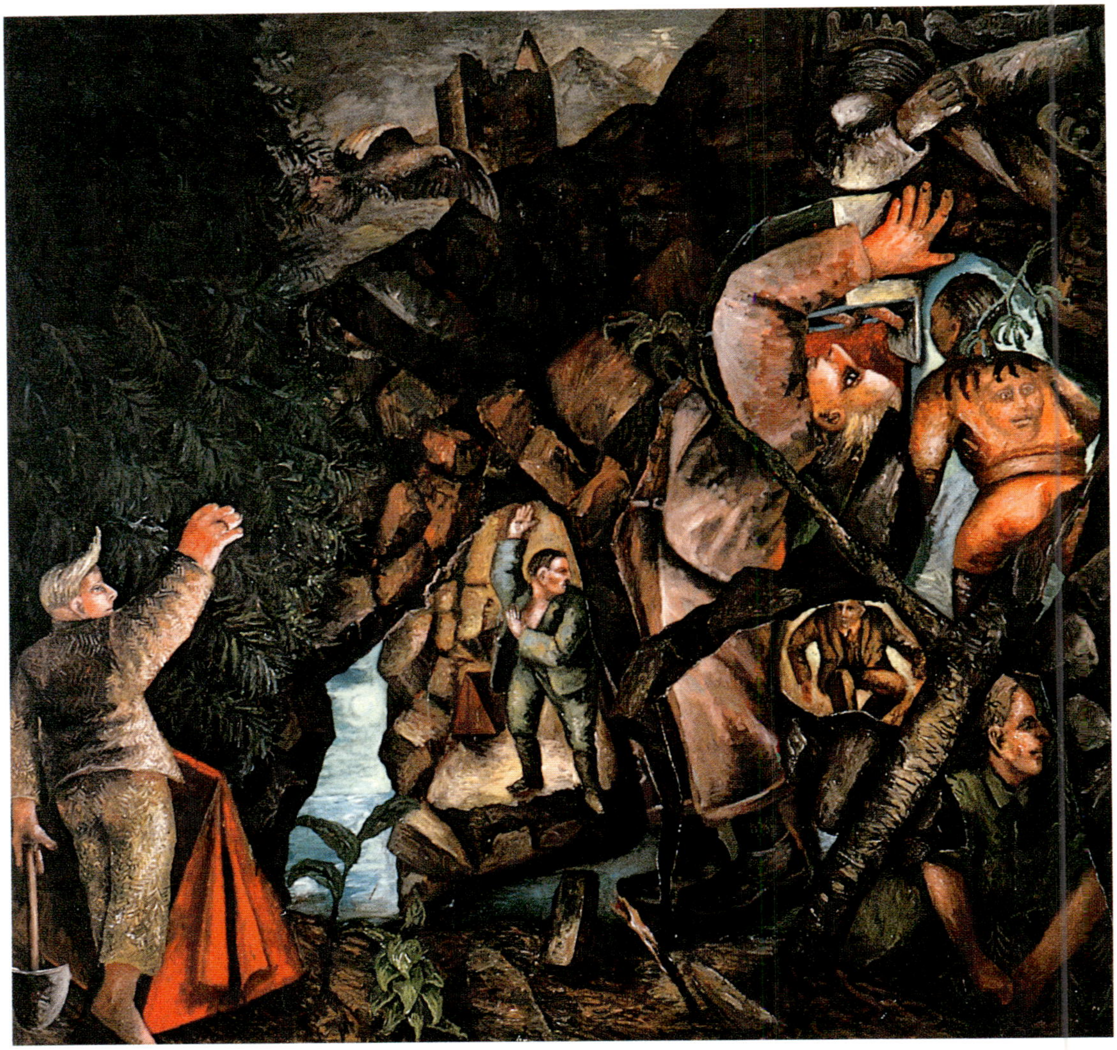

(PLATE 19) *Young Camper Discovering a Grotto in the Ground*, oil on canvas, 284.5 × 287.0 cm, 1984

> The painting dramatises the frustration of all art, the nature of every picture as a Tantalus: the further you investigate its world, the more you are reminded that its promises of pleasure are feigned.[22]

Campbell is always conscious of this and of how here art is only imitating life, but his characters are not and so, as they innocently explore the apparent freedom of the world they inhabit, they run up against its limits, and, unconsciously, burlesque the limitations of the painter's art and so of life itself.

In 1984–5 on a wave of success, Campbell showed in London, Edinburgh and Munich, again with Barbara Toll in New York and in a number of other American cities. Apparently inspired by the freedom of Cubist space, his pictures began to get very crowded, so much so that for his Edinburgh show, he says that he had to paint several pictures with a landscape spaciousness especially to give him room to breathe. These extra pictures all had something of Caspar David Friedrich about them. One, now destroyed, showed a hiker looking out from a mountain top over a wide panorama of clouds and mountains, the fingers of his hand making the outline of a face against the sky. *The Gargoylic Hiker* shows a hiker leaning dizzily out from a rocky outcrop into a wide space of sky and mountain. In *In the Mist Van Helsing Gesturing as Hume (Pl.23)*, a mountaineer half hidden in the mist against a background of dimly visible pines cuts the profile of a human (Hume-like?) face against the sky.

One of the most crowded pictures in the Edinburgh show was *Young Camper Discovering a Grotto in the Ground*. It has seven figures in different scales, each with his own 'grotto' of space. These overlap each other in a strange, illogical mosaic, while in the background the ruined tower of the romantic Scottish landscape proposes a quite different kind of mental and pictorial order. The picture is typical of Campbell's way of working as, in fact, each of these 'grottoes' is a view through to an earlier stage of the painting. *Men who Climb through Attics* of 1985 with the same kind of palimpsest shows the same relationship between the spatial structure of the final painting and the temporal process of its making, a conjunction which the title successfully extends into the additional dimension of narrative. The picture is its own story, a record of the drama in the studio.

Campbell often talks about how his painting, as the record of a process, is the product of his mistakes layered in the painting in this quasi-archaeological way. This is how he described his working process in 1984:

> The painting starts off as one thing and if that doesn't work, I try something else until a memory of all these things is in it, but none of them is particularly true except the one I have chosen to title the work. The picture is a summing up of all the mistakes. It is all that is left.[23]

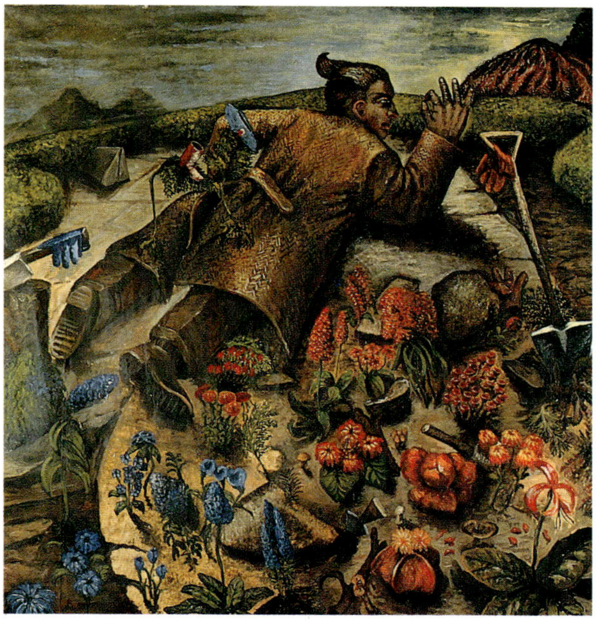

(PLATE 20) *Napoleonic Garden*, oil on canvas, 289.6 × 289.6 cm, 1983

In his pictures painted at this time, the blundering young men are not only painted by him, it is their misfortune to act out his mistakes.

He used very similar words to describe his working process again in 1993. For him, it seems, 'meaning' is both the last stage and the sum of all the stages of a picture and so it is elusive.[24] Part of it is always hidden by this confusion of layers. Meaning slips away. Like Macbeth's dagger, as you move to grasp it, it constantly recedes. But on the other hand, like Derrida's use of language, this elusiveness *is* the meaning. To keep it alive, the painter has to go on inventing and few contemporary painters have been so consistently inventive.

Nevertheless, in spite of this he was anxious not to fall into repetition and mannerism. By 1985, however, not only a

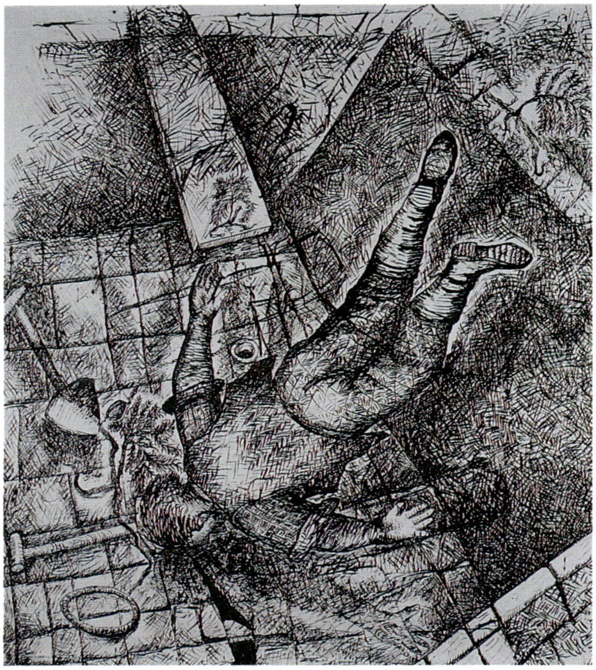

(PLATE 21) *The Fern's Revenge – Pool*, india ink on paper, 271.8 × 248.9 cm, 1984

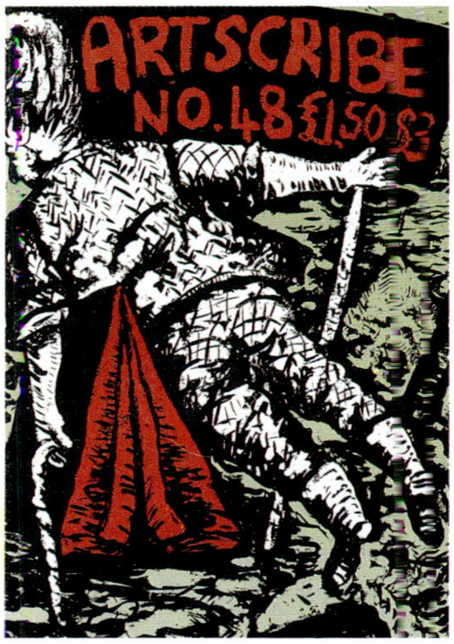

(PLATE 22) Cover of *Artscribe*, 1984

set of characters – the Lost Hiker, Van Helsing, Bertie Wooster and his friends, etc. – had become established, but there was a whole variety of motifs and structures that went with them. These were the crazy architecture of Wee Nook cottage, the piece of plaster from the wall, the animate fern, the grotto and much else. *The Inventor's Garden* of 1984 was a kind of compendium of some of these, like the extraordinary storeroom in *Citizen Kane*.

During the following year, Campbell worked to enlarge this vocabulary. He introduced new characters like Lytton Strachey in *The Dangerous Early and Late Life of Lytton Strachey*, for instance, or James Mason in *The Young James Mason as Egon Samer, the Metamorphosist*. He used devices like the pictures within a picture, for instance, in *In a Landscape a Painting is a Radio, a Sculpture, a Battery* or in *The Re-Illustrated Highland Diaries of Queen Victoria (Pl.24)*. This was a form that looked back to the multiple canvas compositions of the *Hunt* series and forwards to the Third Eye exhibition of 1990, *On Form and Fiction*. In conversation though, he later described the difficulty that he faced at the time, how as the elements that he worked with fitted together more and more smoothly, their world became enclosed. It became more difficult to introduce anything new. Whatever it was, it became immediately conspicuous. It was almost as though he himself was pushed out as his painting assumed a life of its own. On one occasion as early as 1984, looking at his work hung in a show in Chicago, he suddenly felt that he seemed to have used the same horizon in all the pictures.

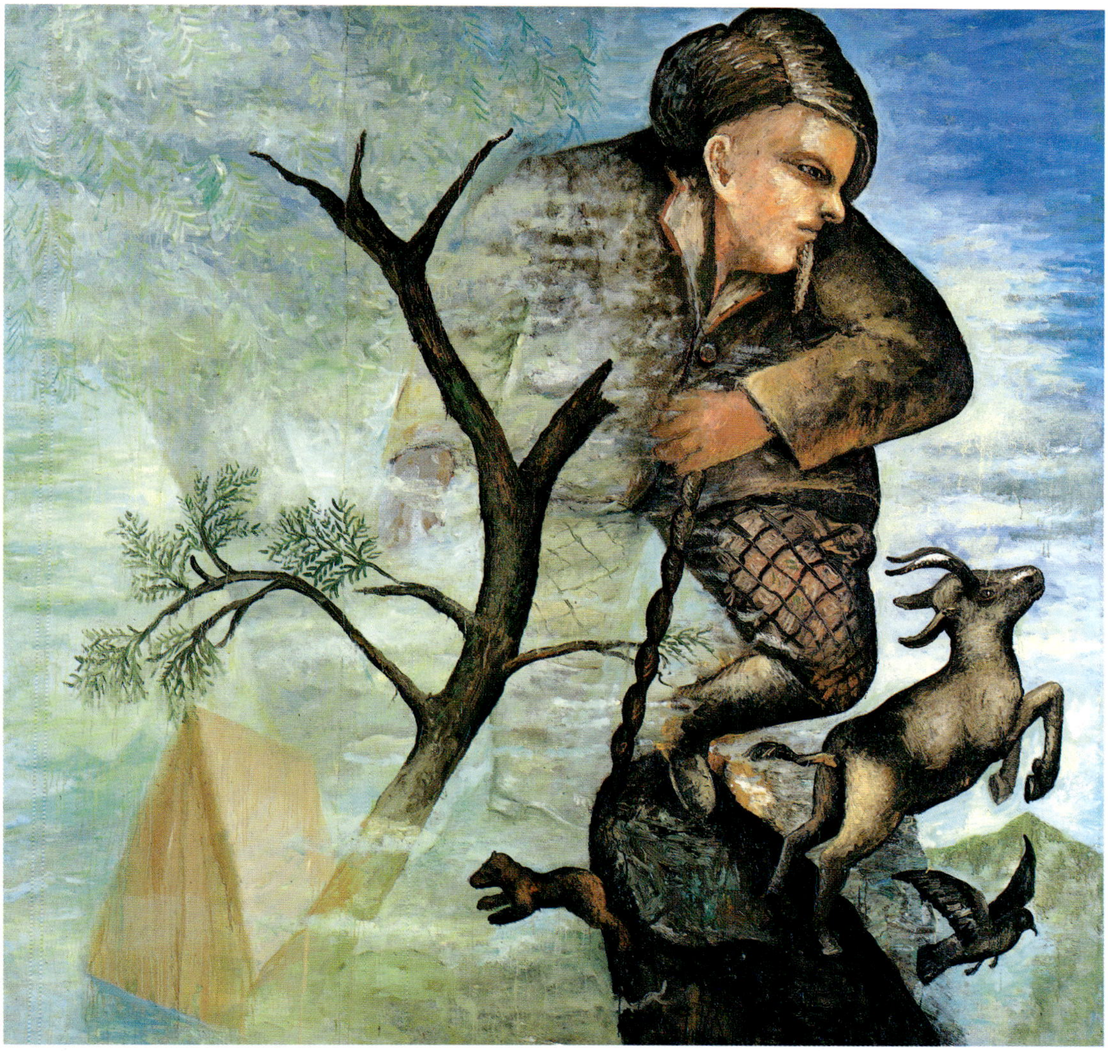

(PLATE 23) *In the Mist Van Helsing Gesturing as Hume*, oil on canvas, 264.2 × 274.3 cm, 1984

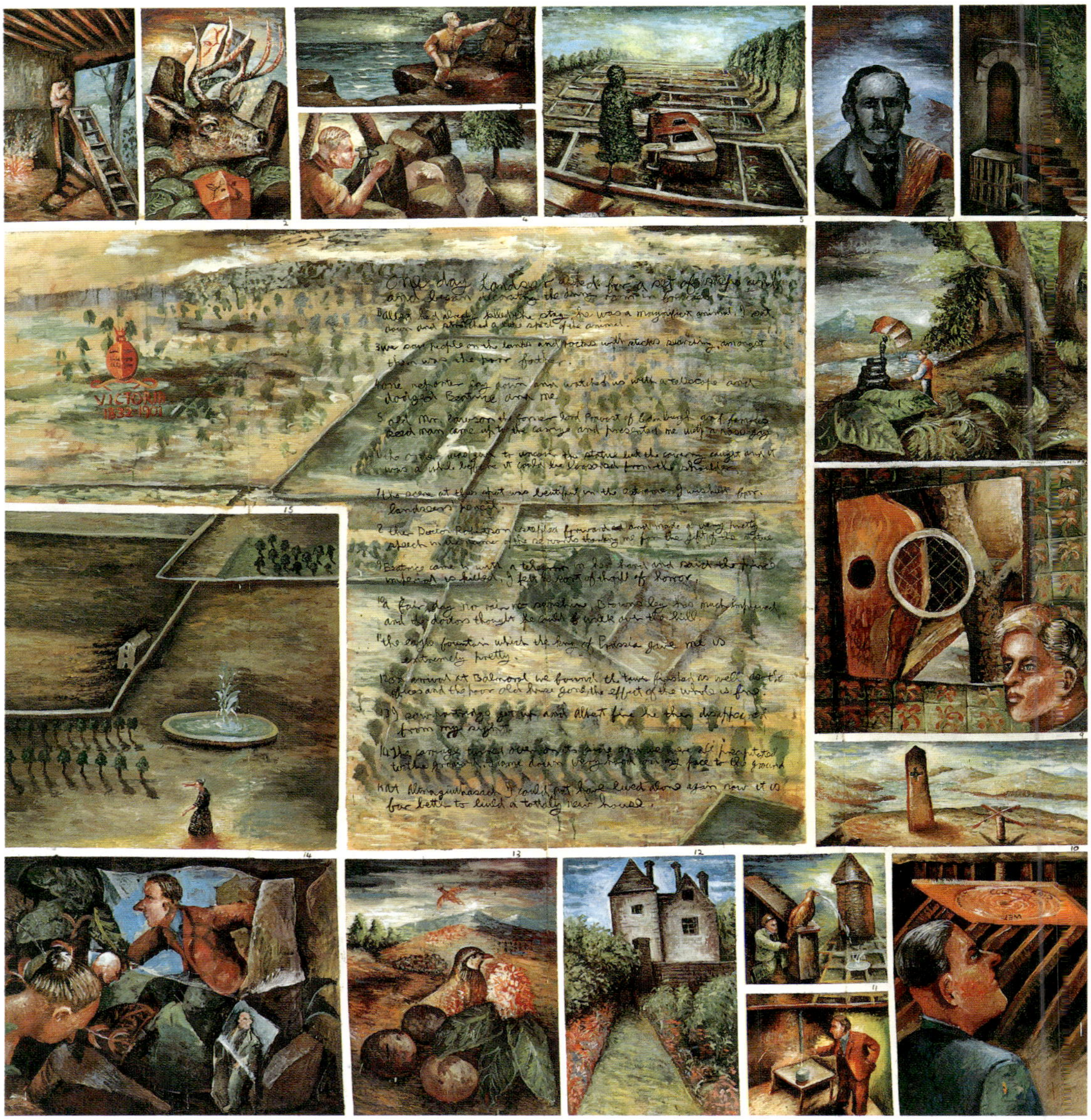

(PLATE 24) *The Re-Illustrated Highland Diaries of Queen Victoria*, gouache on paper, 255.3 × 121.9 cm, 1985

It is perhaps as a result of this kind of anxiety that it is possible to detect a greater self-consciousness in his painting from around 1986, which was also the year that he and his wife decided to return to Scotland. The account he gave in 1987 of his motives for moving reflect this anxiety:

> When I was in New York I felt I could trap myself if I stayed there . . . I wanted to give myself more space coming back to Scotland . . . In New York it was all happening so fast, driven so fast, shows so fast. You could get yourself in an awful mess.[25]

When he does continue with earlier themes at this time, as in *Study for a Portrait of an Agoraphobic Portraying a Claustrophobic (Pl.25)*, the artist's disquiet is tangible. The mood is wilder, more violent and surreal, the handling richer, more agitated and more expressive. In this picture, for instance, the stag attacks and overwhelms the hunter. In *Unlucky at Cards, No Hearts for Hunting (Pl.26)*, Van Helsing, dressed as a hunter or explorer, seems to find himself in similar difficulties with one foot trapped in the stocks in a hostile environment. *A Man with a Floured Head Impersonating a Burning Dovecot (Pl.27)* is equally at a loss in a hostile and incomprehensible world.

It is not surprising that the tremendous excitement about the idea *of* painting that had given his early work such expressive energy and that is still apparent in pictures like these should have been difficult to sustain. Certainly in 1986, there are signs that it is being supplemented by a more self-conscious concern with the ideas *in* painting. In that year, for instance, he created a series of works that illustrated an imaginary correspondence between P. G. Wodehouse and Michel Foucault, *A Life in Letters*. There was also a very large, related painting, *Bonjour M. Foucault*, which was commissioned as an outdoor hoarding for the Tate Gallery, Liverpool, in 1986 *(Pl.28)*.[26]

One does not need to read Foucault very deeply to see the point of contact with Campbell. There was in Foucault an intellectual proposition that matched the artist's own intuitive sense of life's confusion that had been up till now the underlying subject of his paintings. Foucault's task has been to make us aware of the baggage that goes with our institutions and ideas. It serves dark purposes that have shaped our lives, but of which we are usually wholly ignorant. He is explicitly concerned with the relationship between knowledge and morality. Campbell has approached the great tradition in painting in a similar spirit. He has asked how it can be freed from the crippling burdens of fixed and inherited meaning and given new moral validity without actually losing all sight of the possibility of meaning itself, realising, at the same time, that it can only be maintained by constantly extemporising it from the experience of life as the artist lives it.

Wodehouse's Arcady was fragile and Wodehouse's own English certainty partook of the compromised personality of Campbell's Hunt. Foucault, in the inscription on *Idealised Portrait of the Wig'd Foucault (Pl.29)*, writes to Wodehouse, apparently commenting on just this fragility:

> Take a man who imagines himself as glass and if he moves, breaks. Would this in your eyes represent a condition of the malady anglais?

The reference is to Foucault's *Madness and Civilisation* and to an example he gives to illustrate the logic of madness. It is the case of a man who thought he was made of glass. Foucault's argument was that anyone can think they are made of glass. They are only mad if they also believe that in consequence, they are

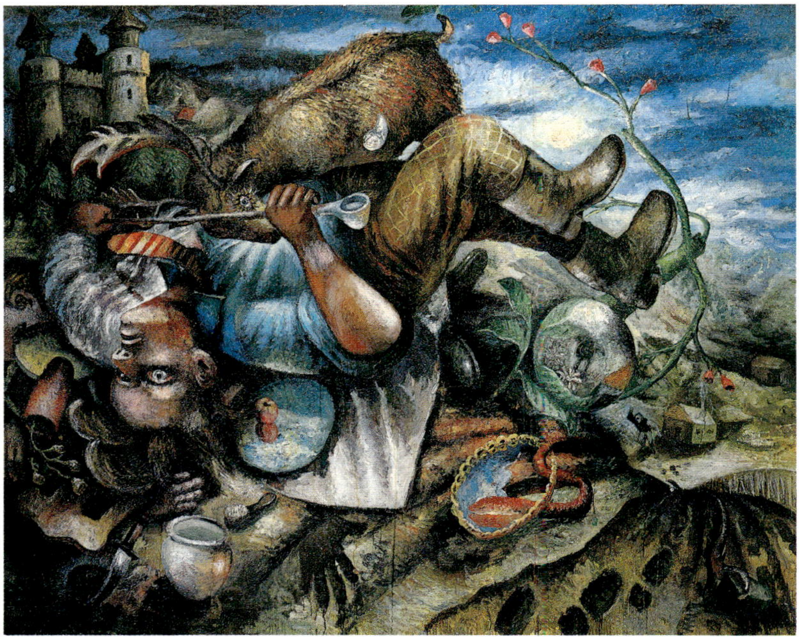

(PLATE 25) *Study for a Portrait of an Agoraphobic Portraying a Claustrophobic*, oil on canvas, 203.2 × 246.4cm, 1986

breakable.[27] The latter belief would follow logically from the former, nevertheless. If you do believe you are made of glass, it is logical also to believe that you are breakable, but Campbell's own belief that art depends on vulnerability could not be better epitomised than by this image of a man of glass.

A glass figure appears in *Bonjour M. Foucault* and in several of the other pictures. In the large picture, for instance, Foucault's own implicit definition of normal reality is confounded as he shakes this glass man's hand and he shatters. Was this the meeting of Foucault and Wodehouse or was the man of glass the artist himself?

The title of this picture is a homage to Courbet's *Bonjour M. Courbet*, the image of the artist as traveller that Campbell had invoked in his earlier *Self-Portrait* installation, though the size of this outdoor painting is closer to Courbet's massive self-portrait, *L'Atelier du Peintre*. Courbet's picture of himself in *Bonjour M. Courbet* personifies the heroic detachment of the artist. Here in Campbell's painting though, detachment seems to imply alienation and so perhaps is not enough. In the background is a Lazar house. It is built like a prison and either lepers or criminals would be appropriate to illustrate Foucault's *Madness and Civilisation*. Foucault himself is wandering in a desolate landscape. At his feet, a blindfolded cricketer falls flat on his face and as he falls, he is pulling down a curtain. In the theatre it would be the key to illusion. Perhaps this implies painting can neither be merely a game, nor can it be a window into some alternative reality. Behind the cricketer, a boxing kangaroo sits up like one of Goya's pedagogic donkeys, symbols of the inanity of learning without wisdom. To the left, belief seems symbolised by a passion-flower. It is on a rather spindly plant stand, bleeding into a collection of chalices. If this is belief, perhaps it is matched by superstition in a collection of turnip lanterns placed on the right, though they are more substantial.

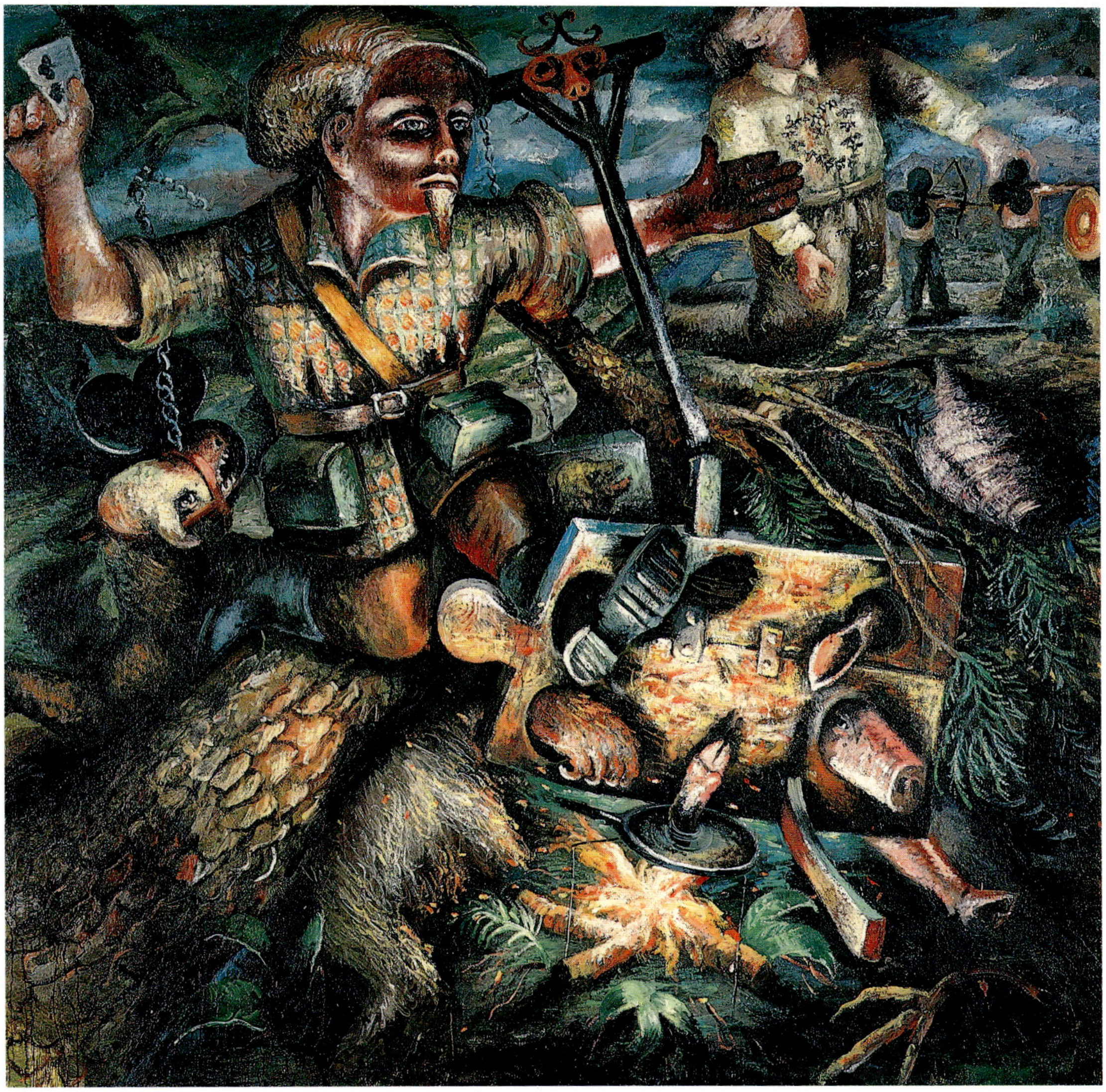

(PLATE 26) *Unlucky at Cards, No Hearts for Hunting*, oil on canvas, 209.5 × 213.4 cm, 1986

In *Idealised Portrait of the Wig'd Foucault*, it is Foucault himself who seems to be made of glass. 'Winged' as much as 'wigged', he is taking off with glass arms and glass hair.[28] In *Recognition by Mirrors (Pl.30)*, the glass figure is identified as a phantom, by its nature likely to be transparent. A hiker threatens its glassy fragility with a rock. Dracula, of course, is a phantom and he is recognised by the absence of his reflection in a glass, which would no doubt also be the case were he, too, made of glass. The caption reads:

> I see no future for this phantom. He has become the slave of a habit. Wodehouse.

Dracula is certainly a phantom who is slave to a habit, but then so are we all in the structures within which we think and see as Foucault and Campbell make us realise. As the 'meaning' extends, it is an elegant

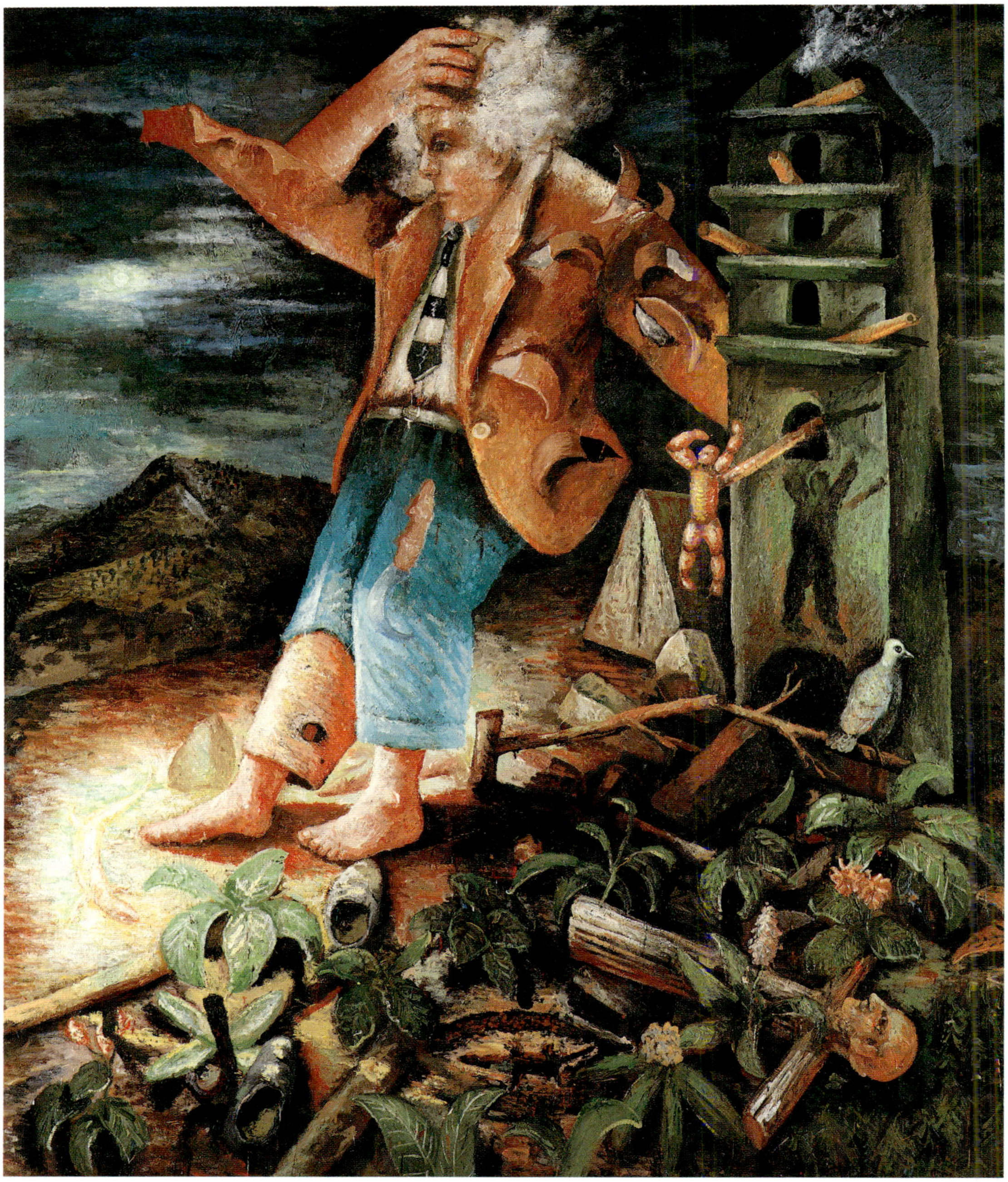

(PLATE 27) *A Man with a Floured Head Impersonating a Burning Dovecot*, oil on canvas, 279.4 × 231.2 cm, 1985

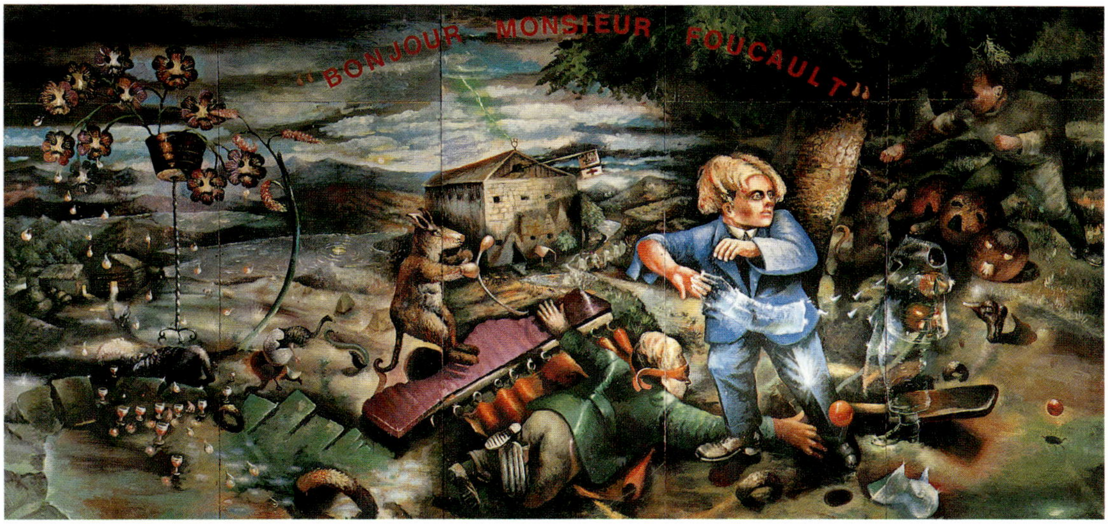

(PLATE 28) *Bonjour M. Foucault*, oil on plywood, 304.8 × 609.6 cm, 1986

and witty illustration of the illusion of transparency and the fragility of meaning, worthy of Foucault himself. (The Wodehouse quotations come from *Performing Flea: a Self-Portrait in Letters*, 1934.)

A parallel theme of the insecurity of knowledge that harked back, via the explorer, to the misfortunes of the Lost Hiker is a painting of a polar bear, sitting on a ship wrecked among the Arctic ice, like Caspar David Friedrich's *Arctic Shipwreck*. The picture is one of this Wodehouse-Foucault series and above the bear, the shape of the ship's mast, coated in ice, suggests the 'Oxford to Salisbury' signpost. The ship has lost its way and that can be a serious matter. The caption reads simply:

Dear Wodehouse,
Vanished,
Michel.

It was Franklin who vanished on his ill-fated expedition to find the North-West Passage in 1845. Inquiry, like that of Franklin or of Foucault, can lead, not to certainty, but to its opposite. This theme of the disruptive effect of knowledge on the artist's sense of security and so by extension on the emotional stability of us all continues in a series of pictures with Darwin as their hero, also painted in 1986–7. A diptych called simply *Darwin* consists of two small portraits. One is of a priest folding his hands in prayer in the mass, the other is an Archimboldo-style face made of vegetables and robustly painted. These two represent the poles of the spiritual and merely physical between which Darwin stretched to breaking point the Victorian psyche and the traditional structures of belief. That this was indeed a breaking point is vividly illustrated by a metaphor of splitting in two pictures, also derived from the story of Darwin. *The Line Belonging to Wallace (Pl.31)* and *Portrait of an Island Splitting* both refer to the discovery by A. F. Wallace of a geographical line in the islands of the Indonesian Archipelago which split the evolutionary history of the species that inhabited them into two quite separate groups. It was a discovery which confirmed Darwin's thesis. In *The Line Belonging to Wallace* the idea is very simply expressed. Two marginally different versions of the same image of our

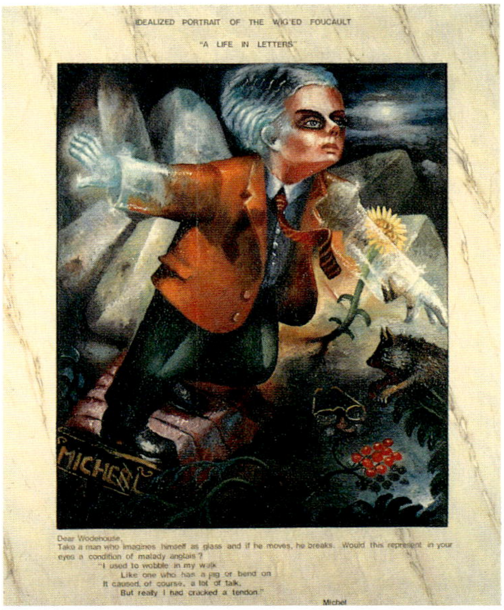

(PLATE 29) *A Life in Letters: Idealised Portrait of the Wig'd Foucault*, oil on canvas, 183 × 150 cm, 1986

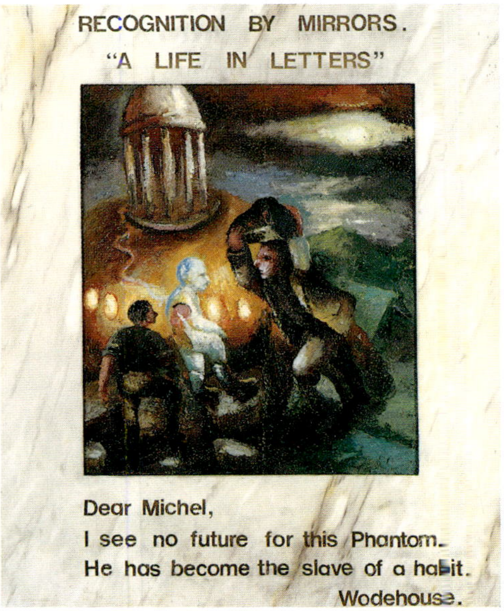

(PLATE 30) *A Life in Letters: Recognition by Mirrors*, oil on canvas, 66.7 × 54.6 cm, 1986

cousins the apes are divided symmetrically by a vertical line.

Painting on a Darwinian Theme (Pl.32) shows the inquirer, Van Helsing, hanging desperately on to the leg of a hiker-mountaineer. He is in turn held by the hair by an ape-man. Their rope is falling into an abyss beneath them and they are only prevented from falling by the ape-man. The gulf beneath them is a cliff over the sea, but it also reveals a section of the geological strata and some skulls on a ledge that suggest the fossils of Darwin's scientific inquiry. Darwin's idea of 'descent' is ironically inverted and suddenly becomes a descent into imminent disaster. A little painting of a man awkwardly poised on the edge of a well, between fire and water called *Man in a Dilemma*, presents a similar situation.

The chain of ideas that links Darwin and Foucault was perhaps most succinctly expressed in the earlier picture, *Wee Nook Cottage*. It illustrates the dangerous and disruptive power of thought, its ability to overthrow our beliefs, to take us to the edge of abysses that we never knew were there and like Frankenstein, even to create monsters. It was Foucault's insight, following in a tradition that derived from Hume and Reid, to recognise that much of what we accept as 'knowledge' is not the bottom line. He showed that what we take for the building blocks of some of our basic assumptions, when examined, present a surface no more solid than that of Wodehouse's English Arcadia. After Foucault, 'knowledge' can no longer be seen as definite and unitary as we assume, but is itself a set of signs which, as Foucault teaches us to read them, reveal the structures of muddled infamy by which power is articulated in our society. They are like the Nazi uniform that seduced Hunt.

This is the intellectual climate of doubt that drives the emotion in Campbell's paintings. How can the artist *describe* anything, if all the means of description and style, the very bones of art itself are already the indentured servants of the ideas and structures of power in this way? This is the programme that thinkers like Foucault set the artists of the late twen-

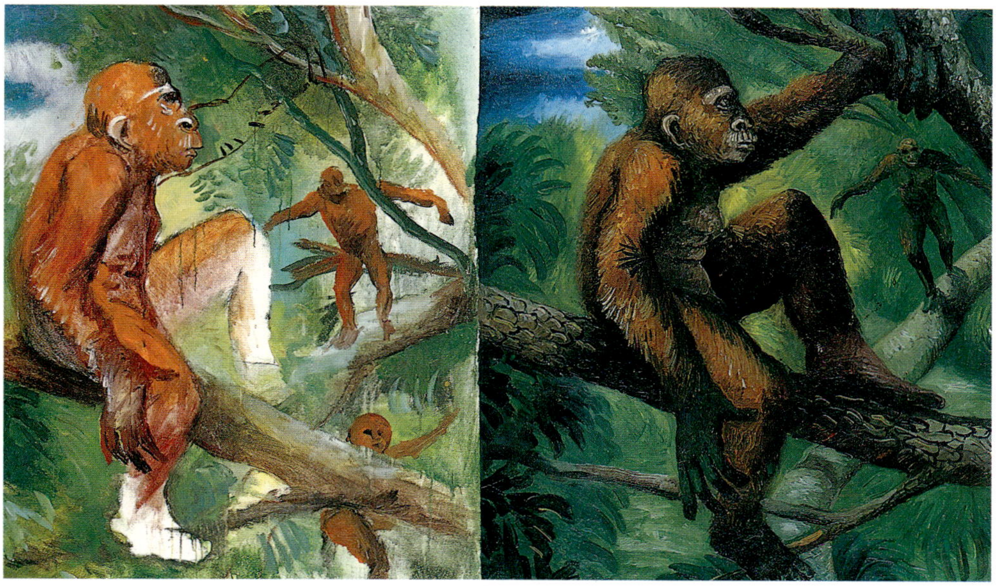

(PLATE 31) *The Line Belonging to Wallace*, oil on canvas, 134.6 × 216 cm, 1987

tieth century. The 'reality' that they had to describe has shifted from the tangible external world and the means by which we know it, to the ramshackle vehicles of thought in which that knowledge is conveyed. These, we must now recognise, far from being a kind of transparent transmitter, have a dynamic of their own which can and has been constantly exploited, but upon which nevertheless all our moral judgments depend. Writing about Campbell, Andrew Wilson quotes Foucault on the correlation between style in art and knowledge as sign:

> There is no such thing as 'pure vision' and it is shot through – and independently of scientific knowledge (conaissance) . . . with the positivity of a knowledge (savoir).[29]

The importance of this correlation between two kinds of fake, the structures of knowledge and the structures of style in painting, is a measure of the enterprise of modern art. All art partakes of style. In so far as it does, must all art therefore be as suspect as Campbell's Hunt, who was seduced by style?

Though this is not the place to do it, one could make a case for the importance of the role of art in preparing the way for Foucault's radical critique of our assumptions. It is, for instance, with Cézanne that one can first see an artist attempting to find a form for the relativism that is central to modern thought in the tradition to which Foucault himself belongs. It was with the Cubists and perhaps even more with Malevich, who did this in terms of specifically moral objectives and within the context of political revolution, that the project of creating *a priori* a completely new set of metaphorical structures for Western thought was formulated. Closer to home though, and contemporary with Cézanne, Mackintosh's library in Glasgow School of Art is a spatial structure in which the distinction between solid and void was for the first time broken down. This distinction was the first principle of Western, classical architecture and it reflected two of the basic categories of the empirical description of the world. Mackintosh questioned its certainty as effectively as Bergson or any contemporary philosopher.

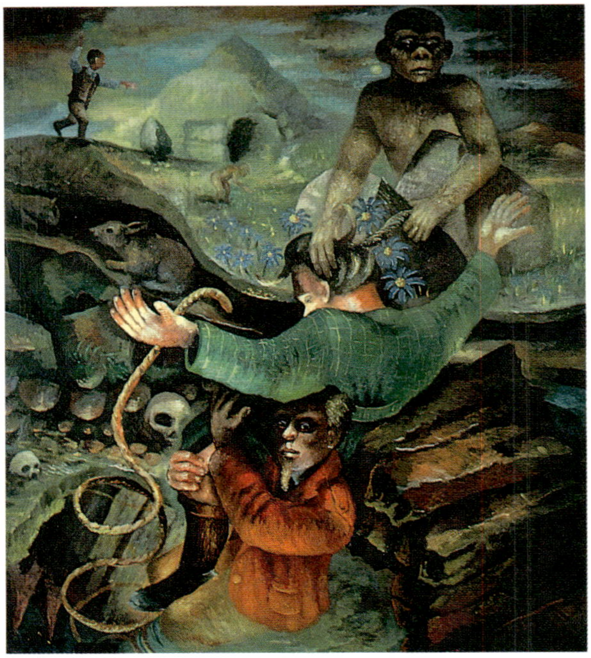

(PLATE 32) *Painting on a Darwinian Theme*, oil on canvas, 183 × 150 cm
1987, (The British Council)

At the same time as he made these remarkable pictures, however, Campbell was moving away from his earlier direct challenge to the monumental tradition. Instead he chose to explore the anxieties and uncertainties of knowledge and our understanding of experience through some of the most straightforwardly comic of his paintings and using a much lighter, more colourful way of painting which was also rather Surrealist in manner. He introduced his pictures in the catalogue of his first exhibition with the Marlborough Gallery in 1987 with a text very much in the Surrealist tradition, Campbell's *Pre-Ramble*. In it he commented on some of the paintings individually. On the theme of *English Landscape with a Disruptive Gene (Pl.33)* he wrote:

> In a large green landscape he (the hero of this essay) sees two hunters walking together in unison looking for something they seem to have lost. They both carry mysterious packages strung over their shoulders and on one of them sat an odd looking individual which seemed to be cloned from a man, a dog and a lobster. He had a human nose, ears, feet and hands and reminded the man of the cheese mites of Wodehouse. He asked the hunters about the unusual manifestation and they explained they were looking for him, seemingly unaware he was sitting upon their packages. He was evidently a disruptive gene . . .[30]

The disruptive gene is a real genetic condition. The visual muddle of the creature suggests its Darwinian pedigree, but given the power of thought to disrupt our equanimity that Campbell identified in Darwin and Foucault, here perhaps it also personifies the artist, carrying his intellectual and imaginative restlessness, his own 'black dog' of feeling, as Pilgrim carries his burden in *Pilgrim's Progress*. It leads him on a fruitless search for something that in the end is hidden in himself.

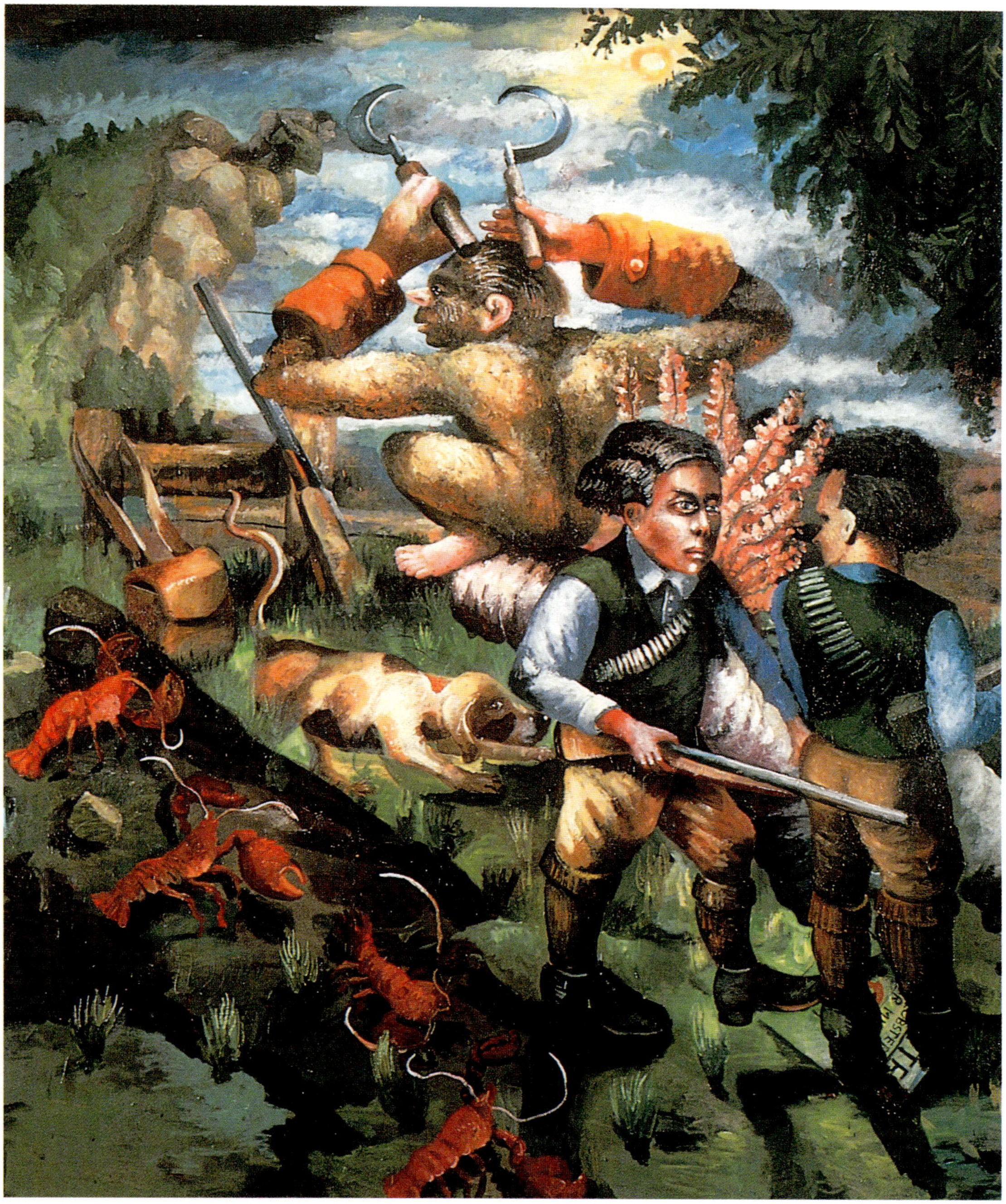

(PLATE 33) *English Landscape with a Disruptive Gene*, oil on canvas, 250 × 236cm, 1987 (The Gulbenkian Foundation)

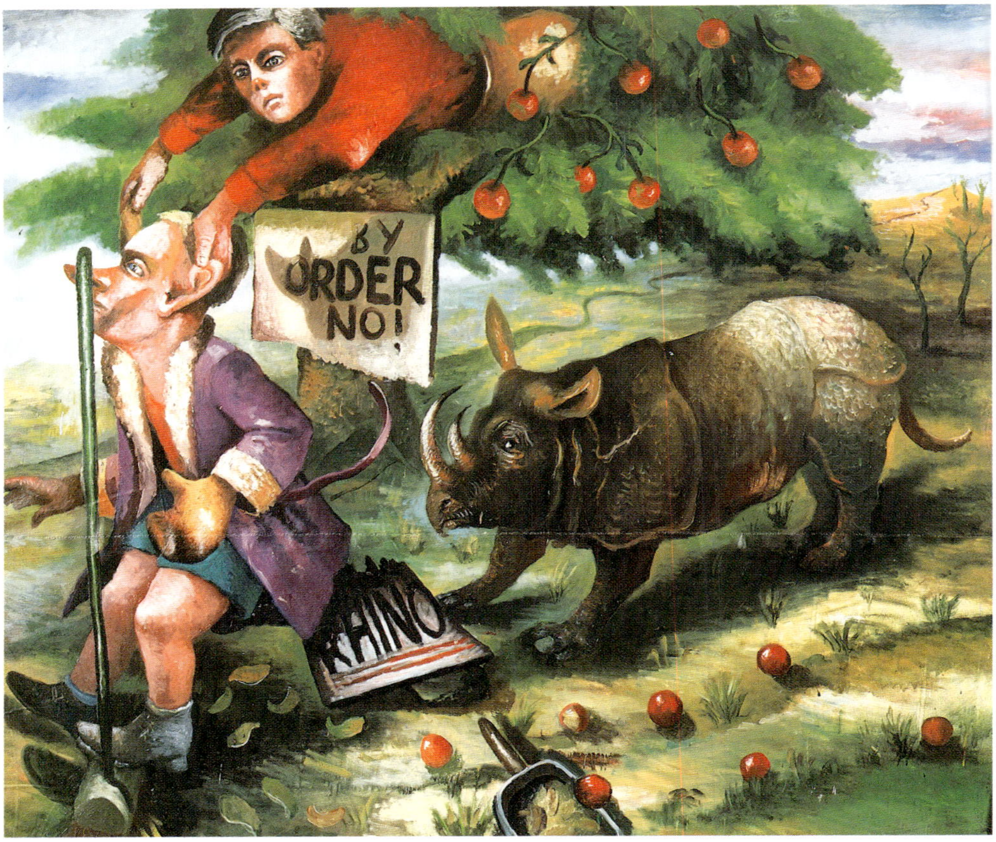

(PLATE 34) *By Order No Rhinos*, oil on canvas, 216 × 236 cm, 1987

Campbell's text continues, describing the misadventures of the same hero in the painting *By Order No Rhinos (Pl.34)*:

> (He) . . . reached a field where a sign said 'By Order No Rhinos'. He considered it permissible to go ahead as he was no rhino; but to his shock out of the blue came a rhino . . . Shocked and dismayed at this apparently careless attitude to rules, he decided to head east . . .

Like the Lost Hiker, the man has made the mistake of believing in signs and is in the position that someone would be in if they tried to follow the sign-post from Oxford to Salisbury in one of Campbell's pictures. He has got it altogether wrong, for in addition he has tripped over a broom and the handle has sprung up to whack him in the face. Something very like the tripping device from the installation *Zoo Opera* is visible by his feet, but tripping and falling in Campbell's work usually seem to represent desire, inspiration, or a shot at freedom in the moment between. Here the trip is reversed. The man does not even enjoy the momentary illusion of freedom. He stays upright and in one place, but gets hit on the head anyway and he is suffering the further indignity of himself turning into a rhinoceros. His very natural assumption that he was 'no rhino' proves false.

The image in *By Order No Rhinos* derives from the classic, comic situation of the unwary hiker and the unseen 'Beware of the Bull' sign. (The charging bull appears separately in *A Life in Letters:*

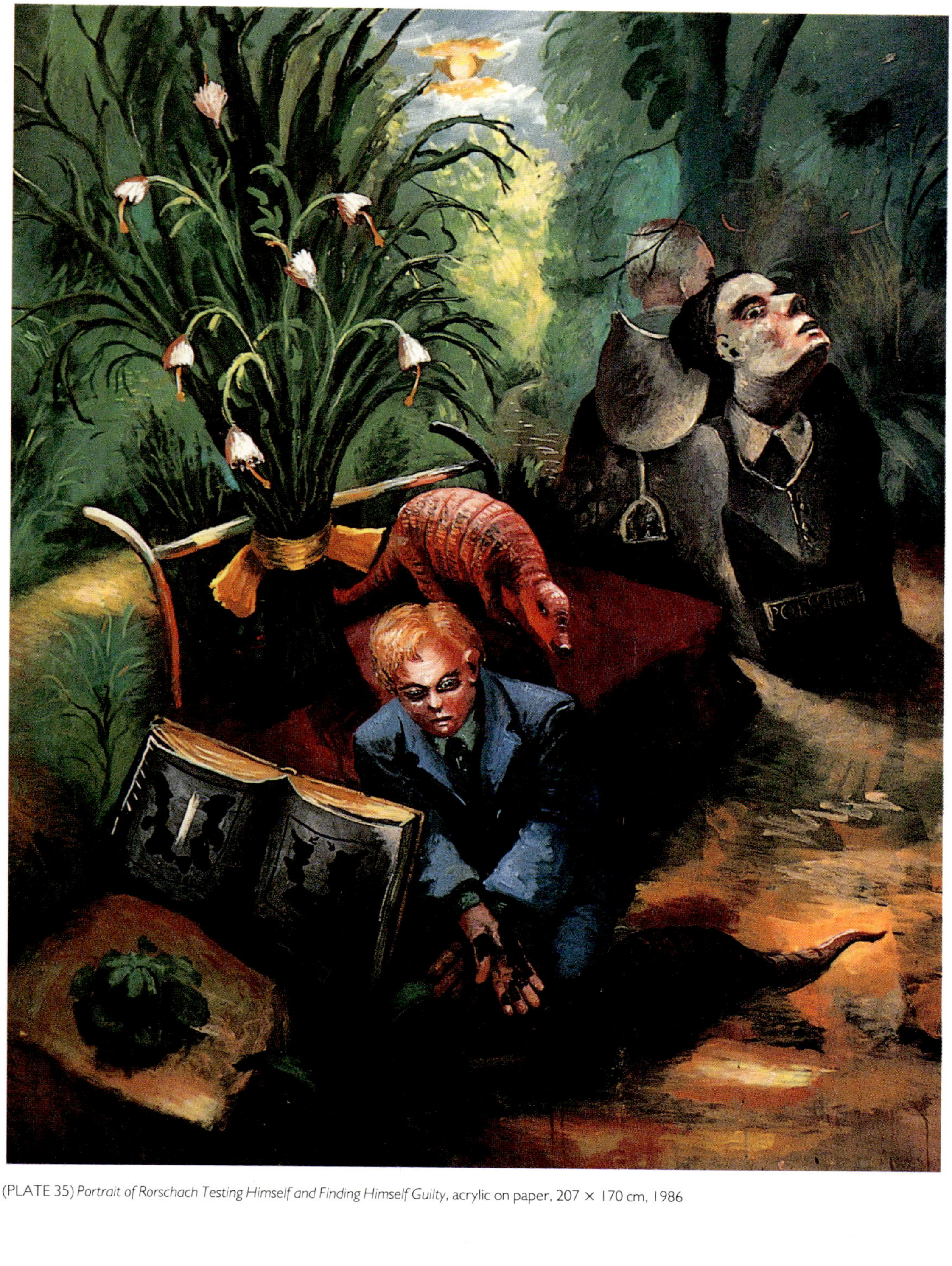

(PLATE 35) *Portrait of Rorschach Testing Himself and Finding Himself Guilty*, acrylic on paper, 207 × 170 cm, 1986

Only the English Kill Themselves in the Lap of Happiness.) The picture is a brilliant comedy of signs, but the paradox, however convoluted, is more explicit than it is implicit in the way it was in Campbell's earlier work. To that extent, it is an illustrative image and although this figure is going through the actions of a clown, he lacks the clumsy innocence which gives a kind of pathos to the clowning of the Lost Hiker and his friends.

The problem of how to work in the field of these ideas without becoming illustrative is a real one. That Campbell was himself concerned about the slippery ground between image and illustration is perhaps suggested in another painting shown in 1987 and painted the previous year, *Portrait of Rorschach Testing Himself and Finding Himself Guilty (Pl.35)*. Rorschach was the inventor of the ink-blot test as a psychiatrist's tool. In the painting, he is kneeling on the ground beside a psychiatrist's couch. His book illustrating two ink-blots is open and he is looking in consternation at a third 'blot', a bloodstain on his hand. Life has intervened in some brutal but unspecified way. Behind Rorschach a hobby horse is labelled 'Rorschach'.

The picture presents a variation on the theme of visual signs. Rorschach's thesis was of course that even though the shape of the ink-blot is completely arbitrary, it reveals meaning as a reflection of the mind interpreting it. Through the guilty bloodstain on Rorschach's hand, the blot becomes explicitly a 'clue'. But what is the crime? Is it the abstraction of the ink-blot and is his whole attempt to represent a state of mind in an abstract way simply off the point? Real life and real feeling break in violently as they always will if art becomes too abstract and polite.

Some of the most memorable images from Campbell's 1987 exhibition were those in which he returned to the simpler imagery of his earlier work, the extraordinary, single figure of the *Travelling Silhouette Collector (Pl.36)*, for instance, which invokes the most primitive form of mimesis, nature's own drawing, the shadow, to make an inimitable pun on the artist's role. Once again he is seen as a traveller, but his business is chasing shadows. With the same felicity, some of the small gouaches combine lapidary simplicity of form with resonances of complexity of meaning in a way that recalls such emblematic images as Peter Breughel's engravings of Flemish proverbs.

In these small works with their strong, simple colouring, Campbell clearly solved the problem of illustration. In *Role Reversal*, a man gives a corpse back to a stork on the rooftop. *Study for Disruptive Gene* makes a similar point to the large painting, *English Landscape with Disruptive Gene*, but does so more economically. Likewise, *Study for the Judges (Pl.37)* can be compared to the painting *Judged by Nature's Law Guilty*. In both there is a punning relationship between the shape of a wild bees' nest and a judge's wig, but in the small gouache, a man stands caught between the wild, romantic(?) bees and the domestic, classical(?) bee hives, but if the bees are the judges, they make no distinction and sting him anyway.

During 1988, Campbell continued to paint pictures of this emblematic kind. *Quelle Heure Est-il?*, for instance, is a play on time, using sundials, a circular garden and the wheels of a bicycle. *Wisdom Torn Apart by Mirrors* uses that ancient emblem, the broken column, to symbolise perhaps the death of traditional wisdom and in the mirrors, its reflection, representation. These problems also return as a main preoccupation. *The Tyranny of Maths (Pl.38)* takes a universal torture of childhood and turns it into a parable on the Platonic idea of representation. A boy has been kept indoors to do

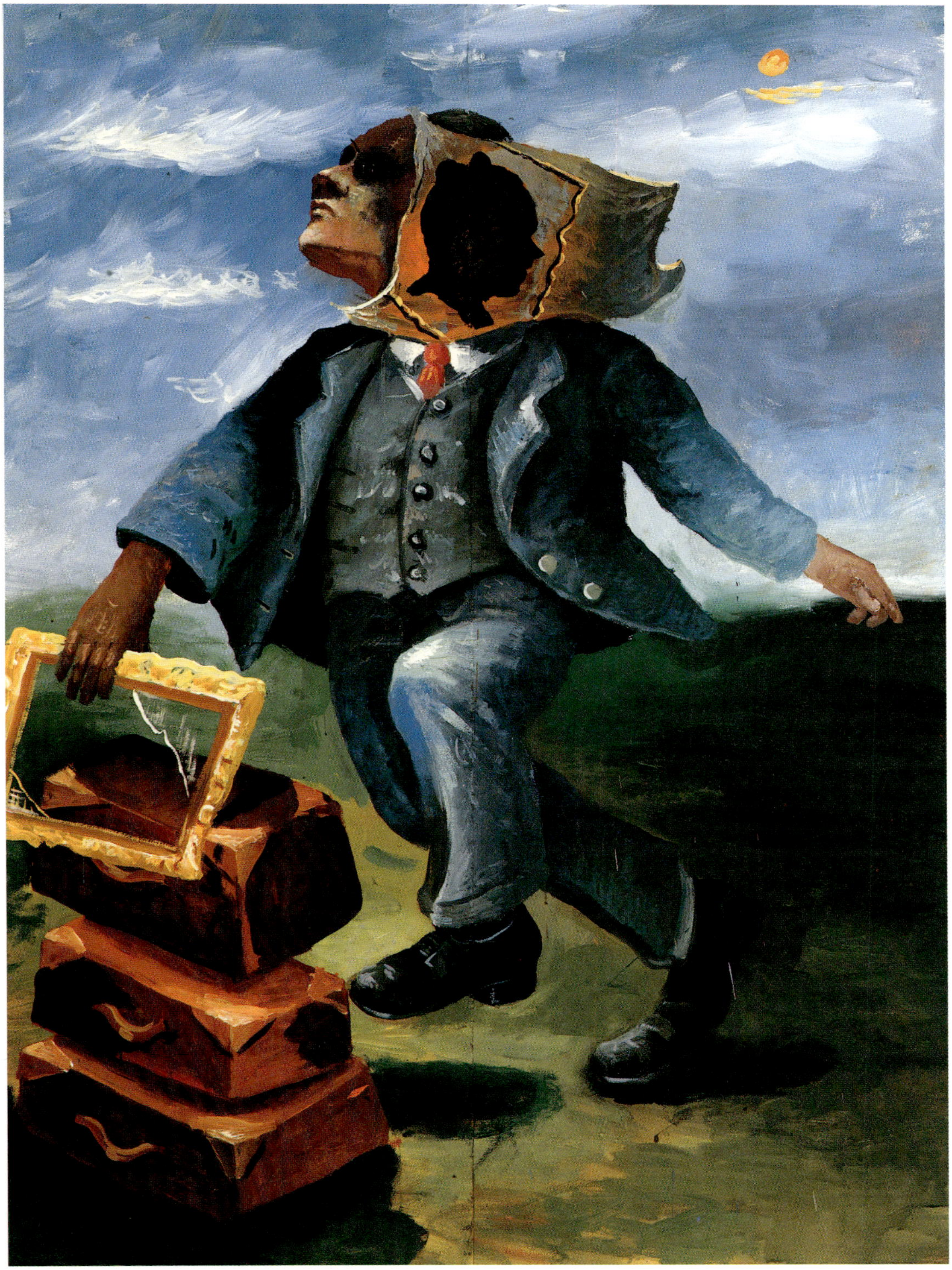

(PLATE 36) *Travelling Silhouette Collector*, acrylic on paper, 190.5 × 139.7 cm, 1987

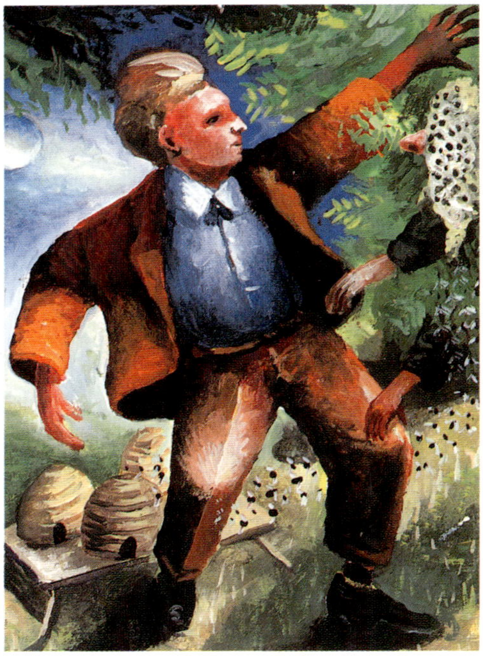

(PLATE 37) *Study for the Judges*, acrylic on paper, 30.5 × 24 cm, 1987

maths, while others play football outside, but it has gone a bit further than usual. He is literally 'tied up'. However, he can see the outside world in a mirror. The mirror represents mimesis, but it puts the boy into the position of the inhabitants of Plato's cave, only able to see reality indirectly.

Remote from the muddle of life, it was mathematics, not art, that was to Plato the means by which we can come closest to the contemplation of the ideal and in the picture on a kind of easel, a drawing approximates maths to art by representing four views of a head as a problem of vectors. The poor boy's position, however, is clearly far from ideal. The football being played outside is a much more convincing vision of art and he is trying surreptitiously to reach a pair of scissors, so perhaps he will escape from art into life. Thus the artist opens an ironic discussion of the distance of both mimesis and the ideal from the world of real experience and from real art too perhaps as we are prompted to wonder if the artist himself wants to escape with the boy from this brain-teasing.

Certainly, in 1988 a new kind of image appeared in the work that Campbell exhibited, but there are echoes in it of some of the installations and performances that he had done at art school almost ten years before. He himself described *Drinks will be Served Over Africa*, 1988, as 'a painting of a modern mime work'. Four pairs of arms appear through a theatre curtain which screens the back of the painting, making it a stage. The fingers of these hands are in various stages of the shadow-play of the rabbit on the wall in which gesture forms one of the most primitive modes of representation, here Surrealistically located in a theatre which is also an aeroplane lounge in the sky. Campbell had used this shadow-play in several pictures before, and long before him, in the eponymous picture, *The Rabbit on the Wall*, Wilkie had used it in the same way to identify the primitive will to representation by mimesis. It eventually evolved into the most elaborate shadow-play of all, the cinema.

There is a much more extensive use of texts in Campbell's paintings of this time and this also refers back to his installations and performances. In *Building Built by a Philosopher who was an Architect for his Sister who was Not*, 1988, for instance, an interior rather reminiscent of Richard Hamilton is divided along its horizontal axis by the text, 'Split Level Adds Interest' and there are other word plays in the picture. The use of strong, simple colour is also a link back to the earlier performances and installations. In *The Aggressiveness of Red and the Passivity of Yellow*, 1987, the role of red is explicitly the same as in performances like *Poised Murder* and *It's Just Violence at the Bar*. The rather giddy, geometric space in that picture is also reminiscent of the way these were staged

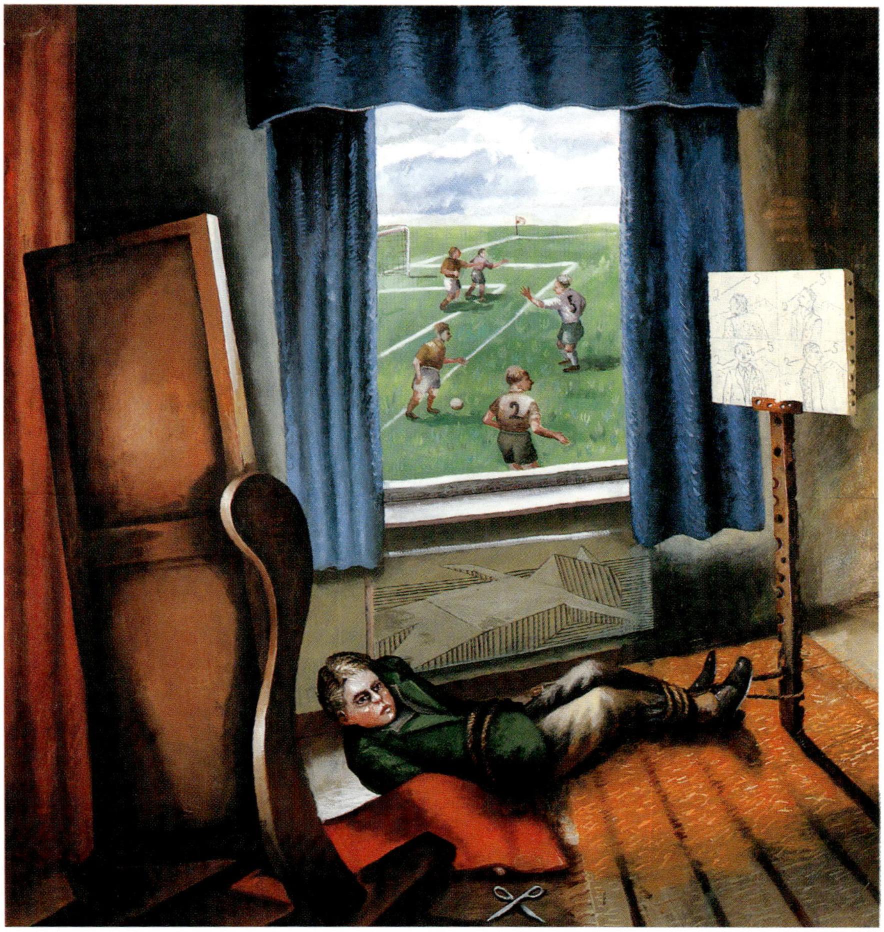

(PLATE 38) *The Tyranny of Maths*, acrylic on paper, 158.1 × 142.2 cm, 1988

and of the structures in installations like *View from the Bridge*. The spindly steel staircase which appears in *The Ship that Died of Shame off the Coast of Africa*, 1988, and several others is also reminiscent of the red painted-steel structures in that installation.

A number of pictures also return to murder as a theme. As it did in his earlier work, murder serves as an image of death conventionalised by the modes of crime fiction, but the ultimate reality nonetheless. The three murders in *Portrait of Three Murders – On this Hangs a Tail (Pl.39)* recall the four murders of *Poised Murder*. The detective reappears in these pictures too, giving some of them the distinctly cinematic flavour that had been such a feature of the performances. In fact Andrew Wilson interprets *Portrait of Three Murders* as referring to three films and film-makers. The telephone stands for Hitchcock and *Dial M for Murder*. Michael Powell's *The Small Back Room* is suggested by the whole space structure and Fritz Lang is represented by the blue door.[31]

Three pictures of 1988–89 in particular seem to take a close, retrospective look at the theme that Campbell had first addressed in *Poised Murder*. These are *Murder Through an Abstraction*, *If the Premise is*

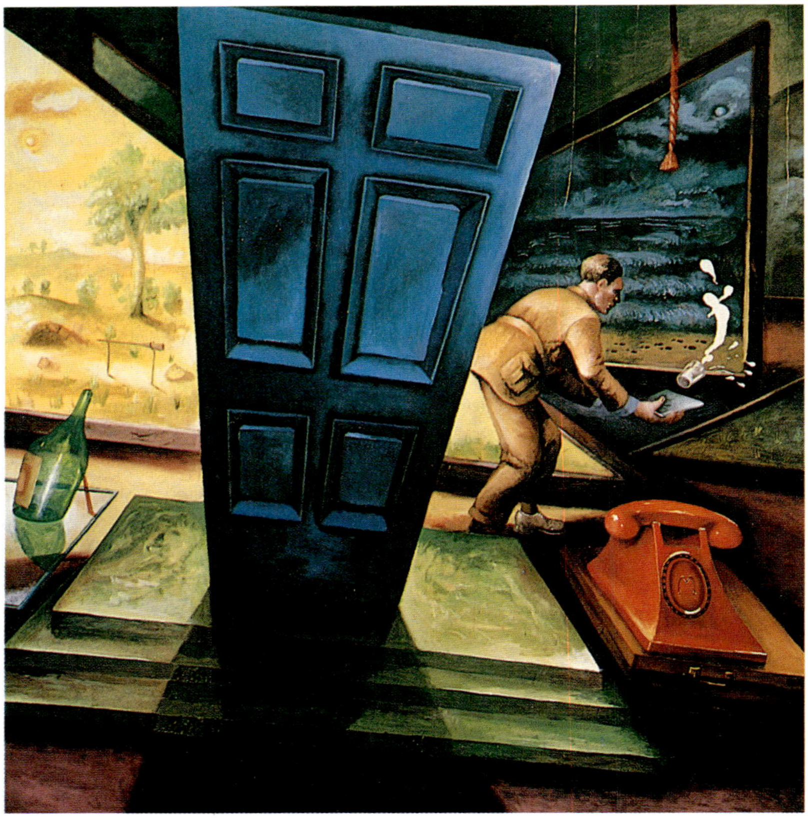

(PLATE 39) *Portrait of Three Murders – On this Hangs a Tail*, oil on canvas, 226.4 × 224.3cm, 1988

Murder Through Abstraction then Abstain from Action (Pl.40) and *Can Abstraction be Taken as Evidence in a Murder Scene?* Each of these reflects in a different way on the inescapably abstract nature of imagery even when dealing with such a subject, but also on the way we break through it. In the first picture, a man in a forties-style double-breasted suit, reaches through a hole in an abstract painting – a Mondrian – to shoot at another man dressed as a mountaineer. Although it is an interior, he is partly supported by a rope as he peers with a candle at some rocks laid out on cloths like jewels in a jeweller's shop. Are they rough diamonds? There are two cut diamonds on the top of the frame of the painting.

The title of the second of these is actually in the form of a crossword puzzle clue. Crosswords exist in the gap that Thomas Reid identified between the two quite distinct characteristics of language: its power to denote the objects and actions of the concrete world of extension and the abstract form of the signs and structures by which it does so. This gap is a wasteland without maps where solid ground can turn into a marsh overnight as it did in the picture, *Hiker in a Landscape Turned into a Marsh Overnight*. Painting exists in this same intermediate area between action and abstraction.

In the background of the picture, *If the Premise is Murder etc.*, a series of visually related, simple words appears along with the stars of a Jasper Johns *Flag* on a transparent curtain. In front of it a sign-

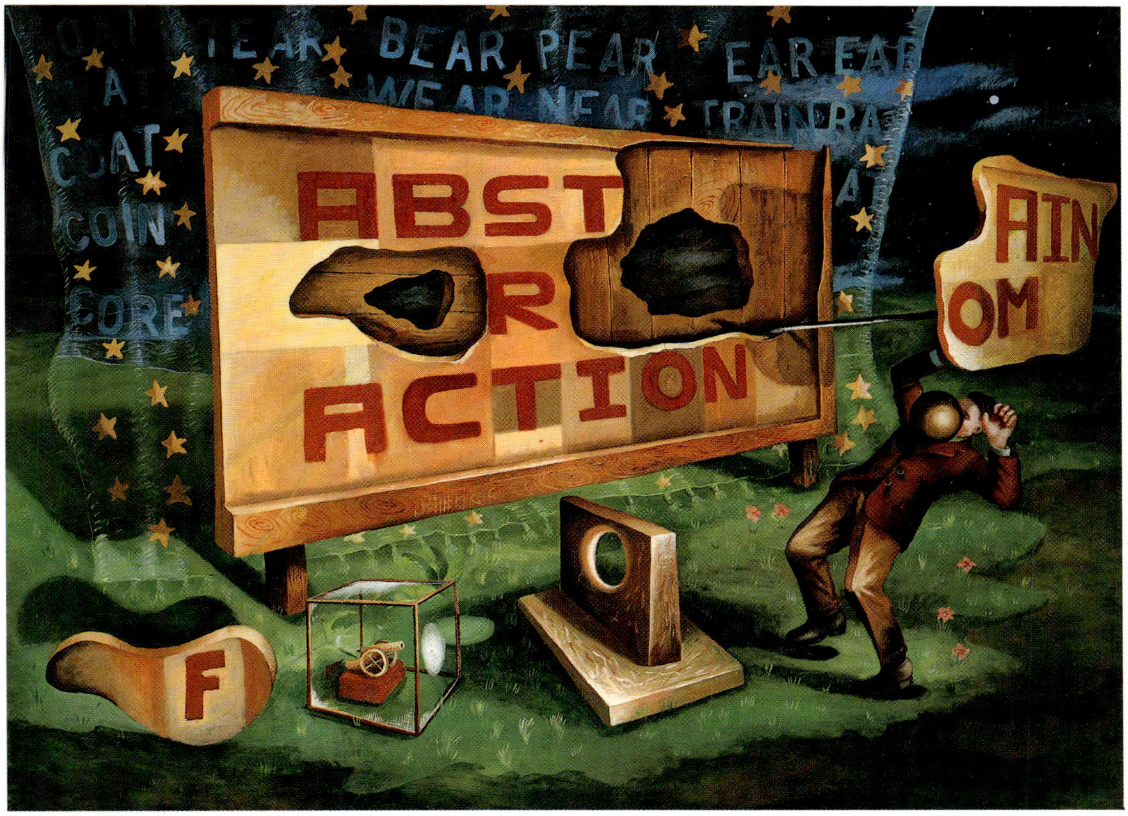

(PLATE 40) *If the Premise is Murder Through Abstraction then Abstain from Action*, oil on canvas, 205.8 × 274.3 cm, 1988 (The British Council)

board doubles as a child's wooden puzzle. It is solid, but it has two holes in it like eyes. The transparent curtain is mimicked by a glass box which has in it a model cannon. Although it is behind glass, it appears nonetheless to have fired a much larger cannonball through an abstract sculpture, thus 'through abstraction'. Its solidity echoes the wooden puzzle behind. The cannonball is knocking a man down and the message seems to be that for all the abstract complexities that beset perception and communication, there is no ambiguity about the way experience can still hit us between the eyes.

In the third painting, a murder is taking place on a wild beach, but in the middle of the picture, a fingerprint is presented on a step-ladder like an abstract work of art. It is the epitome of a 'clue', but it is also an abstract form in nature which can be read and which has a precise and unambiguous meaning. It seems impossible to separate the nature of art and the art of nature.

This was the conundrum that Ruskin tried to solve, though he saw the art of nature rather as the art of God. Ruskin played an important part in the inspiration for Campbell's major show in March 1990 at the Third Eye Centre in Glasgow. In the catalogue, the frontispiece is a plate from Ruskin's second Edinburgh lecture on architecture delivered in 1853. Ruskin's caption is 'a spray of a [Scottish] ash tree and improvement on the same on Greek principles'. In other words, it illustrates the impossibility of improving on natural form by formalising it on abstract principles,

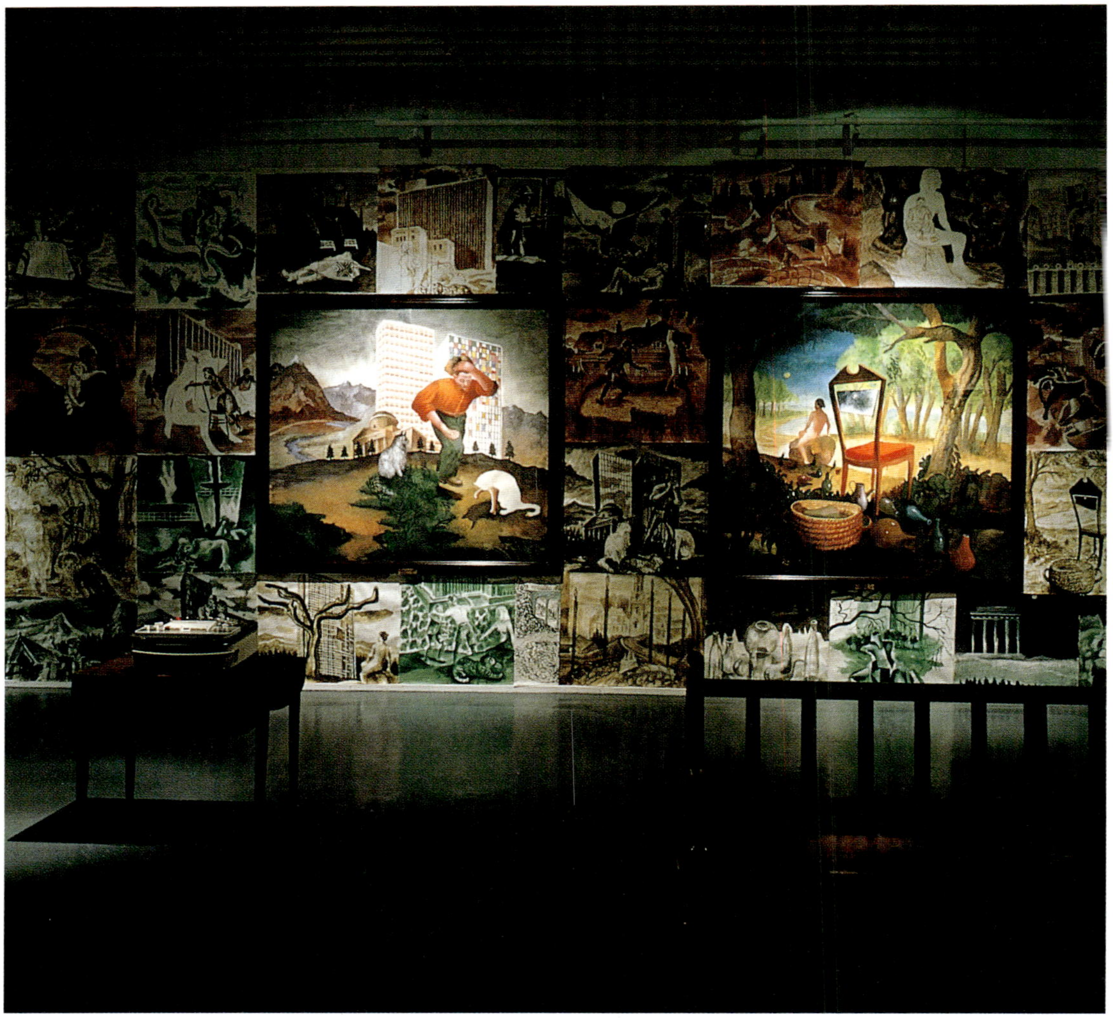

(PLATE 41) *On Form and Fiction*, view of exhibition installation at the Third Eye Centre, Glasgow, 1990

which was also an important theme in Campbell's exhibition. The formalised leaves from this illustration reappear as a detail of the painting *Leaf from a Book by Ruskin*. In the catalogue, there is also a sepia photograph of the artist in an Inverness cape, with stick and hat, standing on a rock above a torrent exactly like *Ruskin in Glenfinlas*, the portrait by Millais.

It was an extraordinary exhibition. Its title was *On Form and Fiction (Pl.41)* and it was really an installation rather than a conventional collection of paintings hanging in a line on a gallery wall. The principal part of the exhibition consisted of twelve paintings on paper, all two metres square and conventionally framed, but these were set in a continuous field of 150 smaller, monochrome works on paper, neither framed nor mounted, but simply pinned to the wall. This was so arranged that each large picture was surrounded by twelve small works on paper. The walls of the gallery were a mosaic of painted surfaces from floor to ceiling, only interrupted by the doors; a whole environment, this was painting, not paintings.

There was music playing. The light in

the gallery was low and each of the twelve large pictures was lit by an individual spotlight. It was an arrangement that clearly recalled, though on a much more ambitious scale, the multiple-canvas installations that Campbell had done at art school some of which, like *Flag*, also incorporated light in a similar way. Now, however, with the space dark and theatrical and the paintings illuminated like cinema screens, painting became cinema.

The stress on the individual images was deliberately reduced by putting a lot of them above or below eye-level in the half-dark, and treating the whole display of more than 150 pictures as a single, continuous flow of images, again rather like a film. As in the cinema, the whole event was the fiction, not just the separate elements from which it was made. The small pictures, and some of the larger ones too, were painted with freedom and an airy lightness. The shift is not surprising and there might well have been something heartfelt about one of the larger paintings, *Men in Pursuit of Simplicity*. In it, two men in a dinghy encounter a huge wave and are almost overwhelmed by it as they sail on an artistic voyage towards a romantically painted sunset. The sail of a second boat in the foreground indicates that they are not alone, but it is also unpainted. The artist talks about the inhibiting perfection that he feels when he confronts simple white canvas. It is already perfect. It does not need to be improved by art. This is one reason why he paints with his canvas unstretched. The young men in the picture, therefore, might have the best chance of finding simplicity by getting out of the picture altogether and leaving the canvas blank.

These pictures do not lack seriousness even while they are humorous, but instead of the complexity of some of Campbell's recent, individual pictures, here the painting is uppermost. He seems to have moved away from the contemplation of the more general problems of the relationship between knowledge and the signs by which it is conveyed which were taking him more and more towards language, back to the exploration of the specific, visual language of art and how to control it, not be controlled by it.

This return to an explicit dialogue with the conventions of painting – how to get inside the fiction once again and use it as a vehicle of expression about something other than itself – had begun earlier. In *Collagist in the Drama – Mort de Pierrot/Très Moderne (Pl.42)*, for instance, he had explored the different levels of reality between a painting of a landscape tapestry and a Seurat-style, pointillist landscape painting. The real tapestry would be made up of innumerable, minute and identical stitches, and the landscape of equally minute, uniform and identical dots. He was to return again later to this question of what constitutes the basic making of a picture. More ironically perhaps, he reflects on his own predicament in *Hunter Looking for his Glasses (Pl.43)* of 1990, developed from one of the smaller works in the Third Eye show. Without his glasses, the hunter cannot see properly, but the resulting double-vision makes the landscape look like a Cézanne and indeed in the foreground, though double, is the Cupid from Cézanne's *Still-Life with Cupid*.

This kind of ironic exploration of the coinage of 'great art' ran through the Third Eye show. In the catalogue, Euan McArthur suggests that the 'ambience' that Campbell created was a deliberate attempt to make a museum atmosphere, the kind that says, 'You are in the presence of great art'. Each of the larger paintings was rather formally framed and had a brass plate on it for instance, but this immediately recognisable cultural proposition was as quickly contradicted by the

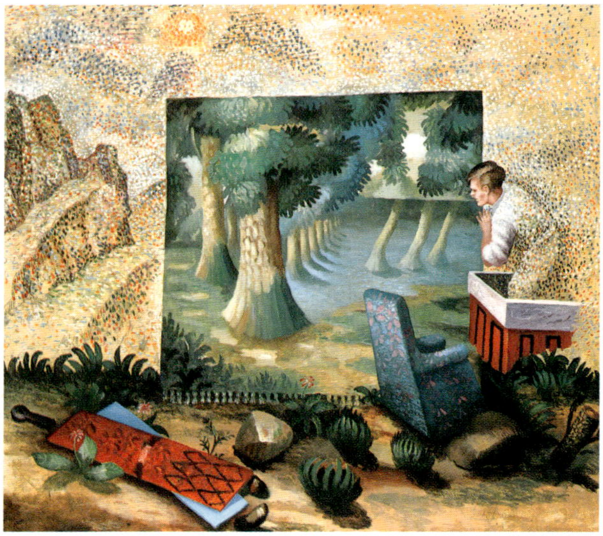

(PLATE 42) *Collagist in the Drama – Mort de Pierrot/Très Moderne*, oil on canvas, 221 × 236.2 cm, 1988

unframed drawings pinned to the walls, the music, the ambiguity of the focus of attention, and the cinematic lighting and sequence of images. In the individual images there was a similar tension between expectations, encouraged by constant use of recognisable signifiers of 'art' and the puncturing of its pretensions.

The female nude, supreme among these signifiers, appeared in these paintings for the first time since the ill-fated picture of Hunt making love (or being made love to) and appears in six of the twelve main pictures. No single image in the iconography of Western art is so charged with the force of convention, or is so tangled in its contradictions as the female nude. For a man at least, it is an image that is almost bound to be close to the centre of his emotional universe and yet no image is treated so much as a convention of 'art'. Kenneth Clarke, accepting this disparity without question and apparently unaware of the abyss it concealed, made a nice distinction between the naked and the nude, but it is a distinction that merely conceals this extraordinary confusion of the conventional and the real. This was a territory in which Ruskin for one got lost. According to legend, it was because he could not reconcile the reality of his wife's body with his expectations nurtured on art that his marriage was unconsummated. There is a nice irony, not lost on Campbell, that it was while Millais was painting Ruskin's portrait at Glenfinlas that he made off with Effie Gray, wife of this unconsummated marriage.

Campbell manages to find a form for the female nude, however, that does not quite fit into either of Kenneth Clarke's categories. She is a slender figure, dated and rather amateurishly painted. In the painting *Portrait of a Nude Encouraging Significant Form (Pl.44)*, she appears in the attitude of washing her hair, leaning over a group of pots left unpainted. Perhaps she is about to transmit to them some of her painted essence. Behind her the classical tone is set by a group of Georgian church spires. *Portrait of a Classical Nude Nervously Sitting (Pl.45)* presents a rather similar situation. Again there is a group of pots in the foreground, though this time they are painted. The nude is sitting on a rock in the distance. The source of her nervousness is that the Georgian chair in the foreground on which she might be expected to be sitting doubles as a guillotine, a reminder of a more brutal reality and also a neo-classical symbol as Ian Hamilton Finlay has made clear. There is a log basket handy to catch the severed heads.

'Significant form' was the catch-phrase of Clive Bell in his book modestly titled *Art*, a kind of Bertie Wooster aesthetics for the country-house modernist, first published in 1914. 'The essential quality in a work of art is significant form',[32] he wrote. He could have been parodying Ruskin's Greeks, but it was an attempt to rationalise the belief that Bell shared with Roger Fry that Cézanne held the answer

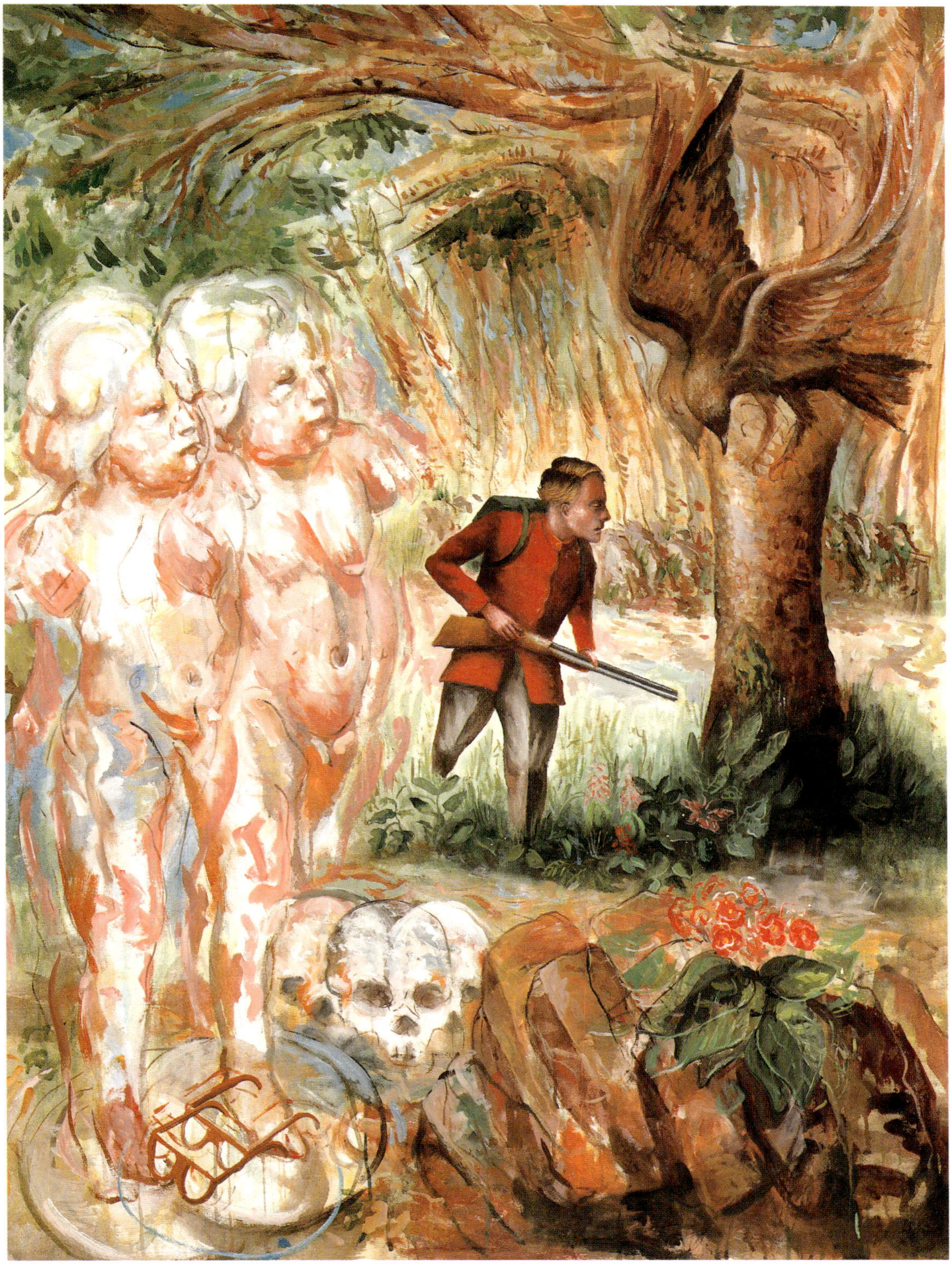

(PLATE 43) *Hunter Looking for his Glasses*, oil on canvas, 159.7 × 116.8 cm, 1990

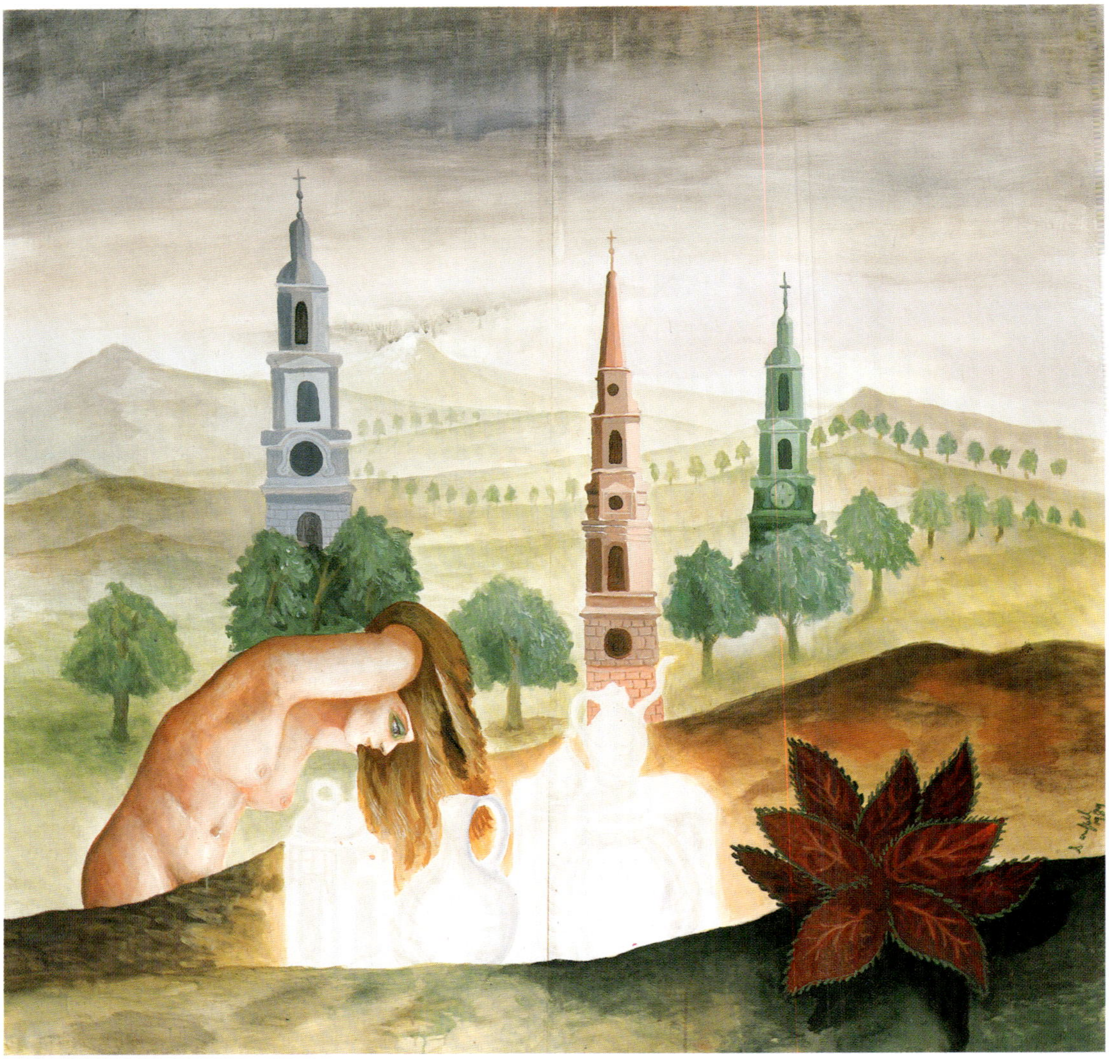

(PLATE 44) *Portrait of a Nude Encouraging Significant Form*, acrylic on paper, 186 × 188.5 cm, 1990

to all the problems of modern art. His attempt to identify a pure aesthetic emotion through this argument led him to some strange conclusions, however. People who 'feel pure aesthetic emotions' he wrote:

> . . . as often as not have no idea what the subject of a picture is. They have never noticed the representative element, and so when they discuss pictures, they talk about the shapes and forms and the relations and quantities of colours. . . . but from these they win an emotion more profound and far more sublime than any that can be given by the description of facts and ideas.[33]

According to this argument, the poor girl in both pictures is to be equated exactly with the pots. In drawings that relate to them, Campbell made this even more explicit. In one, she stands in a Roger Fry style pastiche of a Cézanne landscape. Formally she is virtually indistinguishable

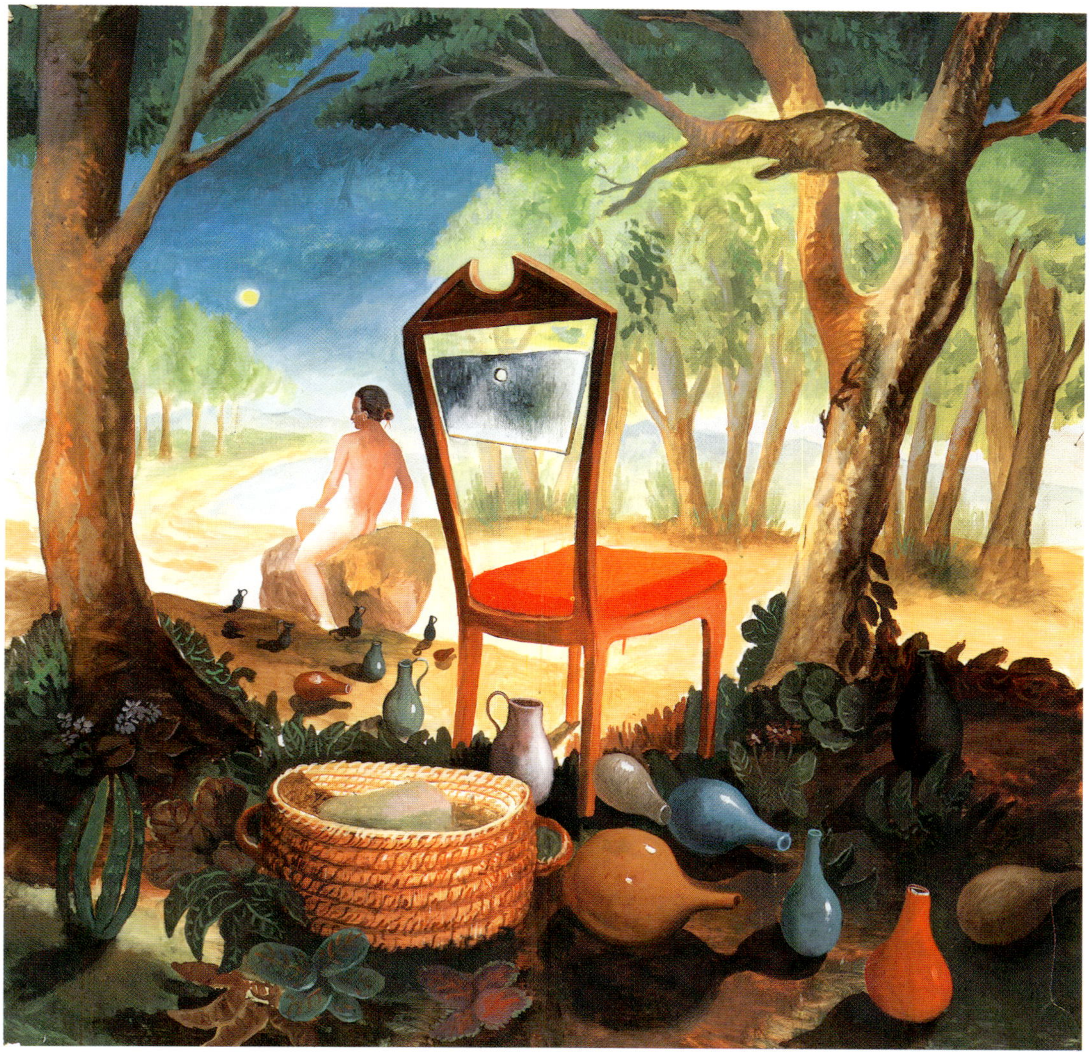

(PLATE 45) *Portrait of a Classical Nude Nervously Sitting*, acrylic on paper, 198.1 × 198.5 cm, 1990

from a group of large, rotund pots in the foreground. (A bent-steel, Bauhaus chair stands in for the Georgian chair in the painting.) In the other drawing *(Pl.46)*, she leans over, or into a hedge, prefiguring Madonna as she presents her buttocks to us, while they are likened to the apples spilt from an upturned basket that is a variation on a small Cézanne still-life in Glasgow. The same basket of fruit appears in a small *Painting Symbolising Autumn*. In the background a figure reminiscent of Breughel's *Harvesters* is shaking the fruit from a tree.

The theme of English twentieth-century aesthetics, its particular struggle with Modernism (and its deluded belief that art itself held the 'answer') seems to be taken up in *Crash Cubism (The Neo-Classical Period) (Pl.47)*. On a trestle railway-bridge of the kind that only appears in Westerns, a man is painted in the style of one of Clive Bell's contemporaries of the Camden Town School such as Harold

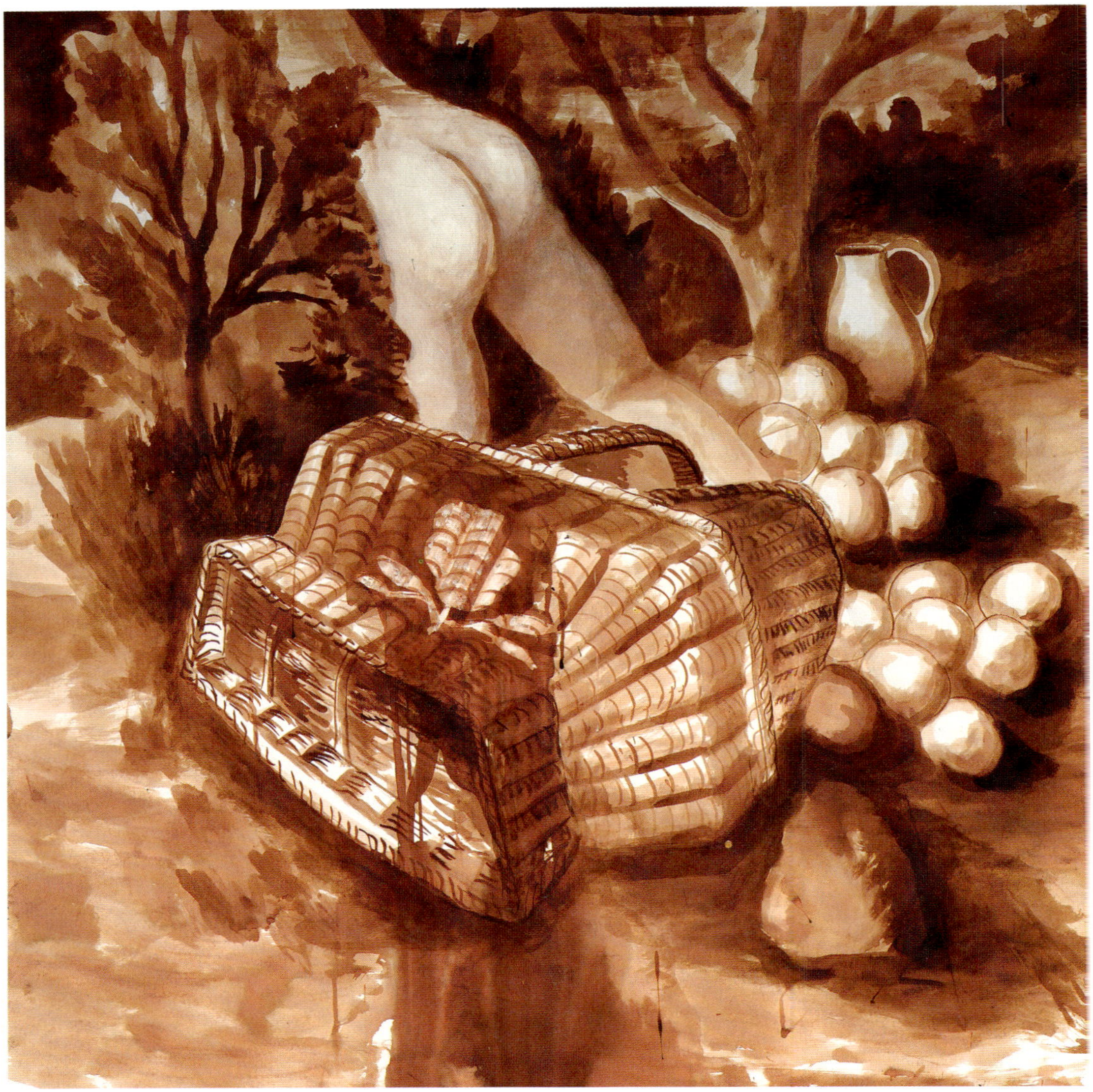

(PLATE 46) *Nude Leaning into a Hedge*, ink on paper, 100 × 100 cm, 1990

Gilman or Spencer Gore. He seems about to be pushed from the bridge by a collage of neo-classical elements in the Cubist style. *An Incident on the Other Side of Mont St Victoire (Pl.48)* also seems to take up this unlikely dialogue of Cézanne and Bertie Wooster. An unpainted Palladian mansion sits on a hillside which is painted in the manner of Cézanne. A man in hat, coat and stick appears to be chasing a girl around the rocks. She is the object of his attention as being clothed, she is recognisably female and human. In the foreground, however, another young man is walking with a girl and her dog. She has no clothes on, but as in this context presumably she is 'nude' and therefore only 'significant form', he appears entirely indifferent to her nakedness as they walk the dog in decorous, suburban fashion.

There was much else in this astonishing and ambitious exhibition. Ajax, for inst-

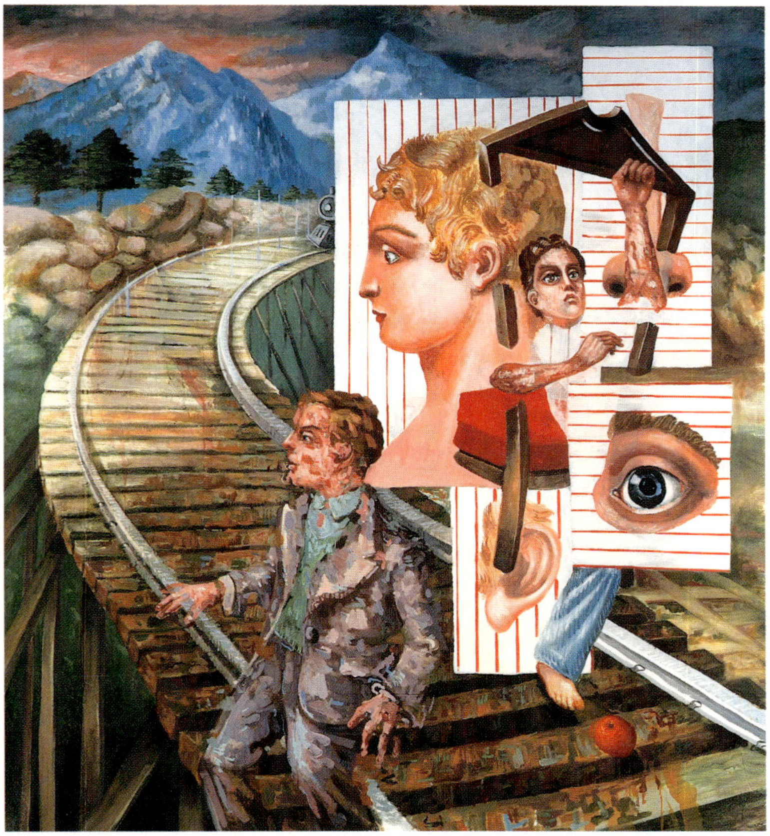

(PLATE 47) *Crash Cubism (The Neo-Classical Period)*, oil on canvas, 182.9 × 162.6 cm, 1990

ance, hero of *Zoo Opera*, was there in his helmet, so was the *Hiker in a Landscape Turned into a Marsh Overnight*. He had perhaps returned home safely only to find that his cat was undergoing a similar though less drastic metamorphosis in *Not You as Well Snowy*. Van Helsing was there too, holding a branch in *The Branch Secretaries* and, if not Dracula, then another fallen angel played a part in *Sad Dirty Little Angel*.

One of several interlocking themes of this show, however, does seem to have been this exploration, starting with Ruskin, of a peculiarly English aesthetic. Much earlier, talking about his interest in British art, Campbell had said:

> This funny way of looking at life, and not continually chasing after style . . . seems British because it has that sense of idiosyncratic attitude – and to use a much misused word 'eccentricity'.[34]

Playing with this kind of eccentricity may have been part of a process of stock-taking for himself, of exasperation with an art that goes around and around, chasing its own tail in the pure insignificance of siginificant form and unable to channel real feeling, but if it was, it was overtaken by a series of traumatic events in his private life.

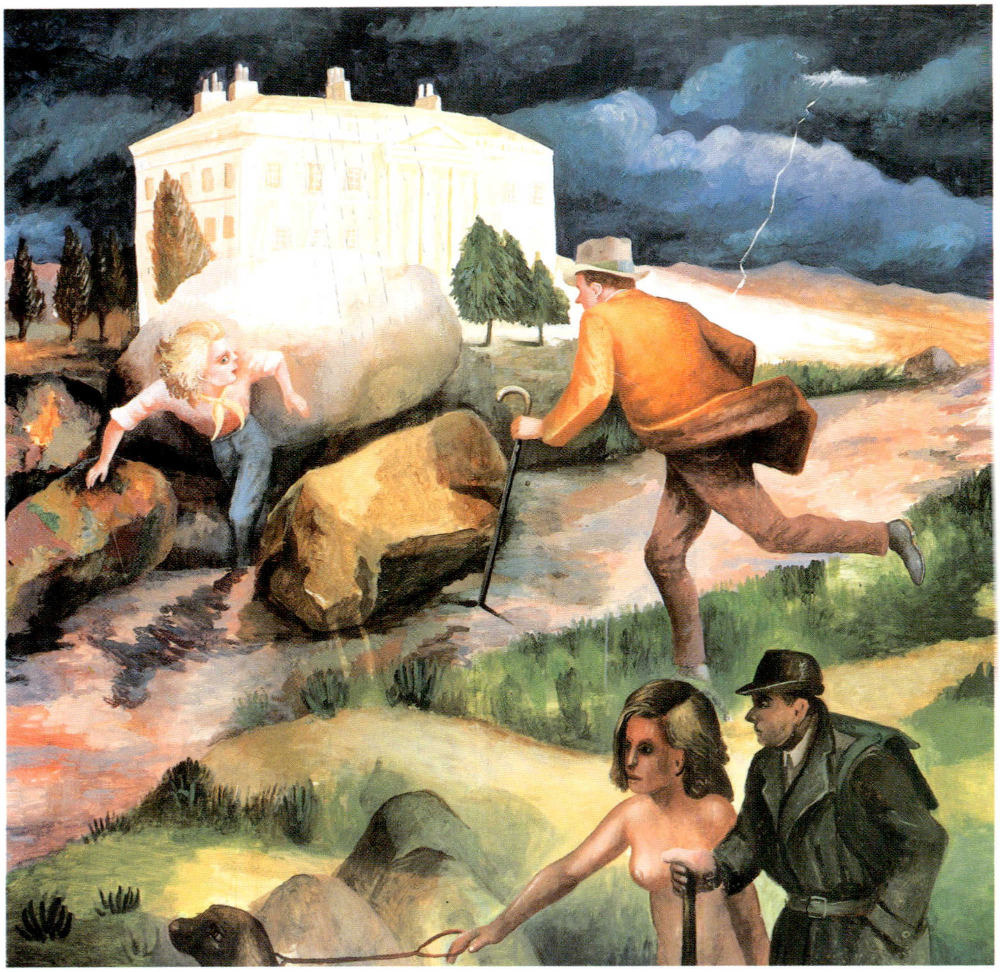

(PLATE 48) *An Incident on the Other Side of Mont St Victoire*, acrylic on paper, 188.5 × 187.5 cm, 1989

In response to these events and in a dark mood, between 1990 and 1991 he made a series of collages. These mattered to him profoundly. It was as though he had to start from scratch again and he struggled with the brutal business of making them till his fingers bled. They took him months of painstaking labour. The Matisse technique of *papier découpé*, which in part they use, was designed to make picture-making easy, but it is as though Campbell deliberately went out of his way to adopt a technique that makes collage difficult. These collages are made up, not just of cut-out paper, but from lengths of coloured string, cut and glued to the surface to create an effect like tapestry, embroidery, or more banally like haircord carpet and turning expression on its head. One of this group, *Penelope at Home Waiting for Dad's Return (Pl.52)*, is almost entirely built up out of lengths of string applied in this way, but if as a group they grew from a mood of despondency, they resolve it too, for although the images in some are rather strange, on the whole they are light and bright.

In *Collagist in the Drama – Mort de Pierrot/Très Moderne* of 1988, with its combination of a Seurat-style landscape and painted tapestry, he had already begun to explore the possibility of modes of representation where the surface is completely neutral, made up additively of equal, non-expressive elements. Now in these collages, the whole process involved a time-consuming and painful immersion in physical labour, building up the picture out of minute, neutral parts. This process was purgative both in intention and effect. He says that it was like making a picture up from its most basic elements. It was a kind of anatomy of painting, a return to first principles. He talks about the guts of it and he was wrestling with the very viscera of his art.

In the Van Helsing-like quest to pin down the clichés of art, technique, like Dracula, can have a misleading, old world charm and a ghostly flamboyance. Campbell had long since given up easel and stretched canvas. Seen as one of the conventions of art, they belong with the smock and beret. He usually paints on a canvas pinned to the wall. Now it seems he wanted to lay the ghost of technique as well.

During 1988 and 1989, he had already made a number of collages which are related to this group. They were not the result of quite such intense and painful labour, but they do stand apart from the paintings that he was doing at the time, even when they share themes with them. *The Balcony Lecture of Kata Phusin (Pl.49)*, for instance, like several of the works in the Third Eye show, is on the theme of Ruskin. Kata Phusin was the pseudonym that Ruskin adopted in *On the Poetry of Architecture*. In the picture, a cut-out silhouette of Ruskin appears to be delivering a lecture to a young man hanging desperately like Buster Keaton from a balcony over a giddy drop. Surprisingly, he seems to be giving some attention to the speaker, though with understandable exasperation. Ruskin's words are written on the collage behind him:

> So there must be in this human form of architecture some equivalent expression for the trouble and wrath of life, for its sorrow and mystery and this it can only give by the depth of gloom, by the frown upon its front.[35]

'Expression for the trouble and wrath of life, . . . its sorrow and mystery' is a ringing Ruskinian phrase that comes close to much that Campbell himself says about the nature of his own art and especially the origin of his later collages. In this painting perhaps this is not obvious, but the young man is the victim of this 'trouble and wrath' nevertheless. The difference between the

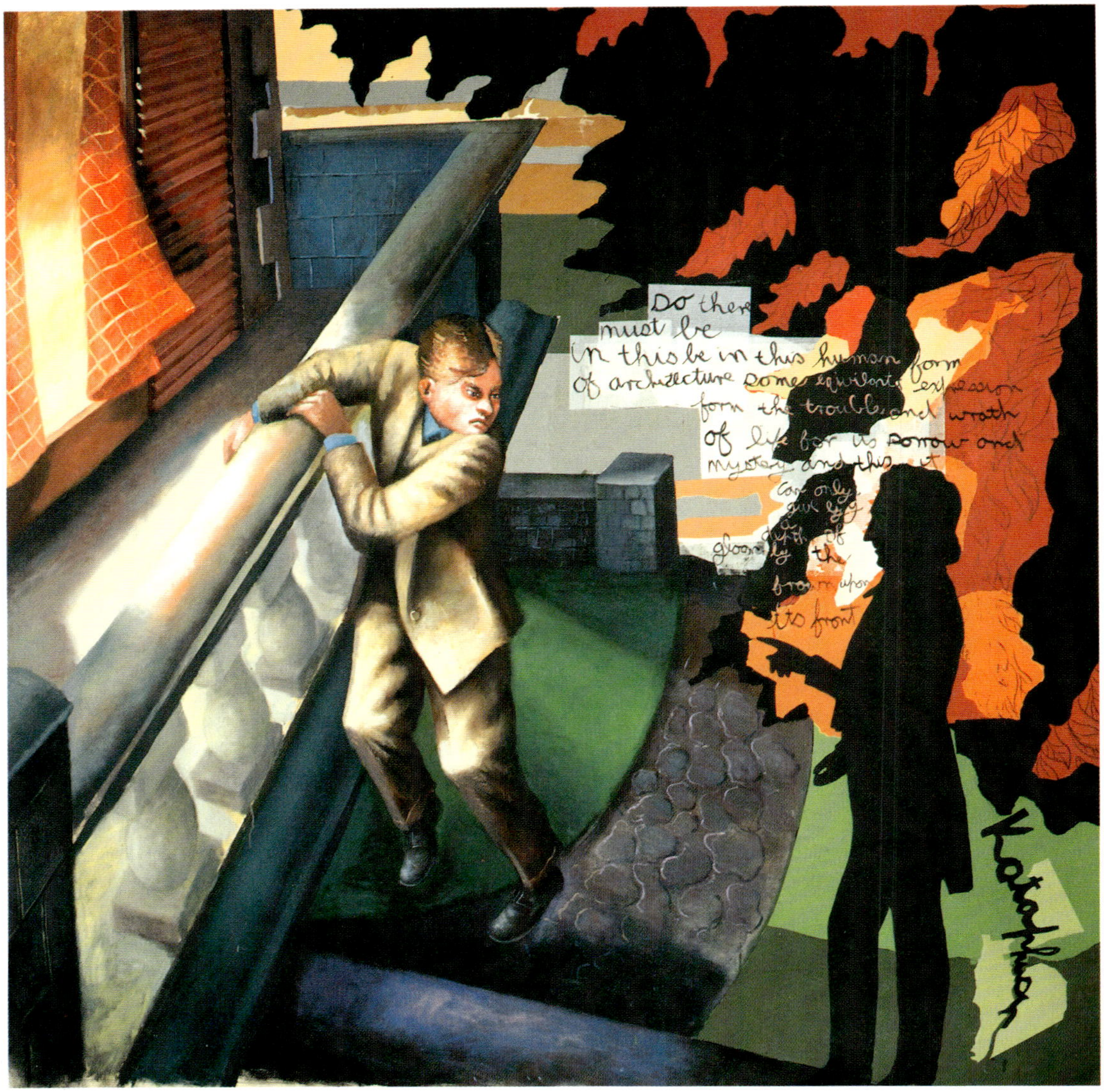

(PLATE 49) *The Balcony Lecture of Kata Phusin*, oil on canvas, 239 × 236 cm, 1989

real urgency of his peril and the abstraction of Ruskin's prose is illustrated by the shift from collage on Ruskin's side of the picture, to the three-dimensional, spatial representation of the young man's predicament.

This collage strikes a more solemn note than some of the more light-hearted reflections on similar themes in the Third Eye show. The same is true of *Portrait of May Milton Between the Studio and the Toilet (Pl.50)*. The most intense of these earlier collages, it takes its title from a picture of the dancer from the Moulin Rouge stuck to the wall in the background of a room that seems to be both kitchen and bathroom. It is an ironic take-off of Munch, but a foreshortened bath in the foreground also recalls Bonnard. Bonnard's iridescent colour here describes bloodstains, however. There is just such a bath in *Last Tango in Paris*, too. Beside

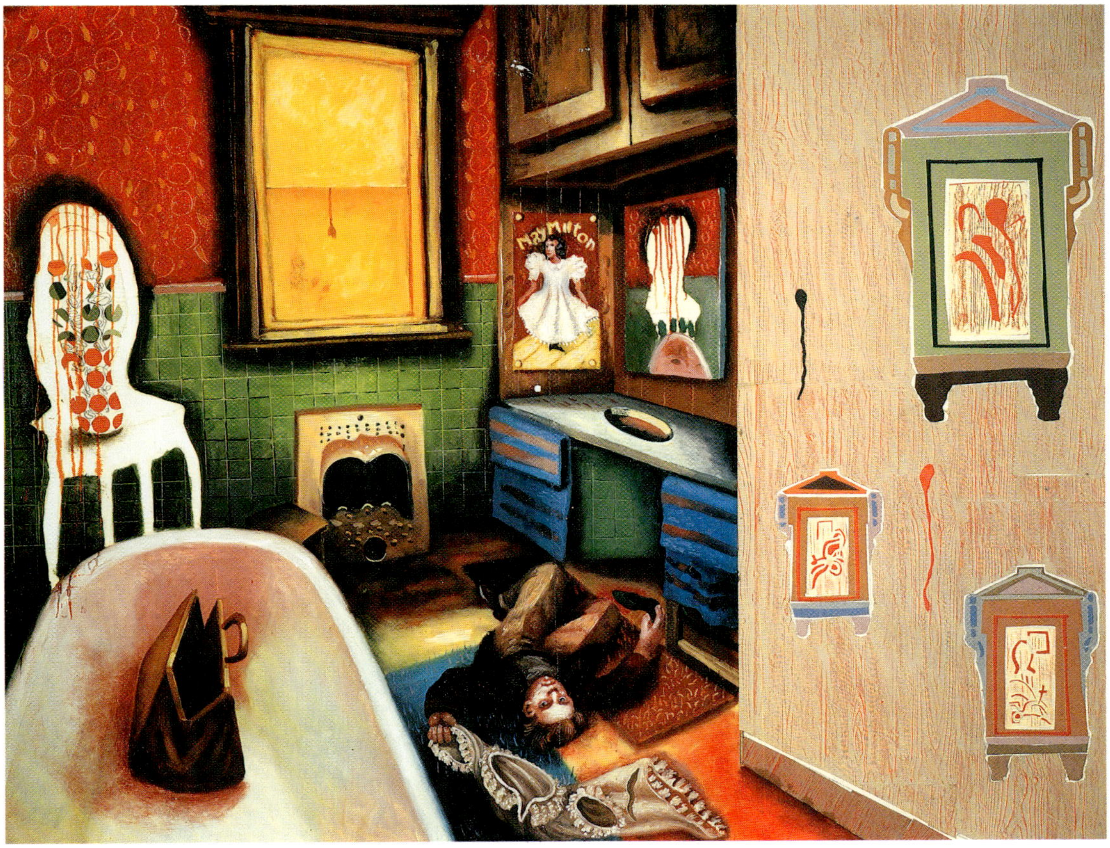

(PLATE 50) *Portrait of May Milton Between the Studio and the Toilet*, oil, collage on canvas, 213.4 × 269.2 cm, 1989

the bath there is a body lying on the floor. It is the body of a man and he has in his hand the dress that May Milton is wearing in the picture. One of her shoes is lying nearby. The intense colour and the mood of mystery in this picture brings it much closer than the other 'murder' pictures of this time to Campbell's performances of ten years earlier. There is a similar reflectiveness in some of the other collages.

The collage technique can also give a lighter, more open picture, however, and there are clear echoes of Matisse in several of this group of earlier collages. Campbell seems to be rejoining his dialogue with the great masters. In *Goat Skull in Italy*, he even joins the inspiration of Picasso to that of Matisse, but he confounds any accusation that he is falling into line by specifically relating Matisse's flat areas of colour to the featureless camouflage of the surface of a 'painting by numbers'.

Looking for Gold in a Forest (Pl.51) takes up this line of argument with Matisse, but it enlarges it to include other kinds of picture-making. A pointillist curtain is hung against a kind of camouflage pattern, Omega-workshop tapestry. The realities merge in the foreground. Is the man there searching for gold in the forest of modes of representation? This does seem to be the artist's own quest as in the later collages where 'tapestry' itself comes to be the means for taking apart and putting together a picture out of its most rudimentary elements. The banality of the

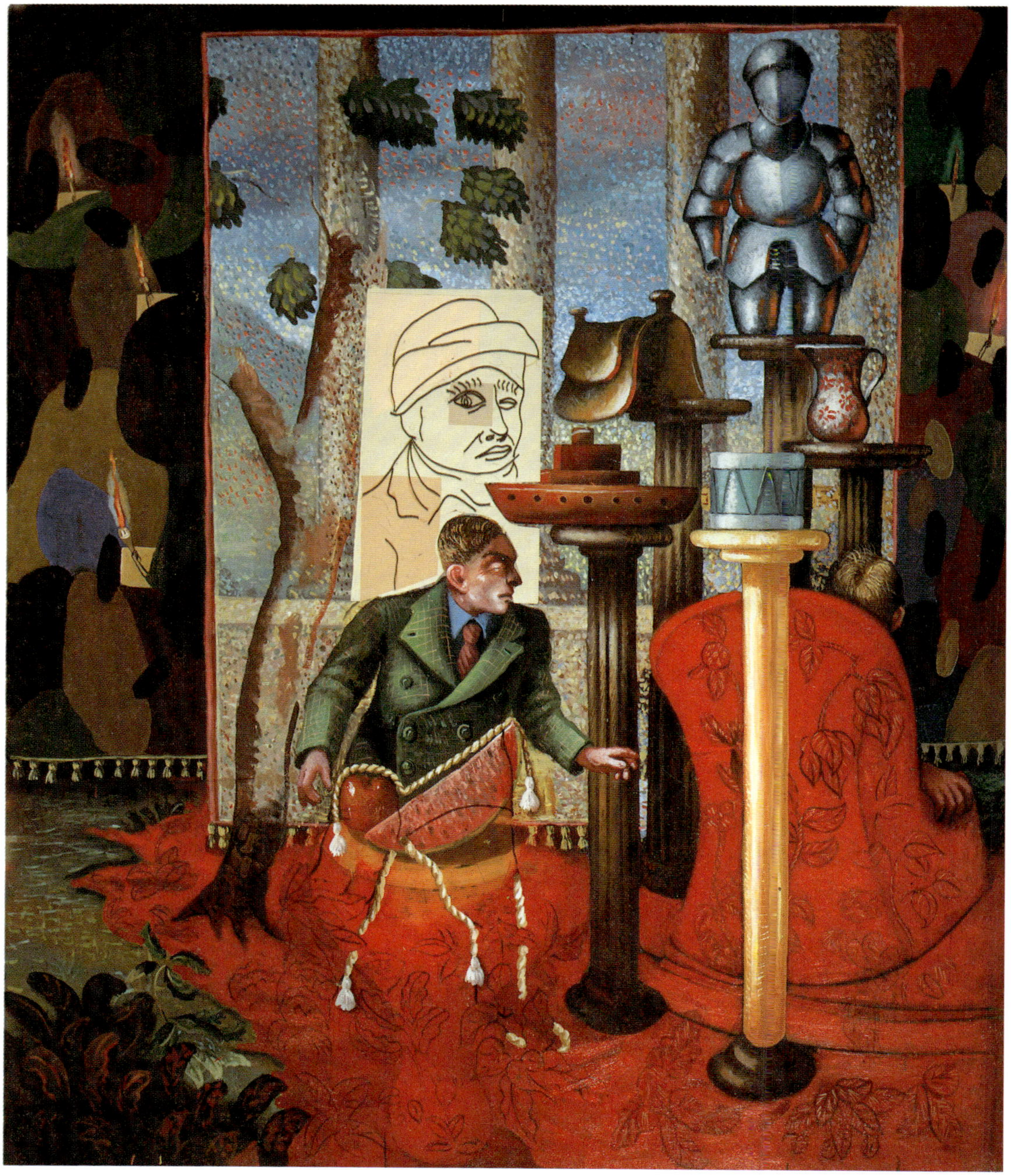

(PLATE 51) *Looking for Gold in a Forest*, oil paint, collage, 239 × 203.2 cm, 1989

surface of the patterns of string in these does seem to be important. It eschews all pretension and paradoxically reaches a kind of beauty.

In proportion to his wish to make something new from the language of painting, the limits of the painter's art are something that Campbell has been more

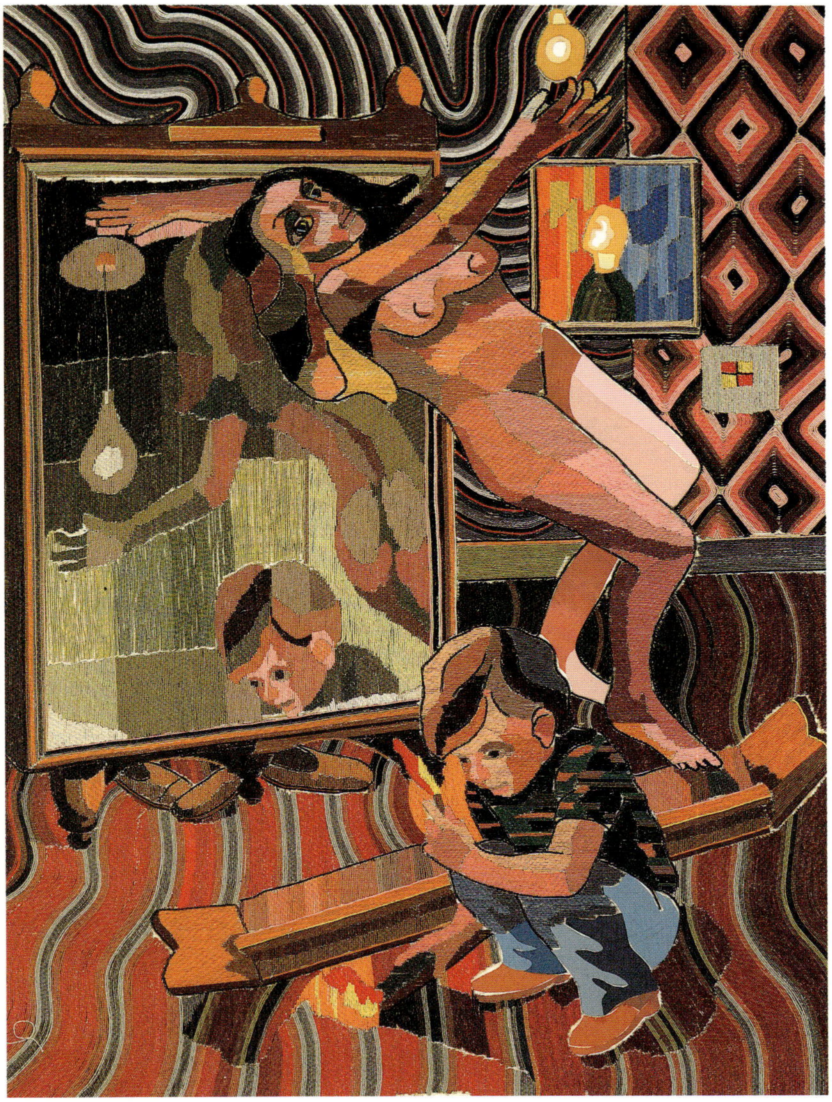

(PLATE 52) *Penelope at Home Waiting for Dad's Return*, collage on canvas, 114 × 158 cm, 1991 (CAT. 36)

aware of than most. Here in this group of collages from 1990–91, he has consciously grappled with them directly. This is what he said about them in conversation with the author:

> I thought people would be attracted by the sheer craziness of building a work up starting with a piece of string. It was only the madness I was interested in. To do the task was all I believed in. I only believed in applying string every day.

The first of them was *The Artist's Chair (Pl.53)*. It is like the space in a Francis Bacon with an empty chair and a bottle from which a cloud is rising like a genie of inspiration. It is simple and immediate and in a way it is typical of them all. They grew in the making. They were not

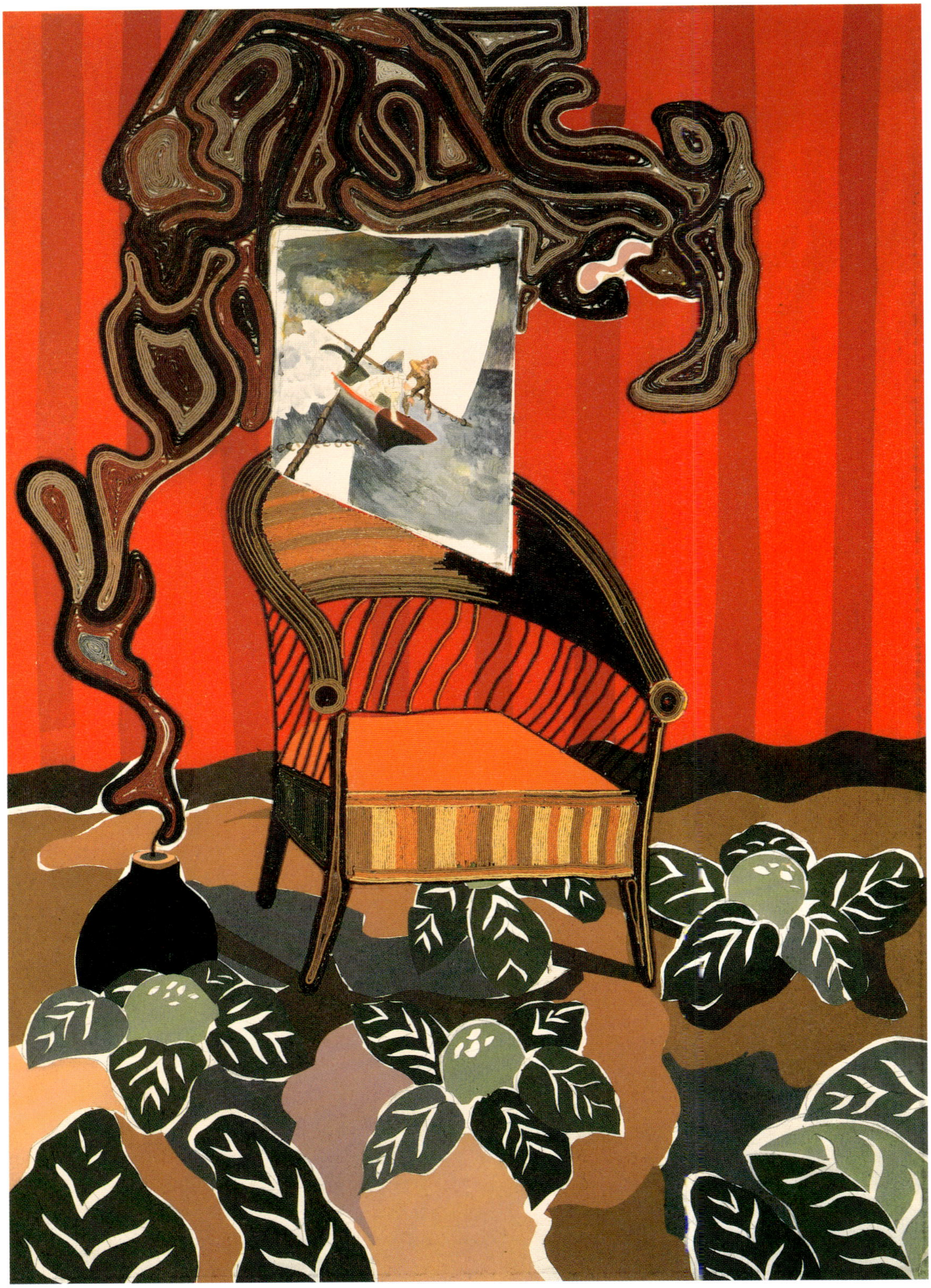

(PLATE 53) *The Artist's Chair*, collage on canvas, 52.4 × 109.2 cm, 1990–91 (CAT. 29)

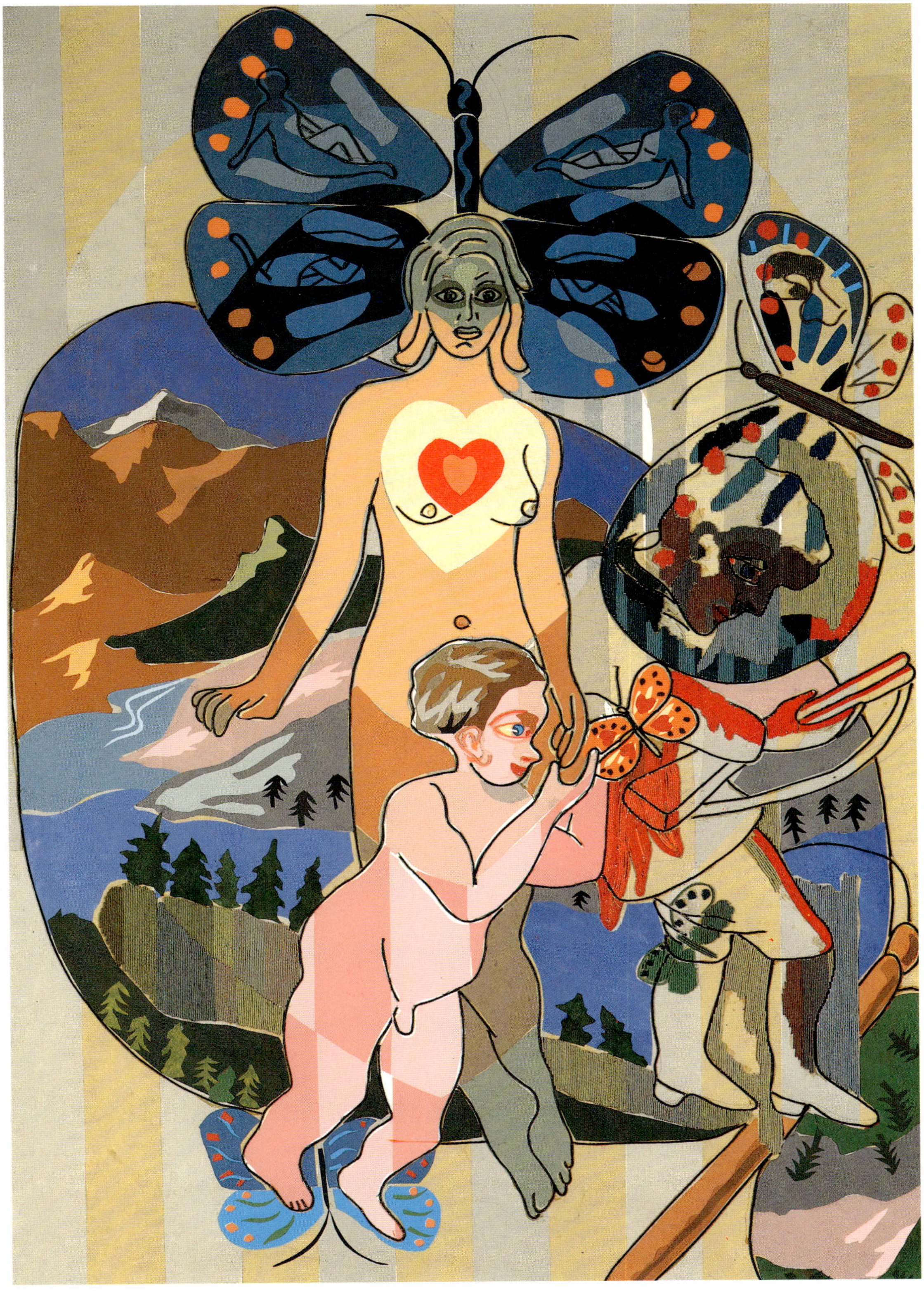

(PLATE 54) *Love*, collage on canvas, 177 × 121 cm, 1991 (CAT. 37)

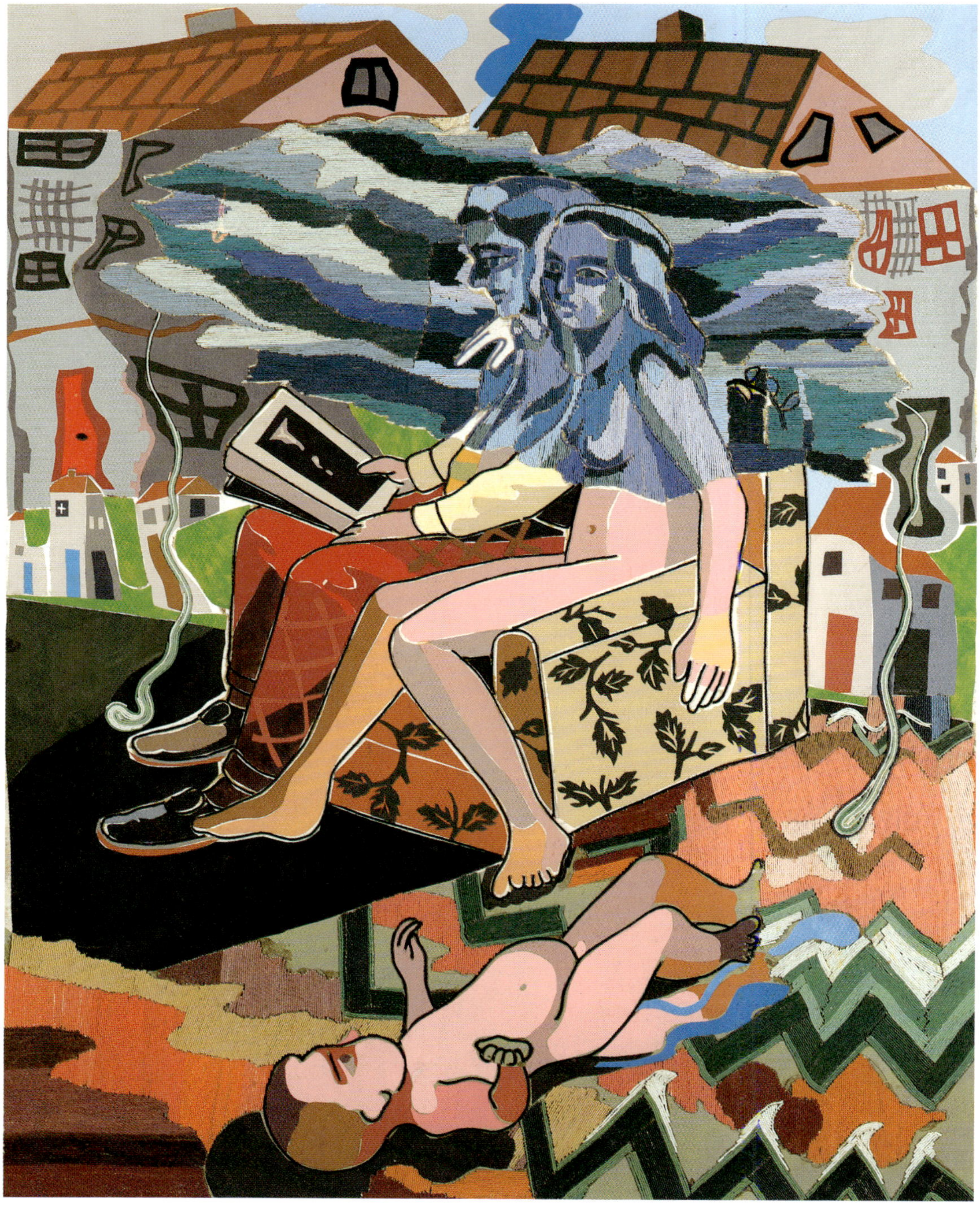

(PLATE 55) *Birth of Eurithia with Drowned Family*, collage on canvas, 150 × 120 cm, 1991 (CAT. 32)

planned beyond the natural evolution of a formal idea just as the cloud rises from the bottle. *Love (Pl.54)*, for instance, is a highly conventionalised Venus and Cupid standing against a giant butterfly's wing and a hunter with a phallic gun lurks behind them. The artist described how he worked the arrangement inwards from a large heart-shape suggested by the butterfly's wing, through a series of concentric shapes to a heart in the centre.

It is a formal image of love's convolutions and many of these collages, put together intuitively, are formal in their impact. *Penelope at Home Waiting for Dad's Return* takes pattern to the edges of the picture and then suspends the figures in the field of force that it creates. In others, a bizarre narrative seems to be acted out *(Pls.55, 56, 57)*. Earlier themes are touched on in this series too. *Dream of the Hunter's Muse (Pl.58)*, for example, refers back to the story of Diana and Actaeon with the hunter, the dead stag and a naked woman in the forest. Here though, she seems at first to have been shot as part of his quarry, but the posy of flowers embroidered at her open knees, the playful cat and the direction of his gaze suggest that it may be she who catches him.

One of the most remarkable of this group is *Fake Ophelia (Pl.59)*. It evokes the tension between convention, which is the basis of all art and which the method used here so unambiguously entails, and representation with its express ambition to transcend convention. The naked body of a woman is lying diagonally across the composition. She is entirely represented by neatly cut lengths of different-coloured string. They are in a dappled pattern like the light on the water. At her head and right arm, where the artist has not drawn round the ends of the string, the slightly blurred effect suggests that she is underwater and ripples circle out from her right arm where it breaks the surface. Like Millais's *Ophelia* with its river-bank flowers painted in the meticulous way that Ruskin admired so much and equated with moral truth,[36] Campbell's Ophelia, too, is surrounded by flowers and leaves. But he uses cut-out, conventional tree and leaf shapes and the flowers are the flowers on a printed, daisy wallpaper. In the top left there is a tapestry-kit picture of a farmstead with a wind pump. In the context, it is strangely beautiful, but it is also ironically Ruskinian. It epitomises the qualities of sincerity and honest labour which he valued so highly and which are paradoxically present in the whole work in spite of its use of conventional forms. They make it just as true as it is fake.

A Small Death in the Family (Pl.60) takes this argument about reality and fakes a stage further. The central figure is inspired by Magritte. In conversation Campbell described it:

> It is Magritte's *Metamorphosis* where [the girl] is made of wood. I thought, if she was made of string, it would be an even better transformation. You know how people say that Jasper Johns took Magritte even further. Well, I thought I would be doing the same, a woman made out of wood, I thought I would turn her actually, physically into string. It takes the absurdity further on down the line.

In a way perhaps all these collages are about metamorphosis. Collage after all partakes of and transforms the real in a different and more direct way than painting does. It is even more a fake than an illusion.

All these collages sprang from strong feeling as he has made clear, but in *A Small Death in the Family* it also seems to be given direct expression. In the collage, a family with a child lying in front of them and a Beatrix Potter rabbit with a wheelbarrow crossing the picture are sitting against a scene from a bullfight. The collage takes up the theme of a number of poetically beautiful etchings in Picasso's *Vollard Suite* where he uses the imagery of Beauty and the Beast. He sees the Beast as the Minotaur and uses his bull-like quality to invoke the savage imagery of the bull-fight, but by the presence of Beauty, he achieves a touching reconciliation of violence and tenderness in pathos.

This quality in *A Small Death in the Family* opens the way towards the paintings that have followed these collages. The collages were a kind of return to first principles, a clearing of the ground. Inspired by strong feeling, they also led to a direct and forceful expression of emotion in the paintings that followed them. Campbell himself says that his painting has always come out of his emotional life and the emotional charge of much of it is clear just through the strength of the presence of the image. The clowning in his work of the mid-eighties was a way of screening this emotion, but it is tangible nonetheless. At the same time, humour and irony were a way of keeping pretension at a distance. In his recent work, however, feeling is once again much closer to the surface.

Campbell began this most recent series of paintings in the latter part of 1991 and completed it in March 1993. In a year-and-a-half he produced almost thirty paintings. These are the paintings that he discusses in the interview that follows. Thirteen are large works on paper; the remainder are canvases. The largest of the latter is more than nine feet square and all of them are close to this in size. It is an extraordinary body of work. Compared to the light, bright colours of the Third Eye show, here the overall feeling is much darker. The paintings are ambitious and successful and they have an immediate and commanding dramatic presence.

In some of the first paintings in this group, the earlier way of working seems actually to be displaced within the picture. In *The Family as Memory (Pl.62)*, for example, one of several 'family' pictures *(Pls.63, 64)*, the family are painted in light colours, but are squeezed behind a white picket-fence by the looming, dark figures of the tribal carvings in the foreground. Looking at the series together, the strong tonal contrasts are immediately apparent. In the interview, the artist makes it clear that he intends this kind of contrast to work both dramatically and morally. In *The Croatian Blouse (Pl.65)*, *Murder Running Through the Woods (Pl.66)*, or *Alice in Ruins (Pl.67)*, it is an explicit contrast of states. The title of the first is a homage to Matisse's *The Rumanian Blouse* and the red spots on the white blouse also take up a motif from Matisse's painting, but the mood in Campbell's picture is very different. It is a brilliantly condensed composition of light framed in darkness. A couple sit in what, as they cannot read the signs, they imagine is an island of calm, but the terrible events portrayed in the darkness that surrounds them are breaking in on their illusory peace. Blood drips on to the girl's blouse as it might in a Hitchcock film. Here the artist takes up again, but now explicitly, the theme that underlay so much of his previous work, innocence confounded by experience, the unreliability of signs and the fragility of illusion. *Murder Running Through the Woods* is a dark reflection on this same theme of violence breaking in on peace. In an island of light, a family are enjoying a *déjeuner sur l'herbe* unaware of the violence that will imminently overwhelm them. However, in spite of the threatening darkness that surrounds her too, Alice keeps her light of hope burning in *Alice in Ruins*.

The latter is an optimistic picture, but a pessimistic world view is apparent in several of the others too. In *Dead Man's Cocktail Party (Pl.68)*, for instance, his-

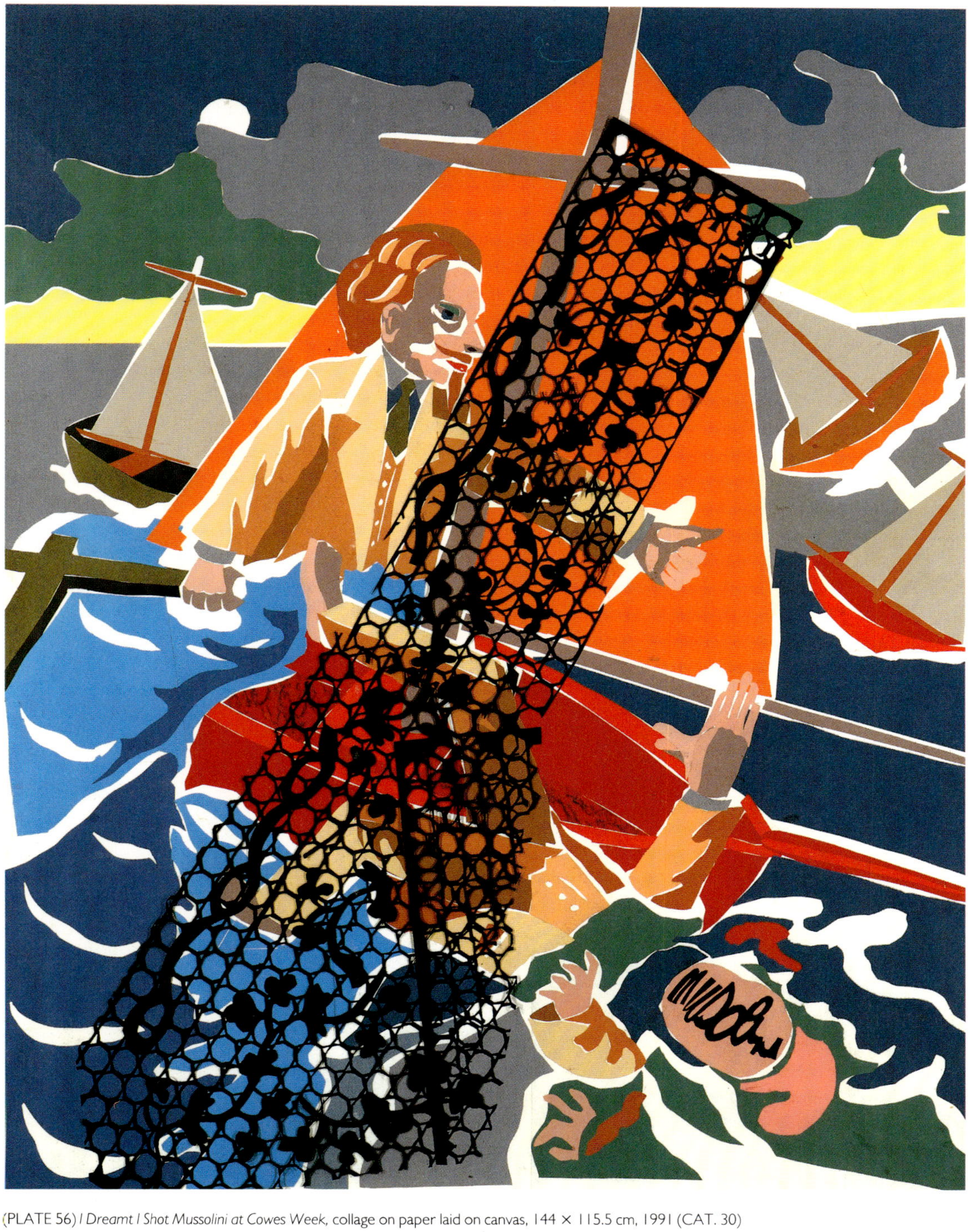

(PLATE 56) *I Dreamt I Shot Mussolini at Cowes Week*, collage on paper laid on canvas, 144 × 115.5 cm, 1991 (CAT. 30)

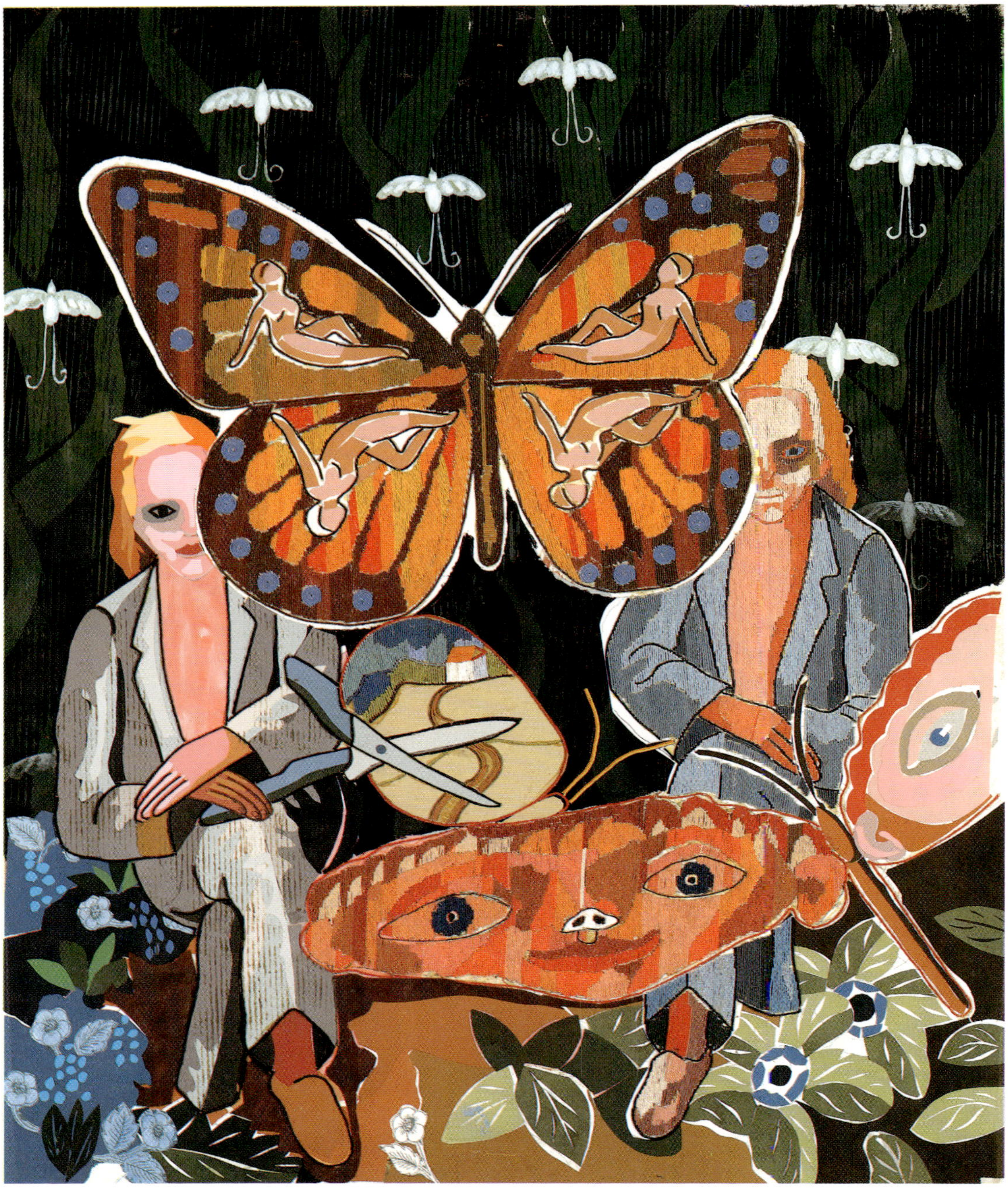

(PLATE 57) *Portrait of Two Cousins with the Same Mother who Left them Alone when she was Seventeen*, collage on canvas, 149 × 121 cm, 1991 (CAT.31)

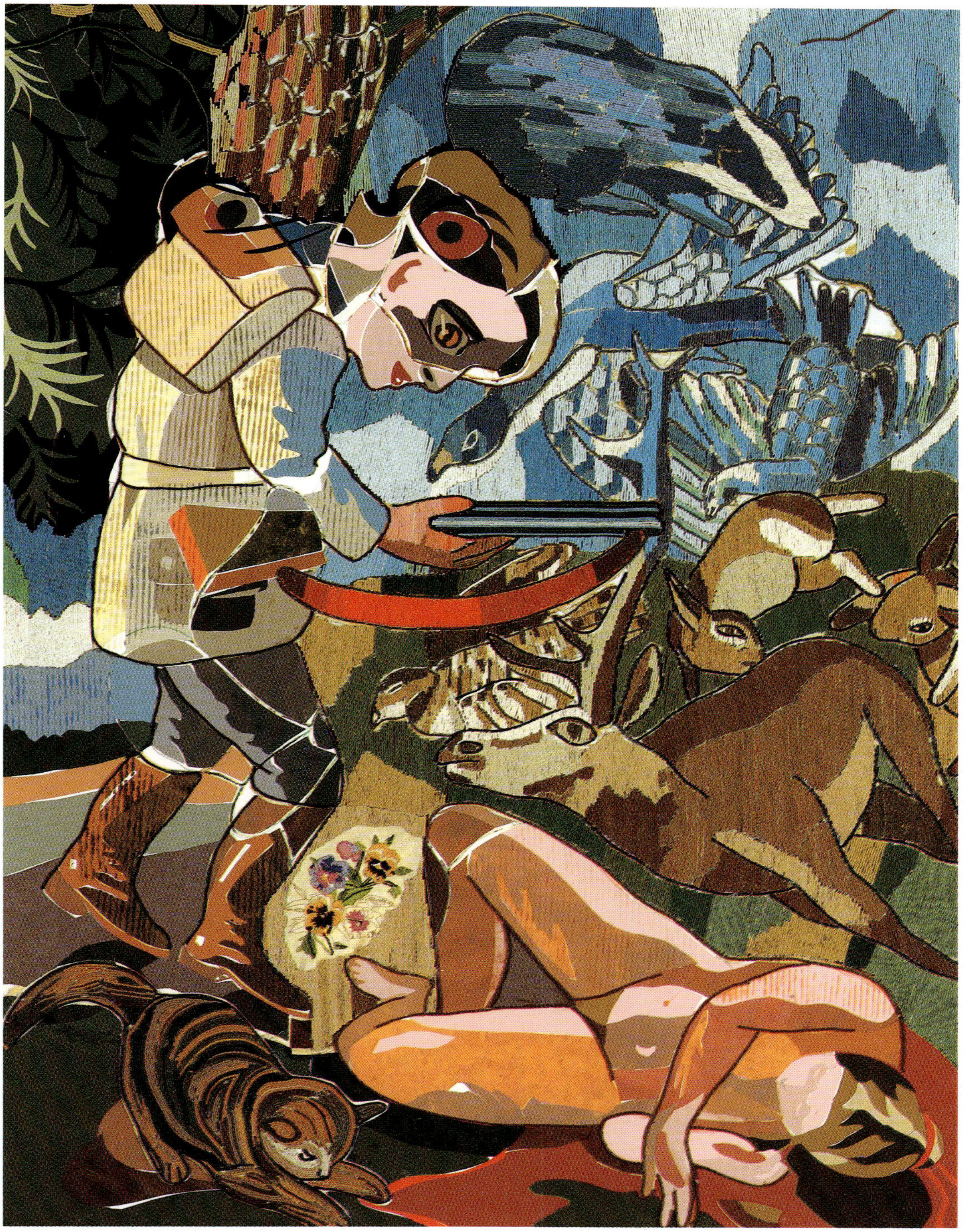

(PLATE 58) *Dream of the Hunter's Muse*, collage on canvas, 146.5 × 111 cm, 1991 (CAT. 38)

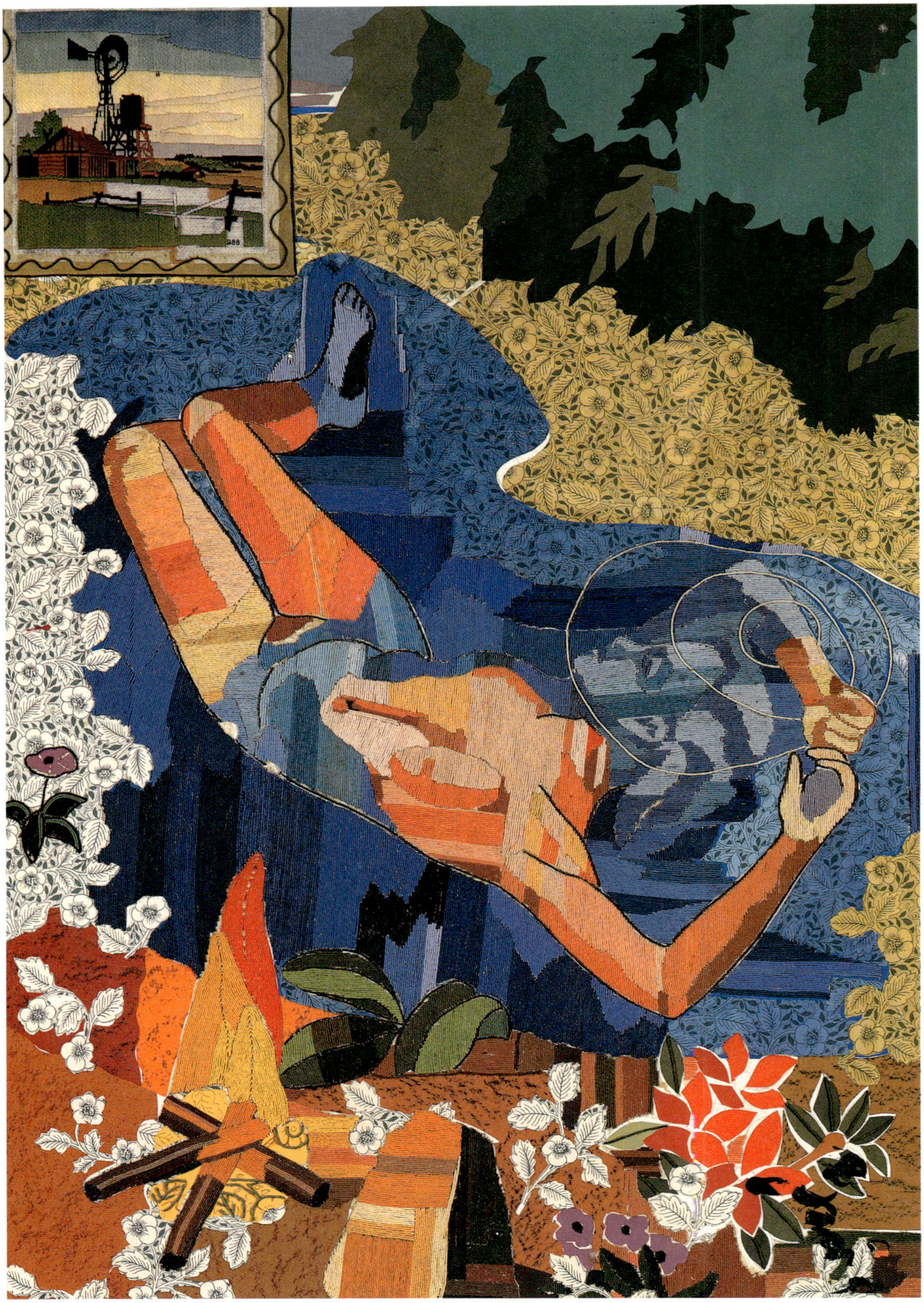

(PLATE 59) *Fake Ophelia*, collage on canvas, 173.5 × 119.5 cm, 1991 (CAT. 34)

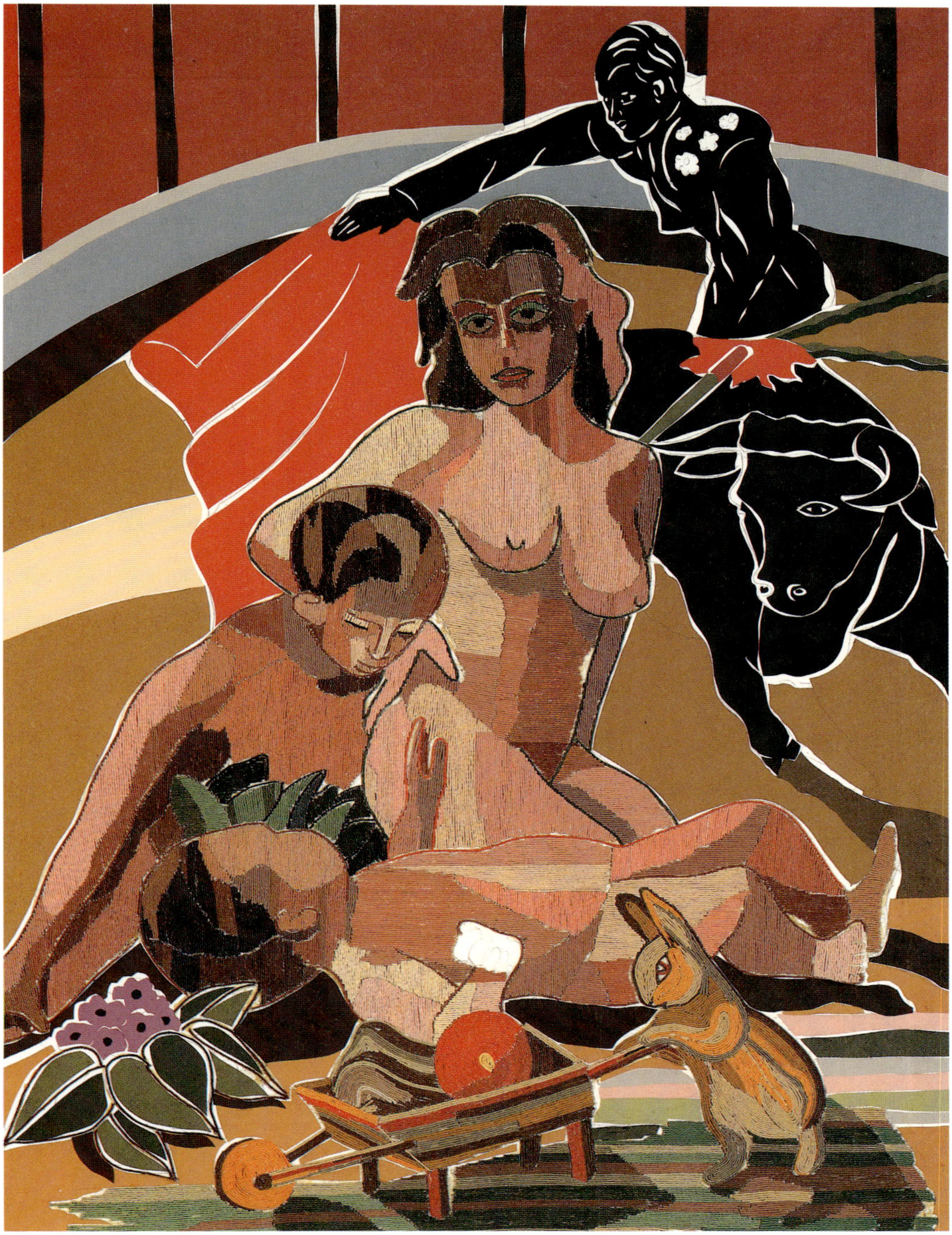

(PLATE 60) *A Small Death in the Family*, collage on canvas, 152 × 115 cm, 1991 (CAT. 35)

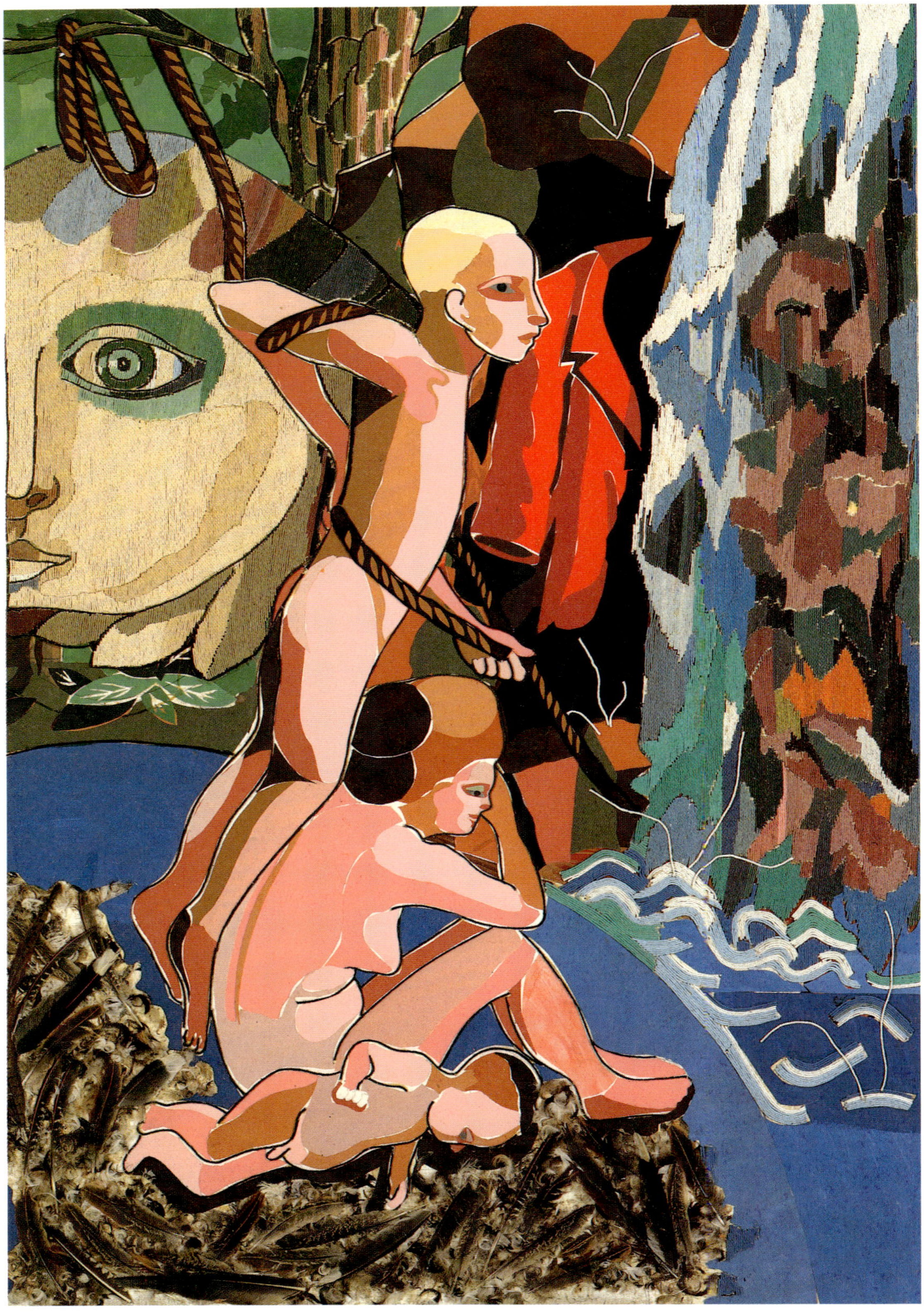

(PLATE 61) *The Family of the Accidental Angel*, collage on canvas, 174 × 121.5 cm, 1991 (CAT. 33)

tory looks on, indifferent to the sufferings of the present. *Painting in Defence of Migrants (Pl.69)* also comments on those sufferings though there is a hint of a gentler world in it too as the migrant birds come to the rescue of the displaced as they might come to the aid of lost children in a fairy tale. The source of all this mischief is represented in *The Spider (Pl.70)* as a malevolent, sexless sprite. The devil himself appears as a saddened observer, gifted, or cursed like the artist with an extra eye in *The Devil's Eye (Pl.71)*.

In all of these pictures, the artist handles different levels of space and depths of narrative reality with extraordinary accomplishment. This process is itself the subject of *The Spider on the Window, Monster in the Land (Pl.72)* which takes its inspiration from an Edgar Allan Poe story, a story which the artist himself suggests in turn took its inspiration from a painting. The picture's theme is levels of reality and our awareness of them, not as an enclosed and self-sufficient game, but rather as in Velasquez's *Las Meninas*, as a way of locating the artist's own position which is somewhere between the mirror and the window.

In these paintings, the artist is not some kind of abstraction, however, a kind of objective and detached commentator like a mirror, or a transparent intermediary like a window. Some of the pictures are directly autobiographical. *Two Years of My Time (Pl.73)* is a very personal reflection on the passage of time, symbolised in the waterfall and more eccentrically by the unused Christmas presents, the pots of Brylcreem piling up year by year. The beautiful and poetic painting, *The Poetess (Pl.74)*, was inspired by a plastic sack found on a picnic. It first suggested water, then Cézanne's *Bathers* and then an image of drowning.

Drowning also appears in two of the other paintings. *The Drowned (Pl.75)* is like a poem as the artist imagines the ghosts of drowned people returning to play on the beach in the evening. *The Dream of St Sebastian (Pl.76)* is an altogether darker image, however. It offers a reflection on ideas that have had a constant place in the artist's work. The picture, he says, represents the moment of going under in sleep or in death. Death has often appeared in his work, but usually by being presented as murder, it is conventionalised as it is in crime fiction. Here it is confronted more directly. St Sebastian, Campbell says, fascinates him because he is half in love with death. This is implicit in the beauty that is an essential part of the iconography of St Sebastian. It is like Keats's yearning in the 'Ode to a Nightingale' where death and beauty meet. This temptation is itself the subject of *St Sebastian – Curtain (Pl.77)*, where in an ordinary interior, for a man in a reverie a net curtain turns into a waterfall and from its top, St Sebastian beckons the dreamer.

The Dream of St Sebastian draws on memories of the *Raft of the Medusa*, a painting that is itself very ambiguous about the artistic relationship between death and beauty, but like Géricault's, Campbell's picture matches the ambition of its theme with the scale of its realisation. It is a figure composition in the true grand manner and it is not surprising to find echoes of Titian and Cézanne in the extraordinary pyramid of seven naked figures.

St Sebastian's female equivalent, Andromeda, is the inspiration for the figure in *Penelope Rescued from her Suitors (Pl.78)* and men come to her aid as Perseus comes to the rescue of Andromeda. In the interview, the artist expresses some disquiet about this picture because it is too sexy and a little perverse, but in being so, it is in the main line of the iconography of Western art. There are countless versions of *Perseus and Andromeda* on the walls of the most respectable museums. As effec-

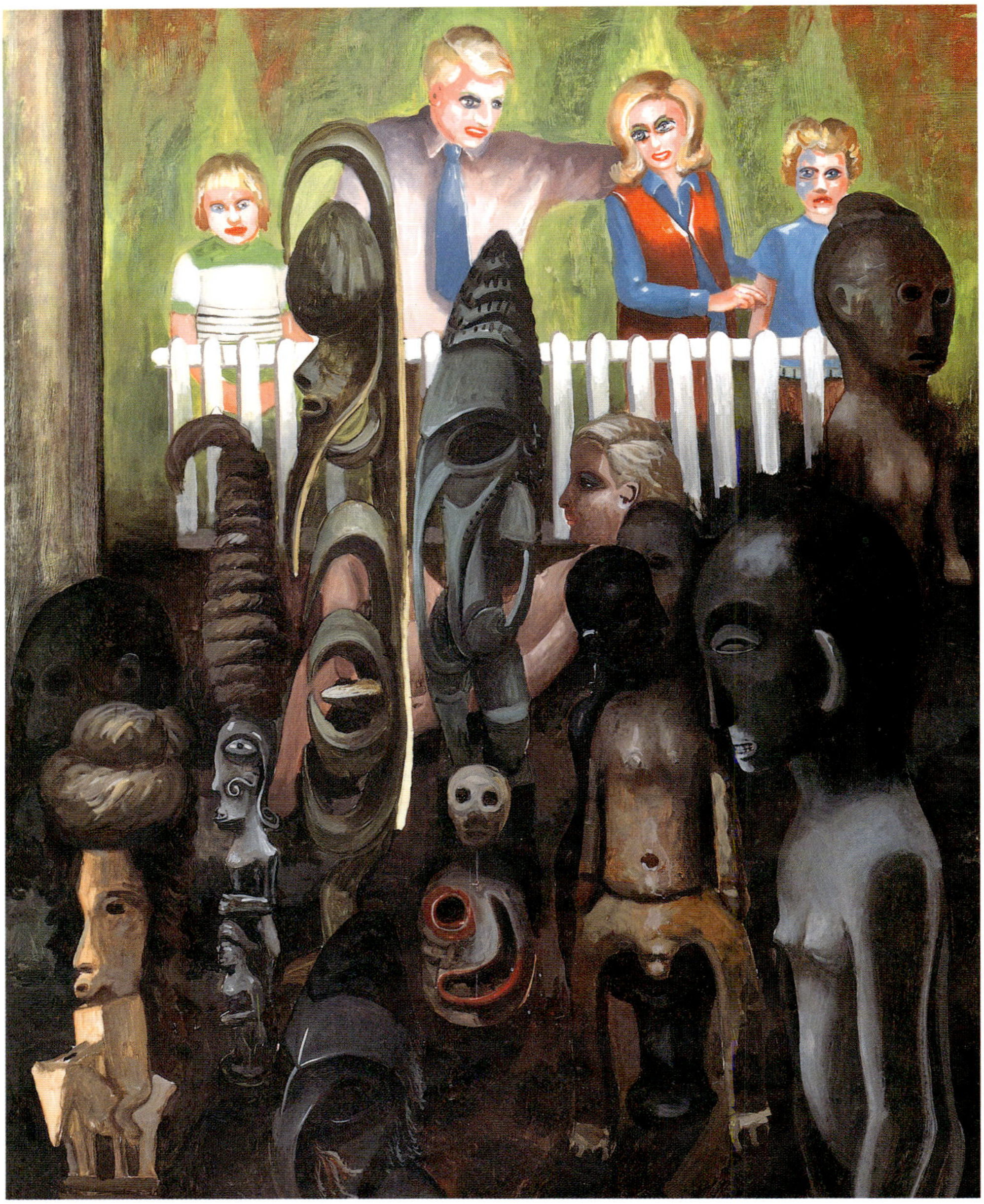

(PLATE 62) *The Family as Memory*, acrylic on paper, 193 × 147.3 cm, 1992 (CAT. 24)

tively as he does with St Sebastian therefore, the artist questions the unspoken motives that underlie the iconography of Western art whose mirror image is the violence and dispossession which he himself comments on so forcefully in some of the other paintings in this series.

Nevertheless, Campbell suggests that *Penelope* is the picture which should have Pinocchio hung alongside it. In the story, Pinocchio's nose grew each time he told a lie. As we saw much earlier in this discussion, Pinocchio is like Hunt, a kind of *doppelganger* of the artist. He was made of wood and so belonged in the world of art, but in spite of the fact that he

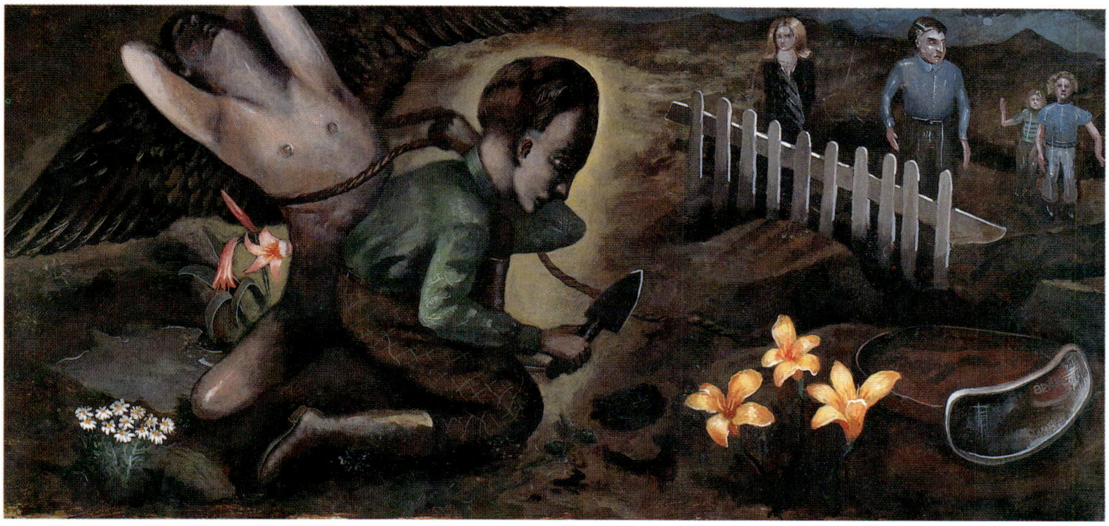

(PLATE 63) *The Family as Memory II*, acrylic on paper, 91.4 × 195 cm, 1992 (CAT. 25)

was himself an artifact, like Hunt, Pinocchio was all too fallibly human and suffered for it. Campbell wants to put his Pinocchio pictures alongside his other paintings so that his nose can serve as a kind of litmus paper to reveal a lie. His presence, paradoxically therefore, bears witness to the artist's search in his art for some kind of truth and in a strange way it aligns him with Ruskin.

There are three Pinocchio pictures in the present series. *Pinocchio, the Habit of the Shrike (Pl.79)* refers to the shrike as the butcher bird with its habit of impaling its victims on thorns as sharp as Pinocchio's nose. *Pinocchio in Chains (Pl.80)* shows him as he appears in his home town in Umbria as a prisoner. He is behind a picket-fence which Campbell explains in his account of the 'Family' pictures, he has adapted from Indonesian funerary art where it is a symbol of the barrier between the living and the dead. The implication of our viewpoint here is that it is Pinocchio who is living and the spectator beyond the fence who is in the land of the dead. In the third picture and the strangest one, *Pinocchio in Exile, Alone (Pl.81)*, surely we recognise clearly the *doppelganger* in a kind of strange self-portrait:

> I like him when he is old and pissed off, on his own, just standing there. He is sad by the sea with a glass. There is nothing very much there. He is waiting to become a myth.

Campbell would not be the artist he is if he could not focus so economically as he does in this picture how provisional all our certainties must be in an inextricable tangle of truth and falsehood.

Pictures like *The Croatian Blouse*, *In Defence of Migrants*, or *The Spider* remind us of Breughel's response to the insecurity and violence of his time. Looking back over Campbell's career so far, when so many of his contemporaries have seemed impotent in the face of this same anxiety and instability and able only to discourse on art to art, he has broken this circle of impotence and given these things expression. These latest pictures will surely become icons of their time, not because of their topicality, which will inevitably fade, but because by their strength as images they successfully articulate something universal *(Pls.82-87)*.

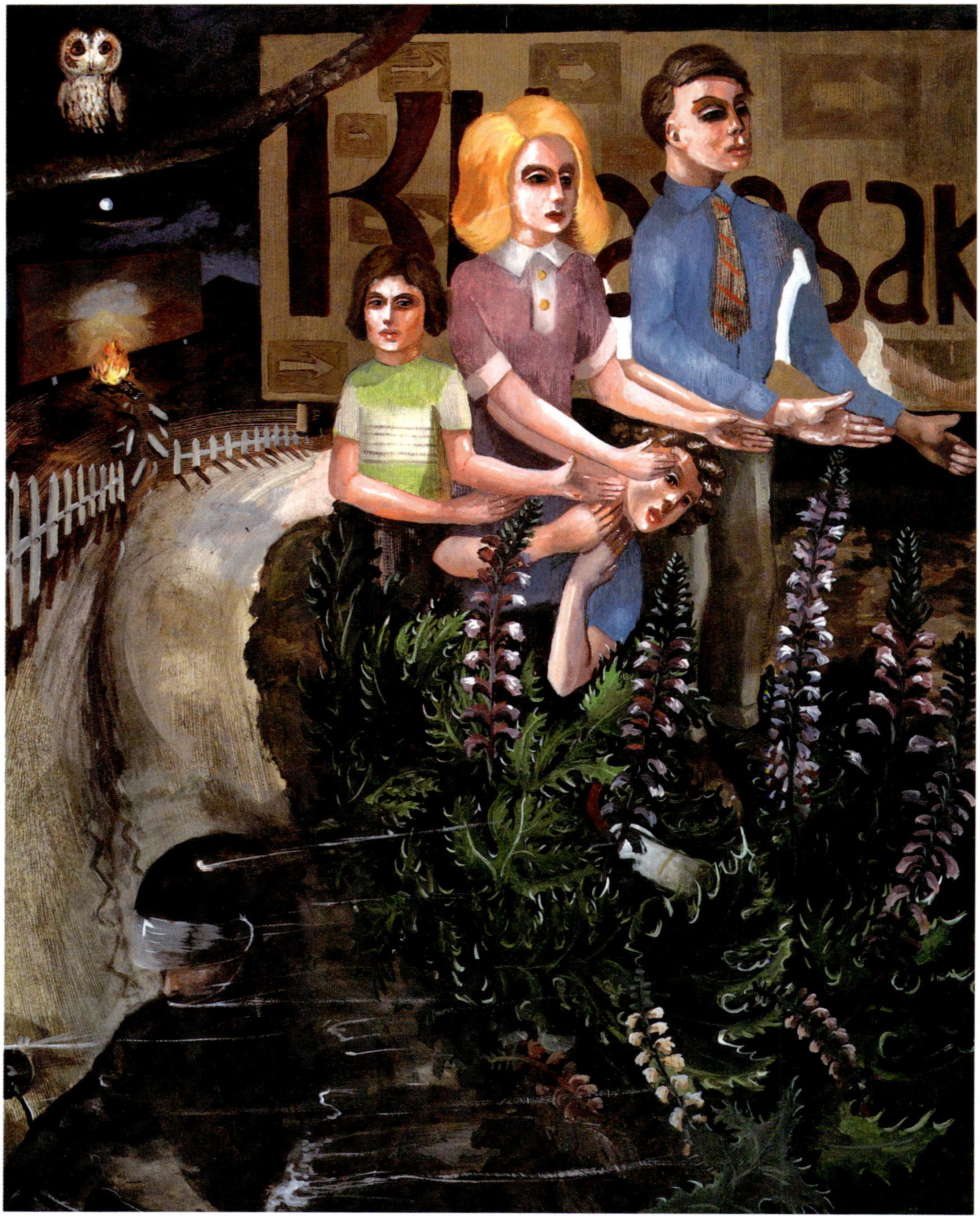

(PLATE 64) *The Family as Motorbike Road Sign*, acrylic on paper, 179.4 × 138.8 cm, 1992–93 (CAT. 26)

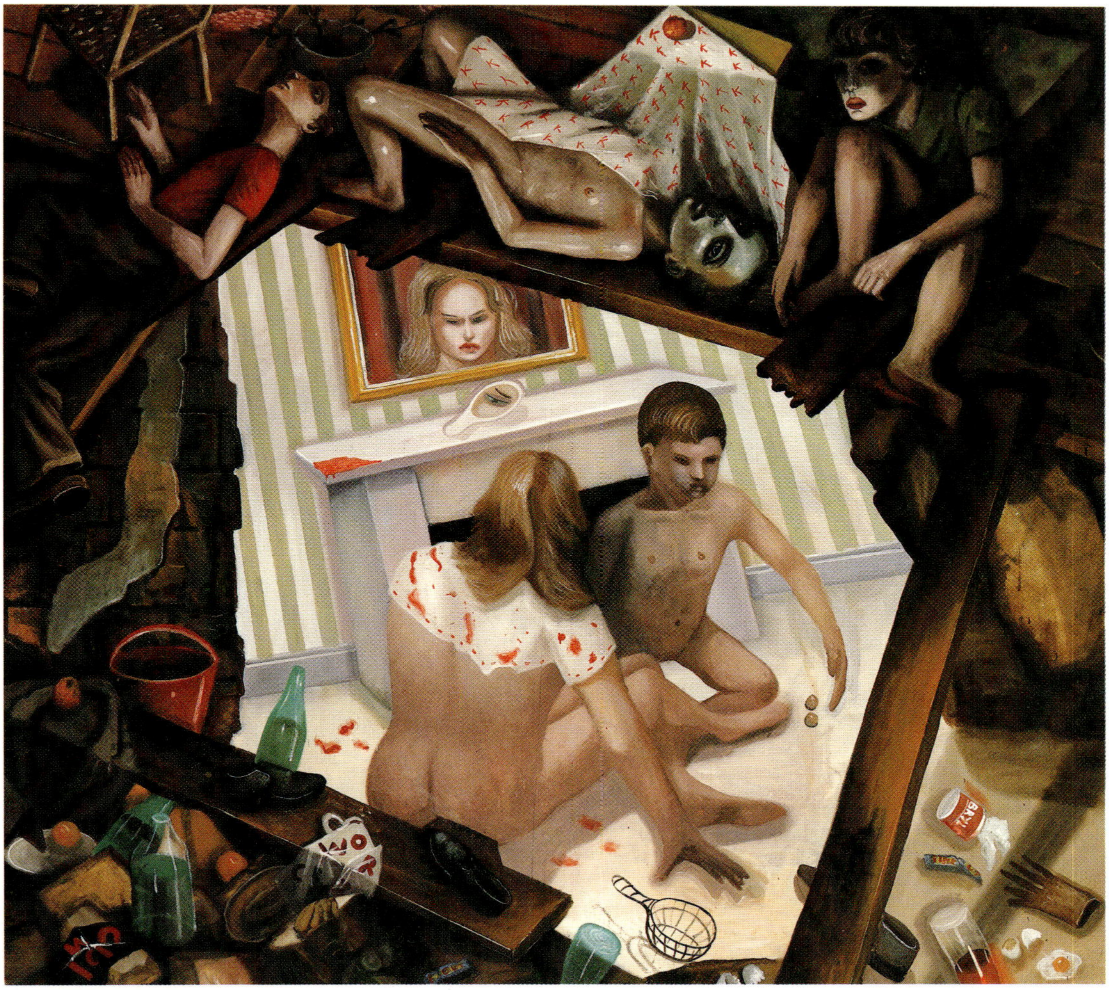

(PLATE 65) *The Croatian Blouse*, acrylic on canvas, 210.8 × 226.7 cm, 1992 (CAT. 2)

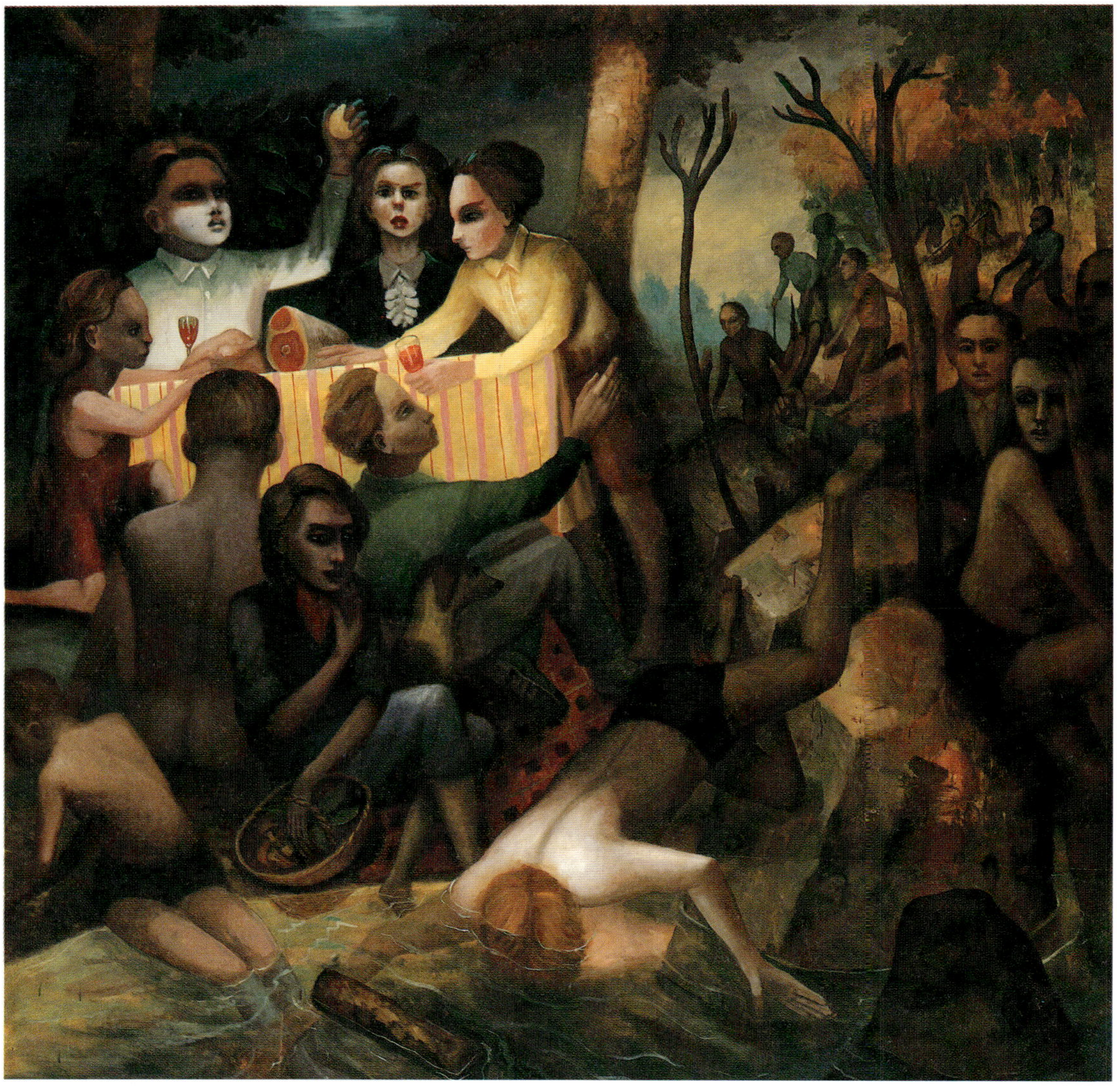

(PLATE 66) *Murder Running Through the Woods*, oil on canvas, 249.2 × 243.9 cm, 1993 (CAT. 13)

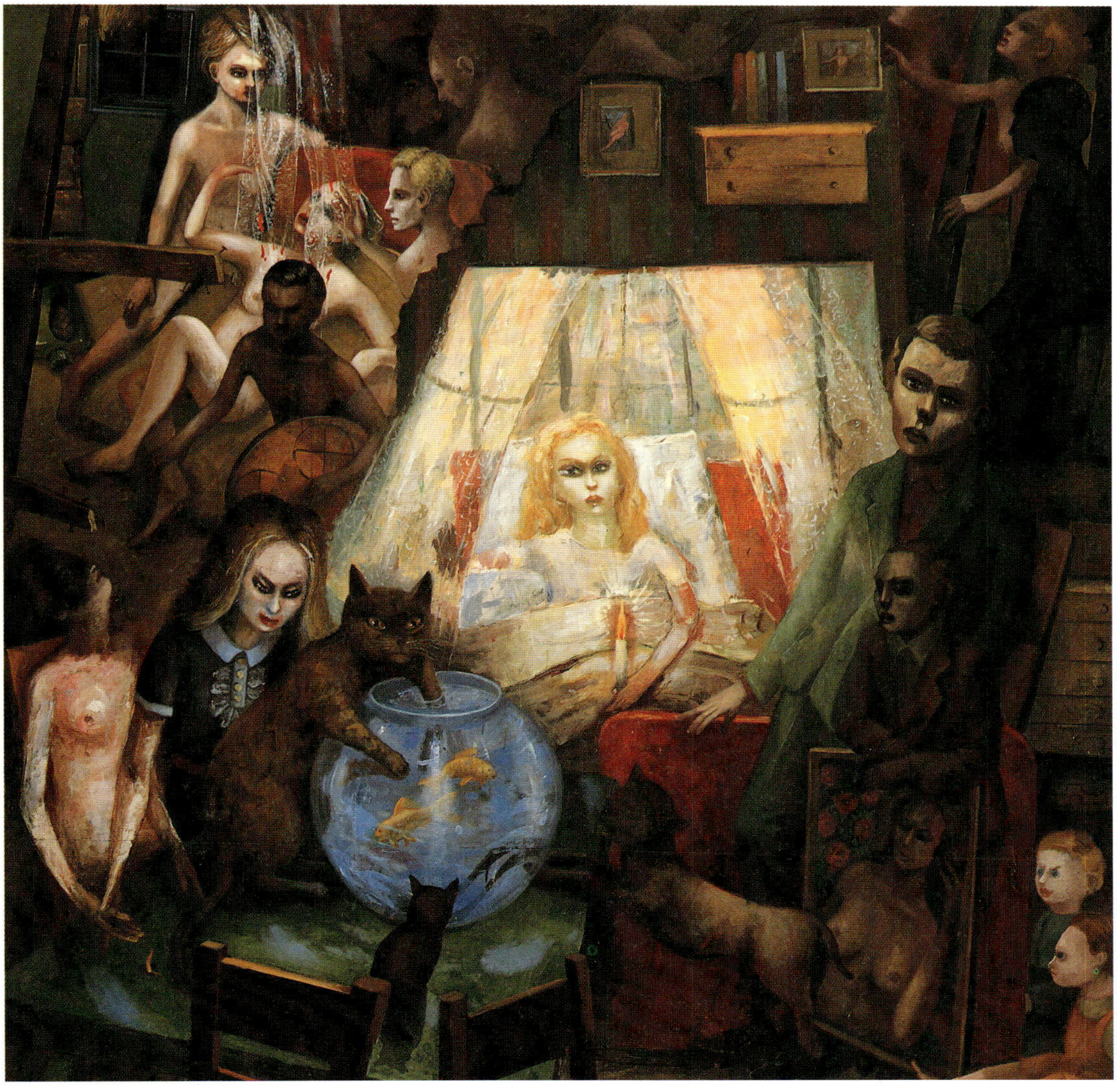

(PLATE 67) *Alice in Ruins*, oil on canvas, 269.9 × 263.7 cm, 1992–93 (CAT. 11)

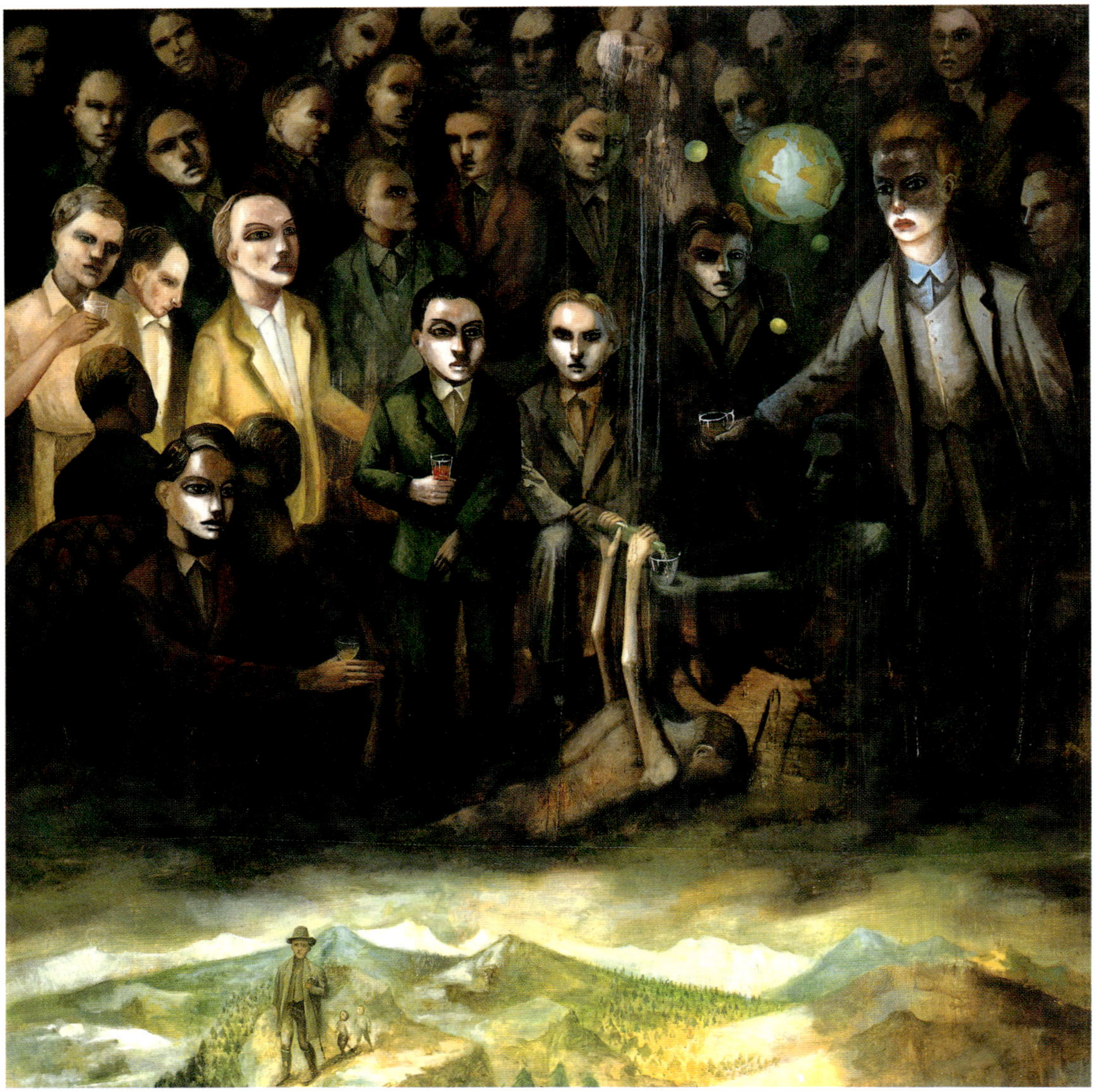

(PLATE 68) *Dead Man's Cocktail Party*, oil on canvas, 283.5 × 269.2 cm, 1992–93 (CAT. 10)

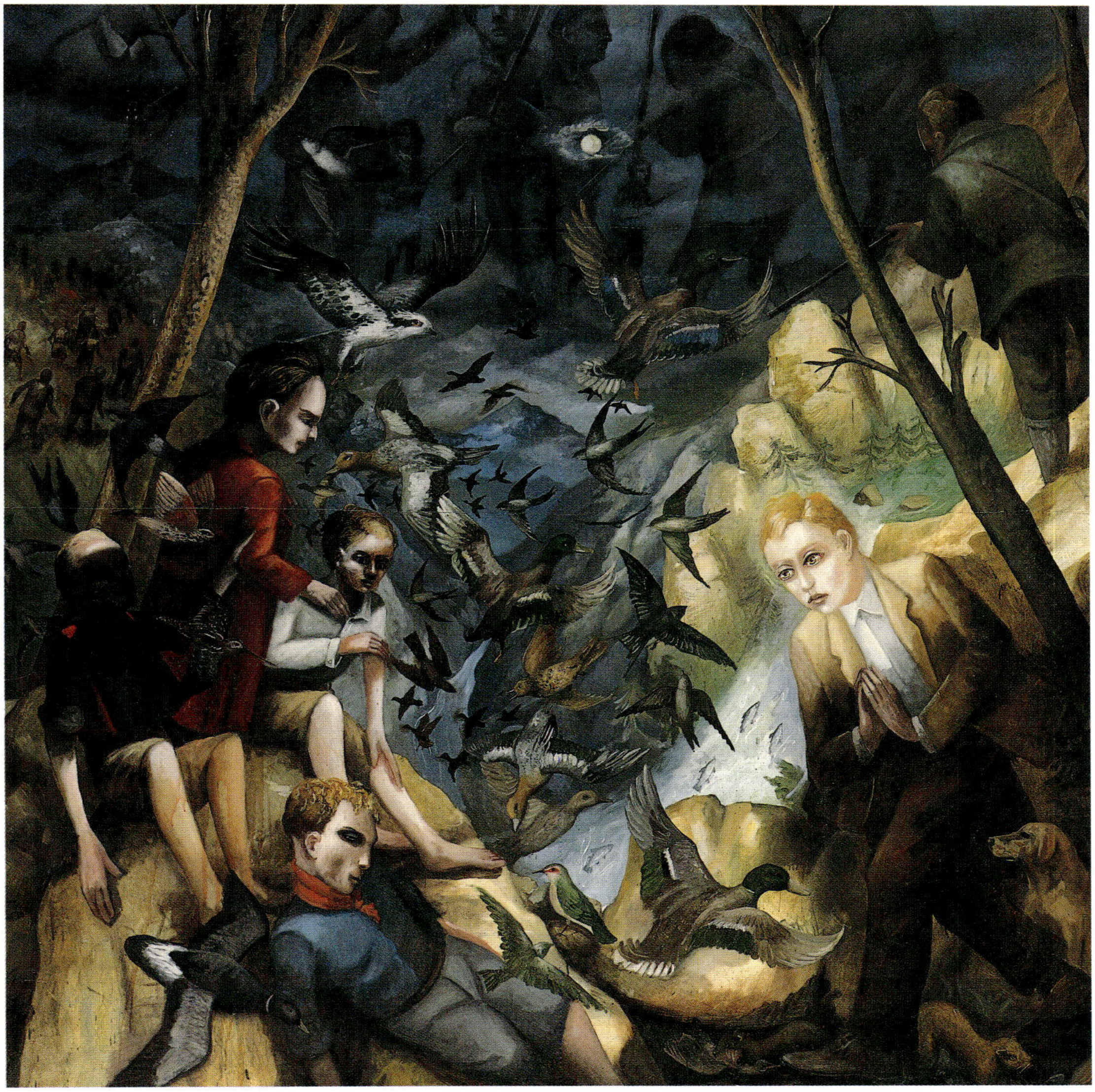

(PLATE 69) *Painting in Defence of Migrants*, oil on canvas, 272.4 × 256.5 cm, 1993 (CAT. 14)

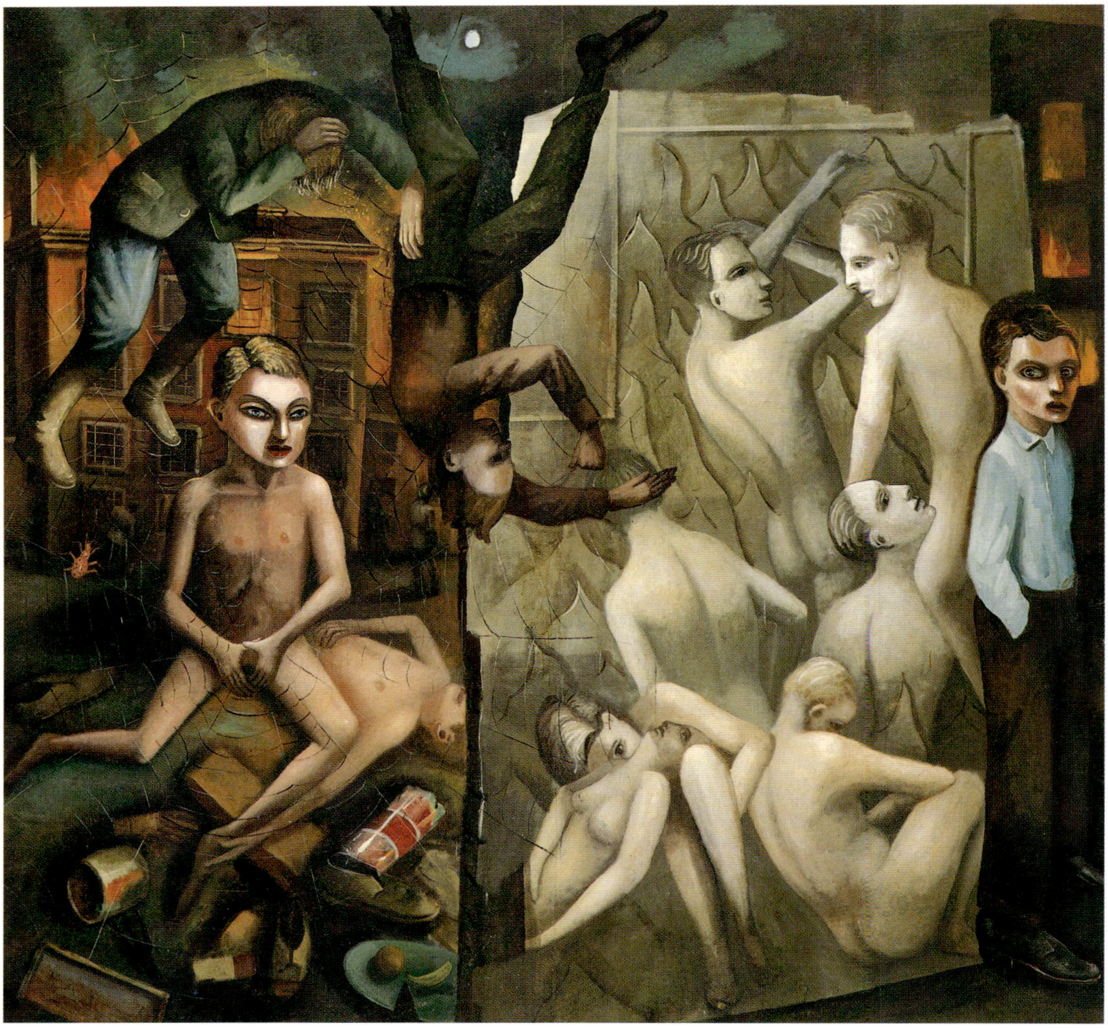

(PLATE 70) *The Spider*, oil on canvas, 221.5 × 234.3 cm, 1992–93 (CAT. 5)

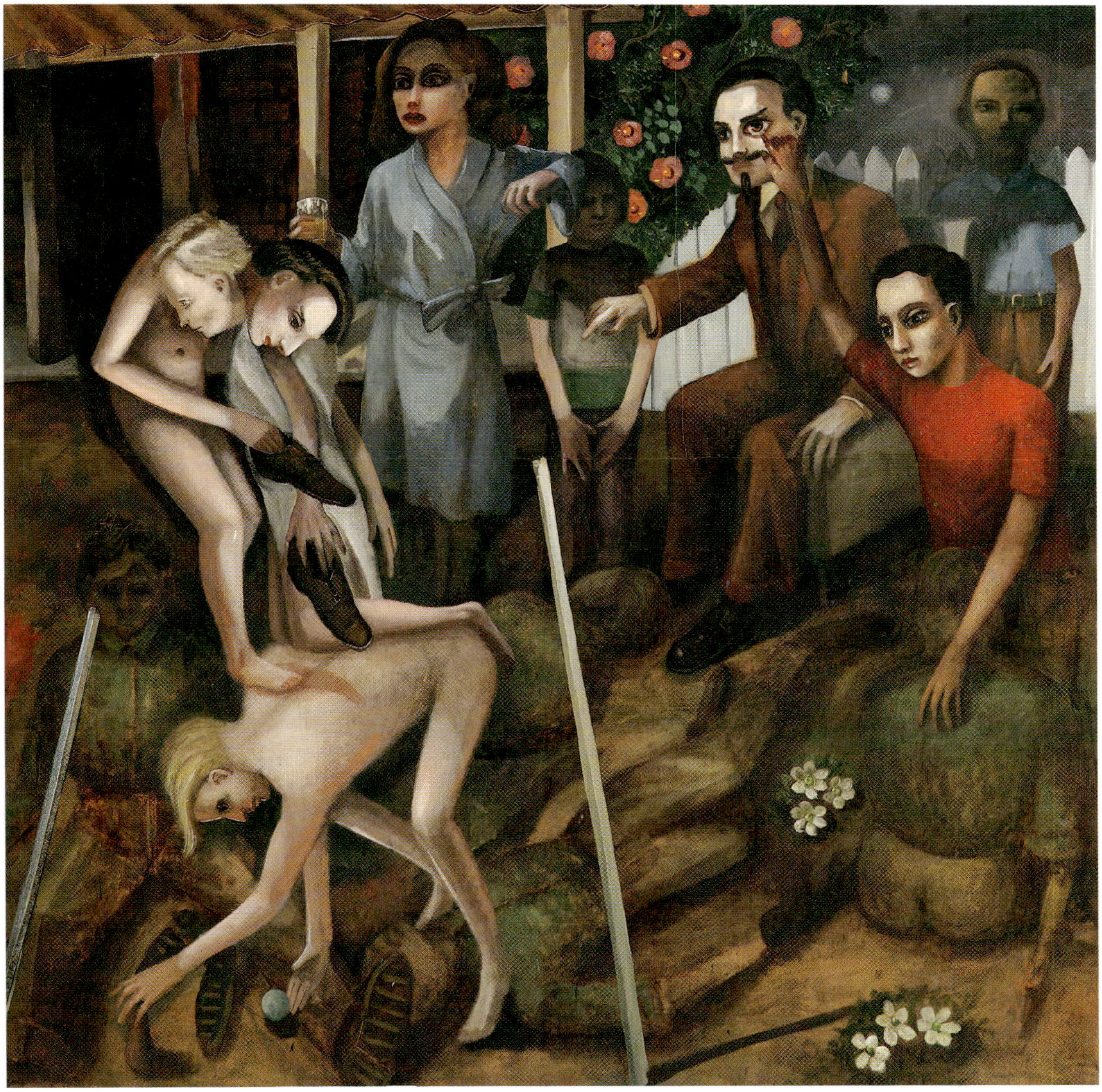

(PLATE 71) *The Devil's Eye*, oil on canvas, 218.7 × 211.4 cm, 1992–93 (CAT. 9)

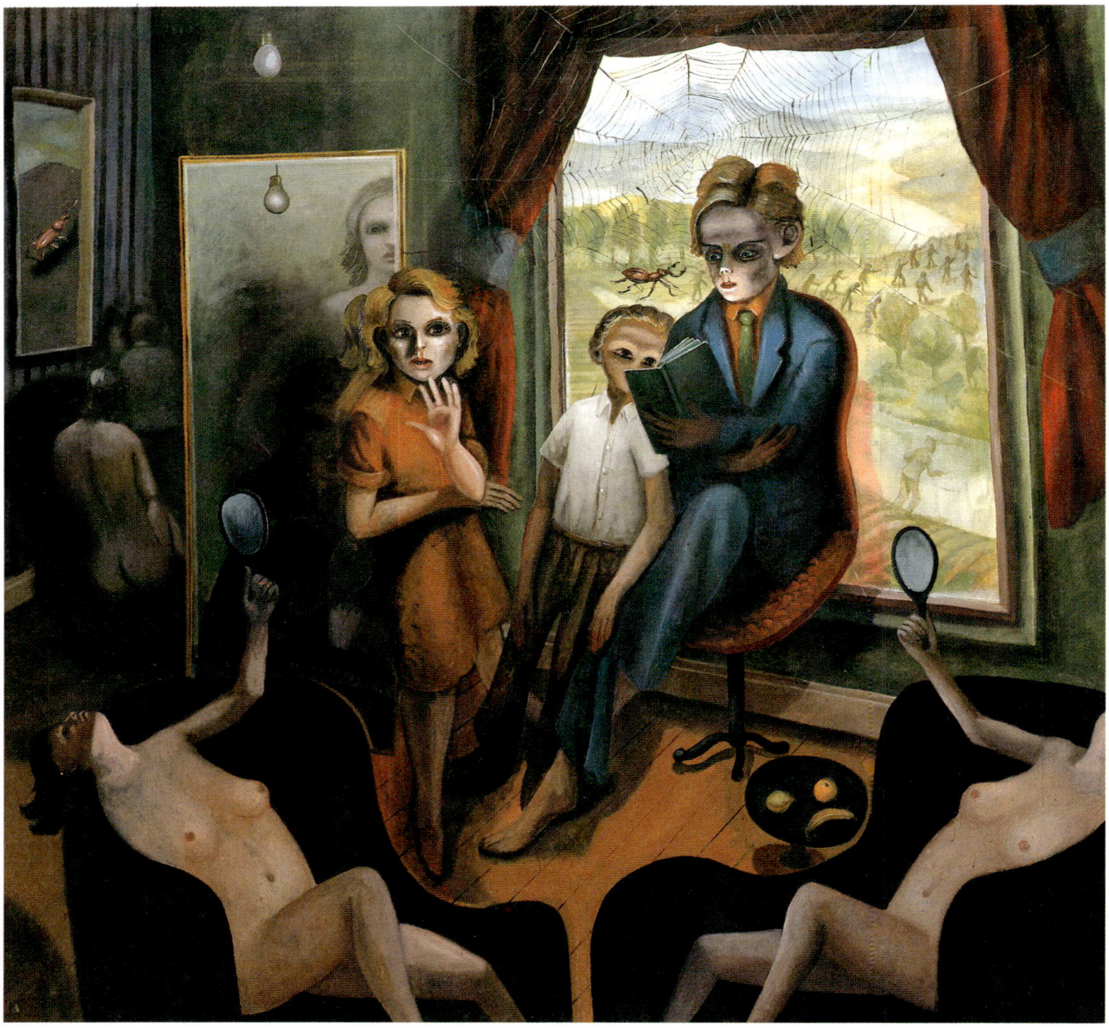

(PLATE 72) *Spider on the Window, Monster in the Land*, oil on canvas, 220.4 × 232.7 cm, 1992–93 (CAT. 4)

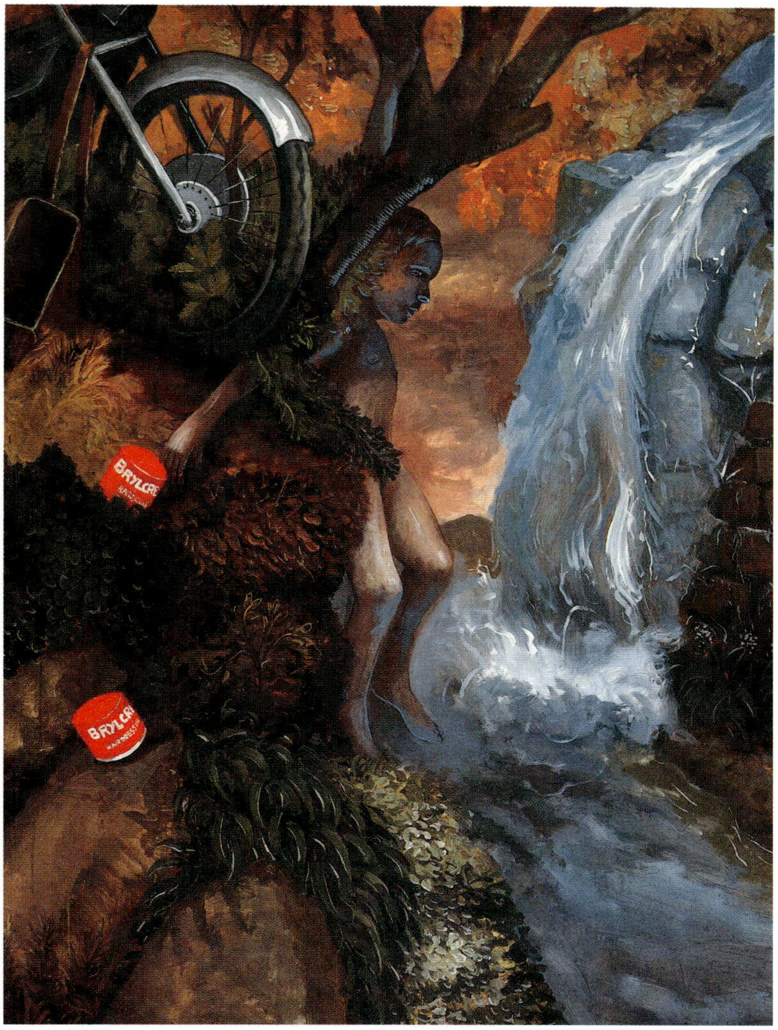

(PLATE 73) *Two Years of my Time*, acrylic on paper, 185.5 × 144.2 cm, 1992 (CAT. 21)

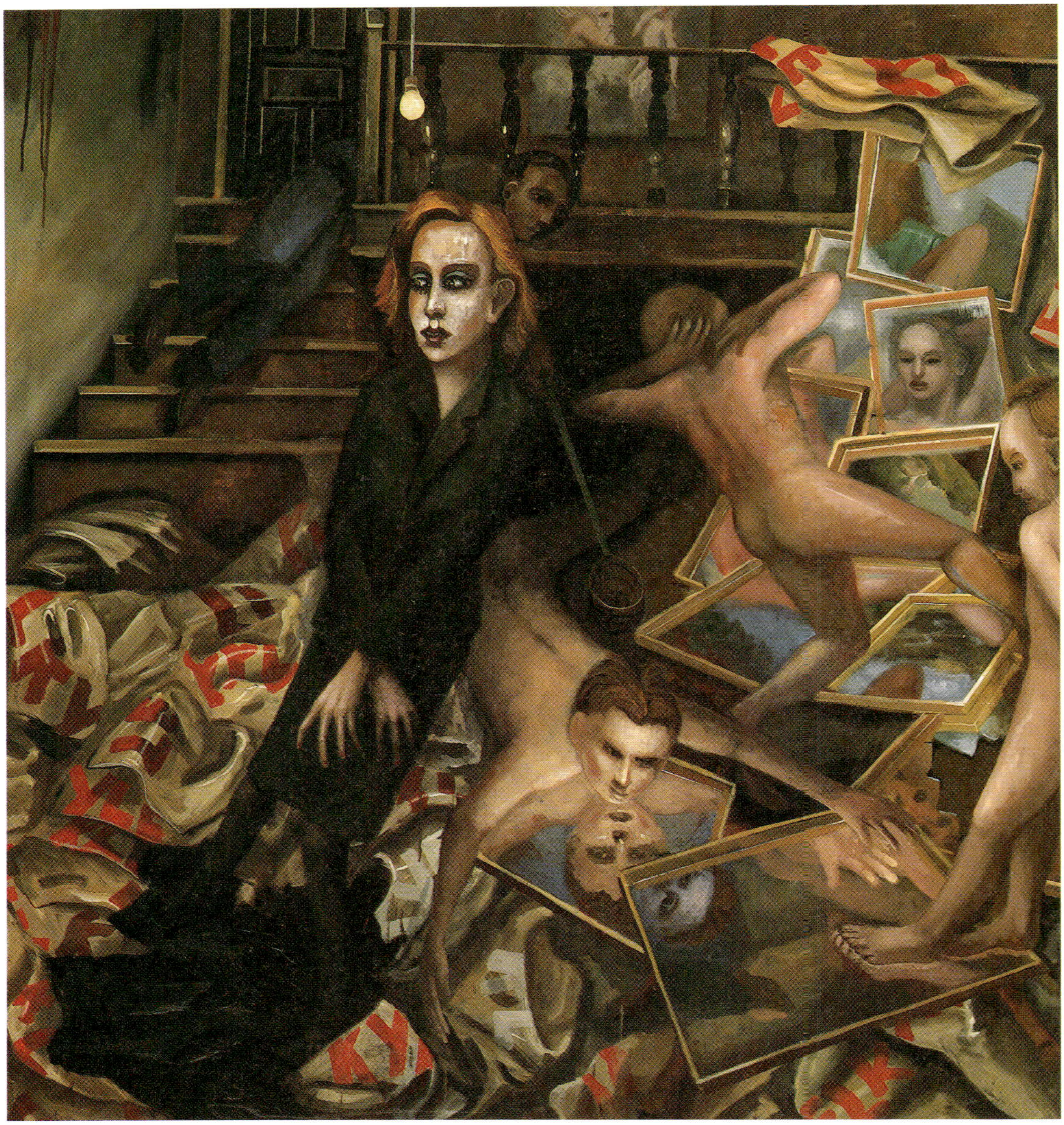

(PLATE 74) *The Poetess*, oil on canvas, 211.1 × 199.7 cm, 1992–93 (CAT. 12)

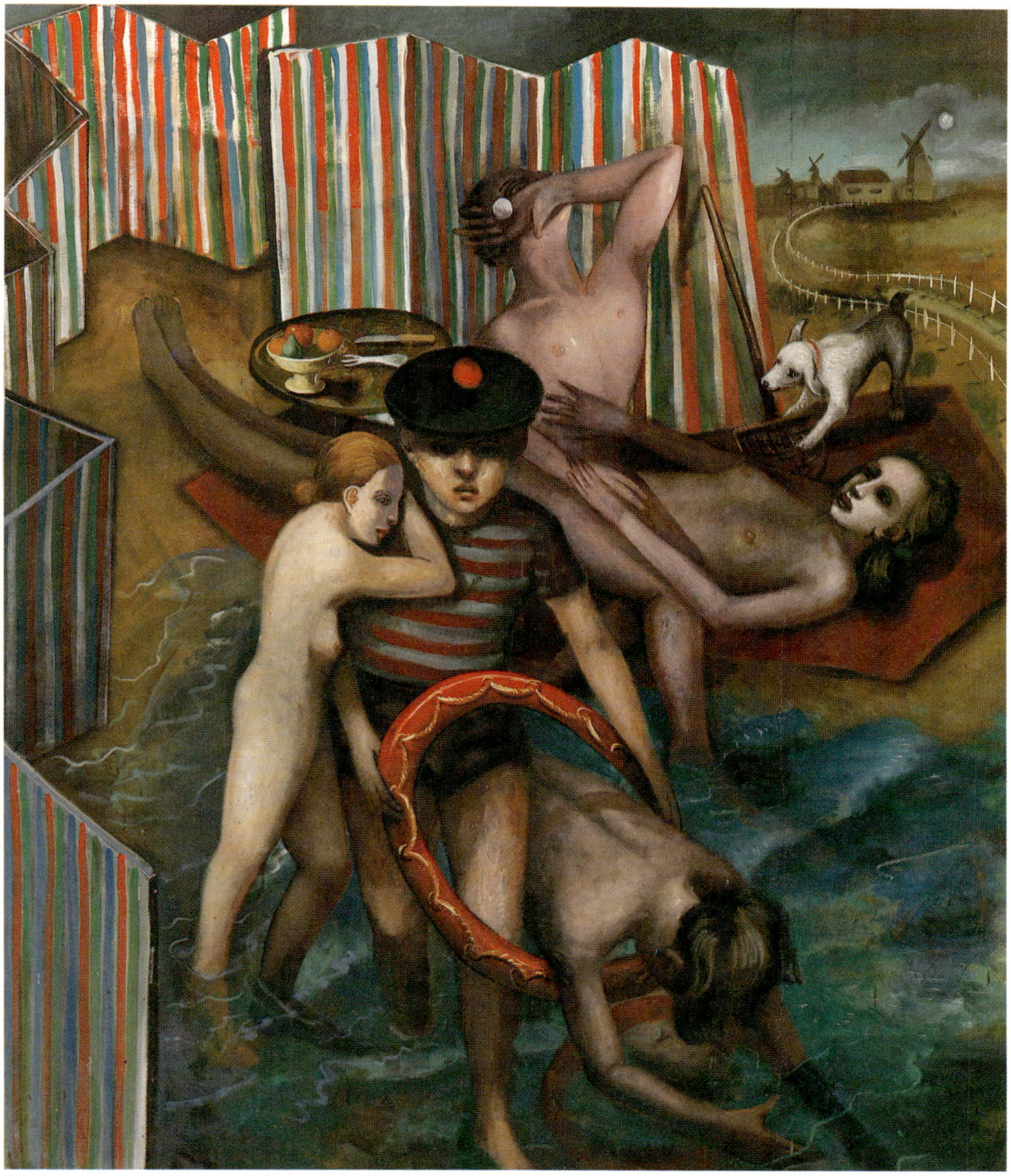

(PLATE 75) *The Drowned*, oil on canvas, 208.5 × 175.5 cm, 1992 (CAT. 1)

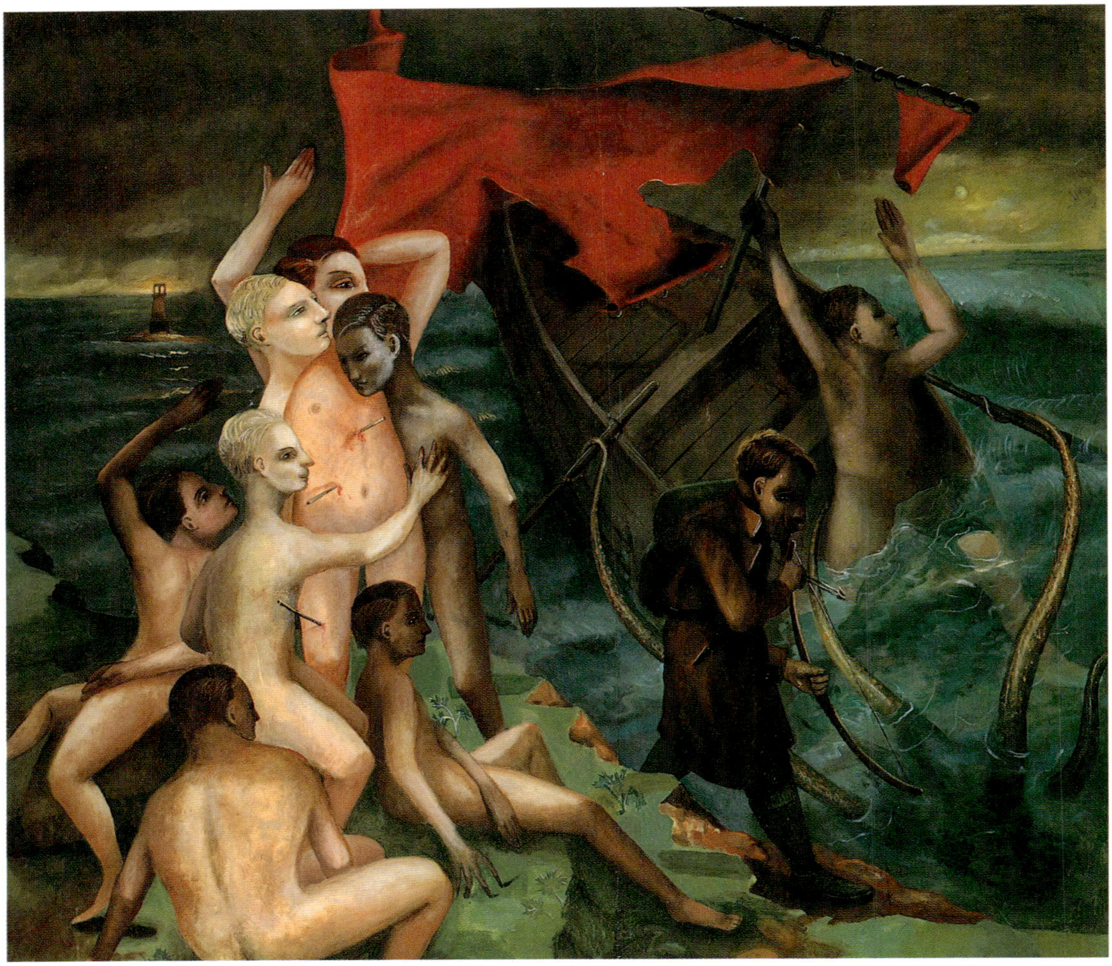

(PLATE 76) *The Dream of St Sebastian*, oil on canvas, 218.7 × 244.5 cm, 1992 (CAT. 6)

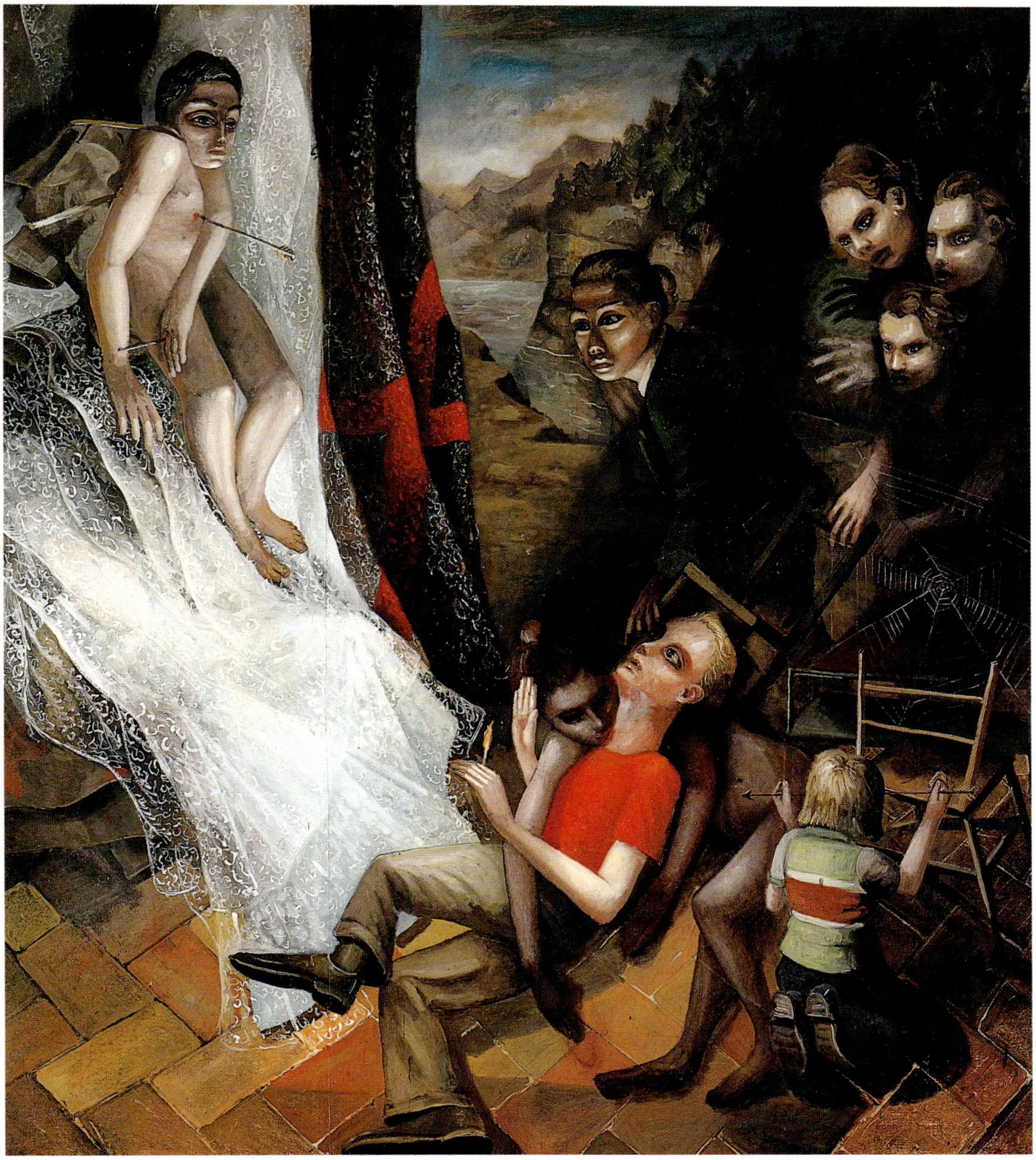

(PLATE 77) *St Sebastian – Curtain*, oil on canvas, 220 × 193 cm, 1992 (CAT.7)

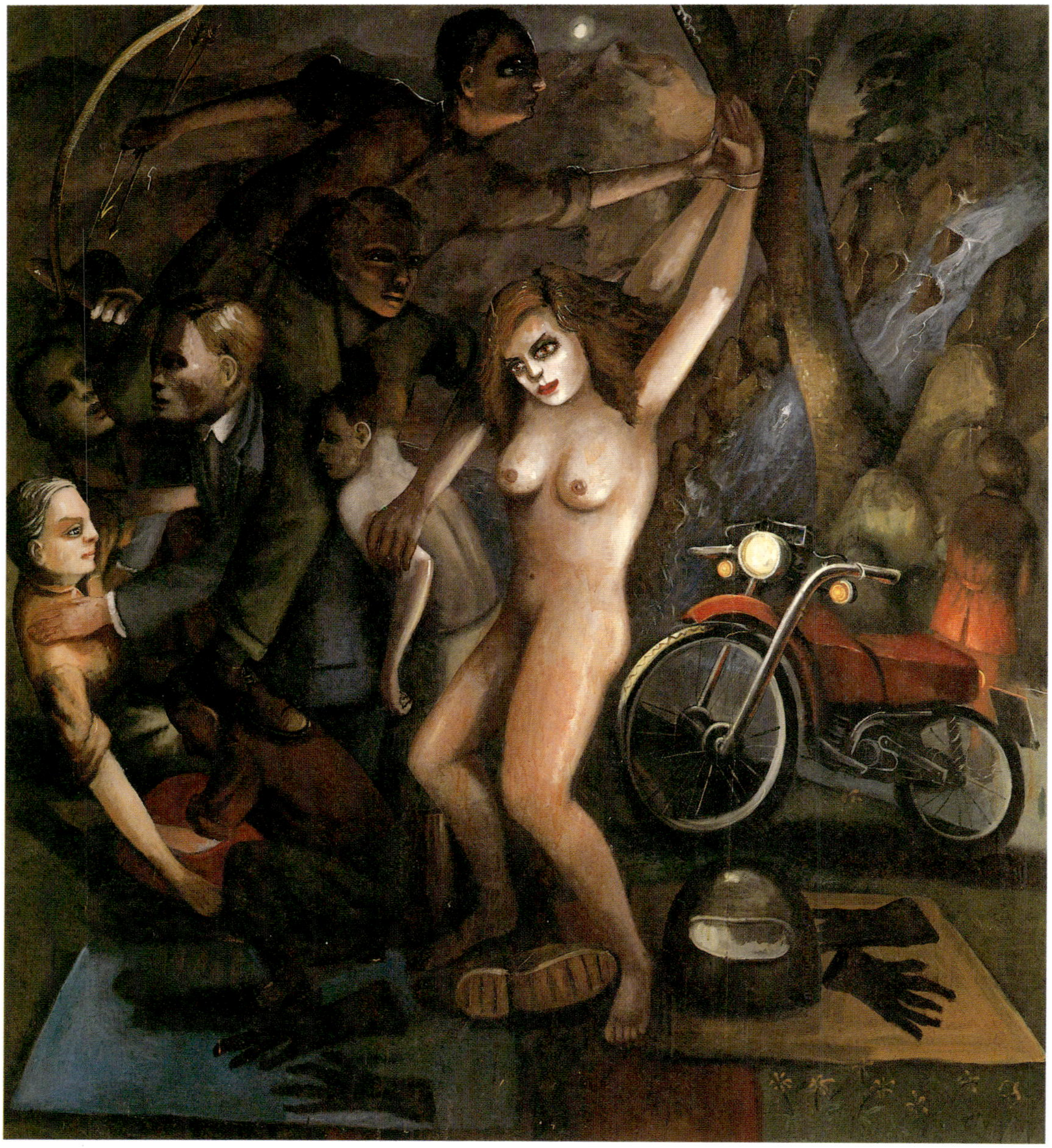

(PLATE 78) *Penelope Rescued from her Suitors*, oil on canvas, 218.7 × 194.6 cm, 1992–93 (CAT. 8)

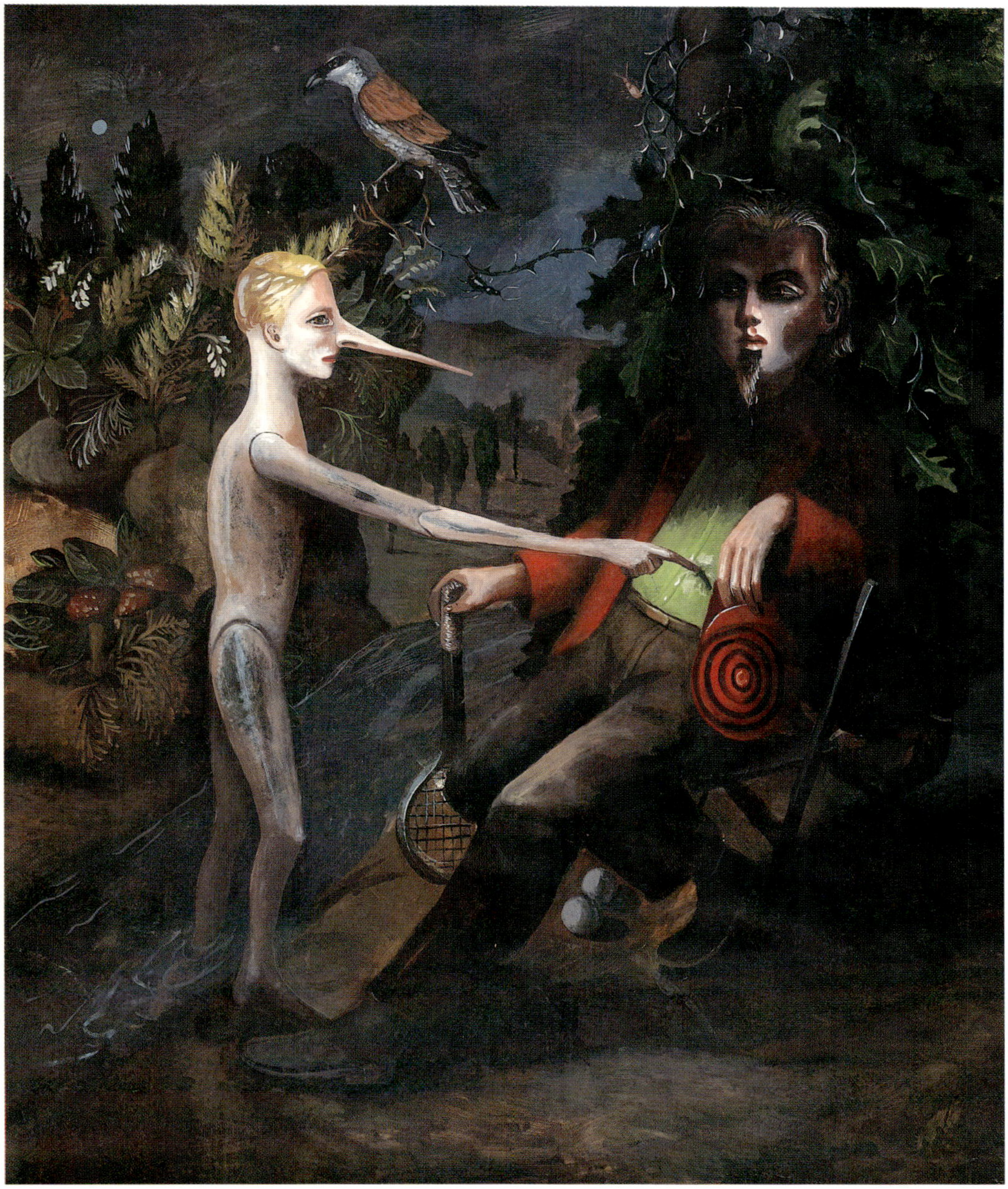

(PLATE 79) *Pinocchio, the Habit of the Shrike*, acrylic on paper, 178 × 149.2, 1992 (CAT. 16)

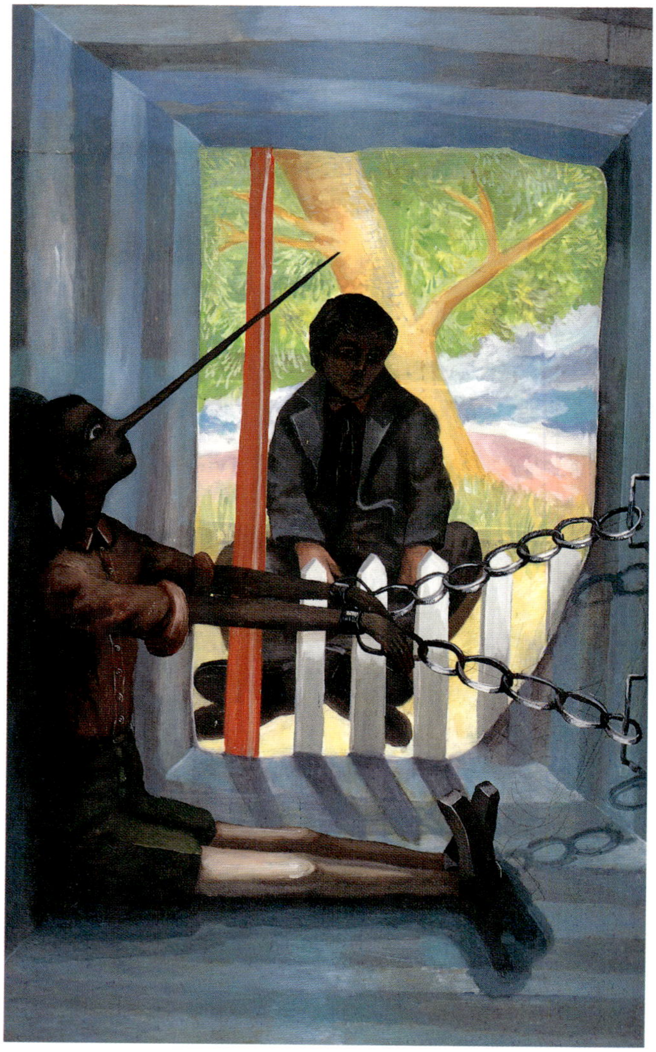

(PLATE 80) *Pinocchio in Chains*, acrylic on paper, 175.2 × 106 cm, 1992 (CAT. 17)

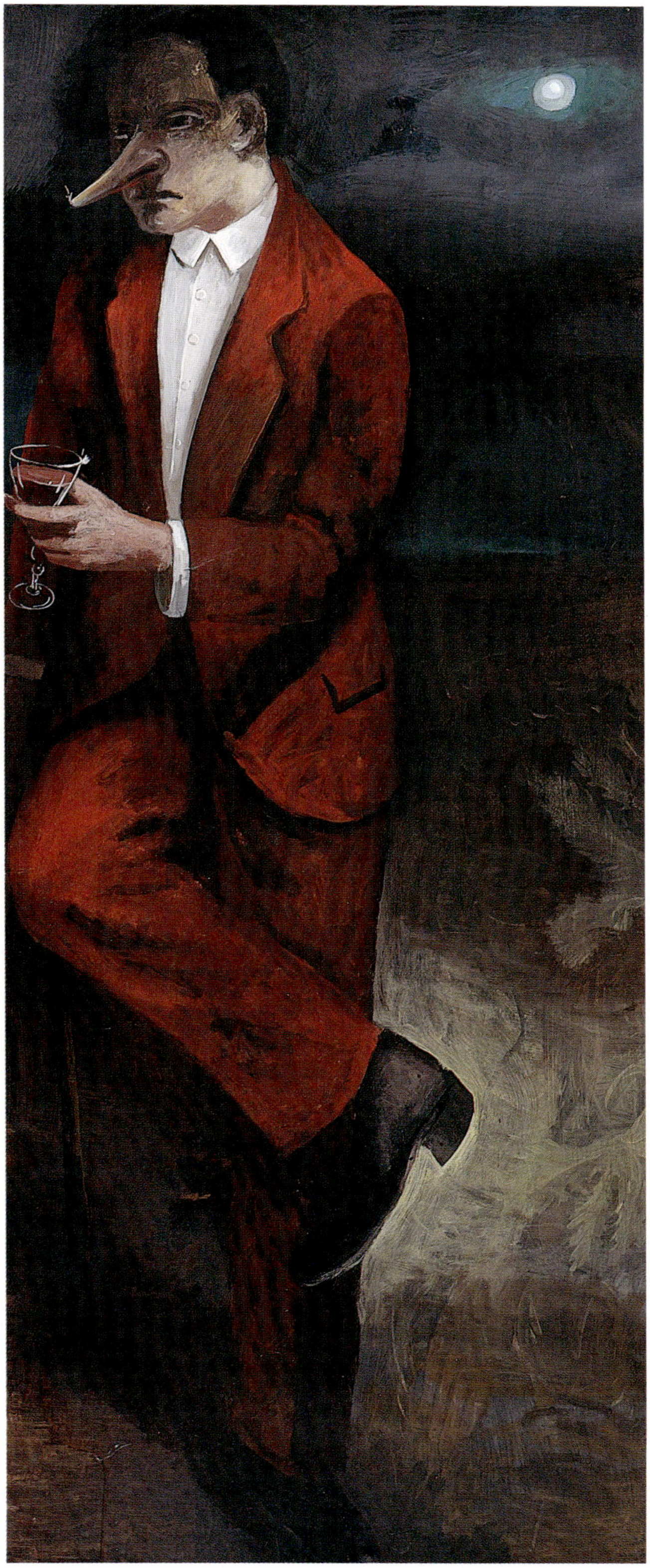

(PLATE 81) *Pinocchio in Exile, Alone*, acrylic on paper, 162.5 × 66.3 cm, 1992 (CAT. 18)

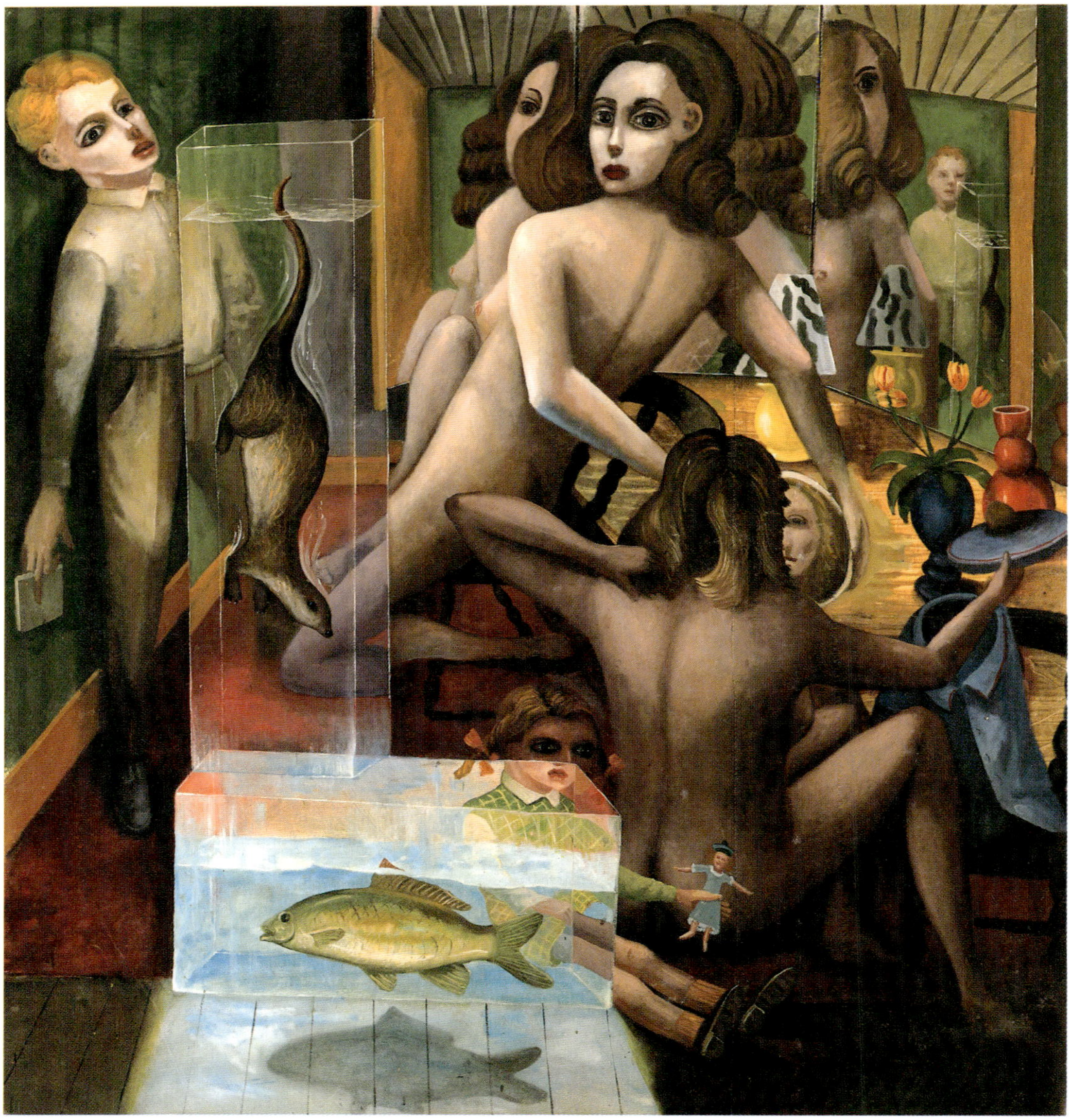

(PLATE 82) *Two Women and Otter*, oil on canvas, 216.2 × 199.4 cm, 1992 (CAT. 3)

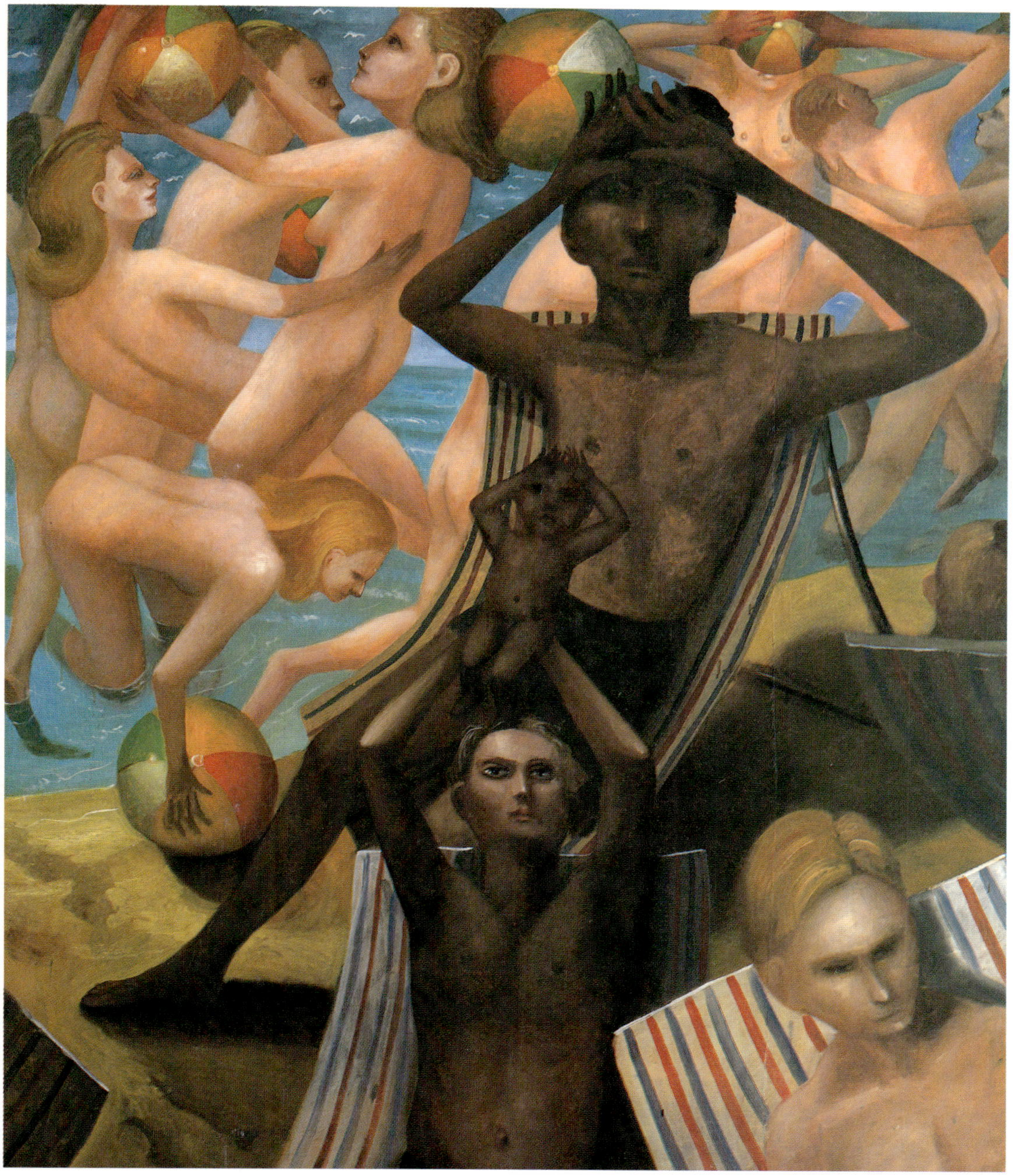

(PLATE 83) *Born Under a Cloud*, oil on canvas, 215 × 181.6 cm, 1993 (CAT. 15)

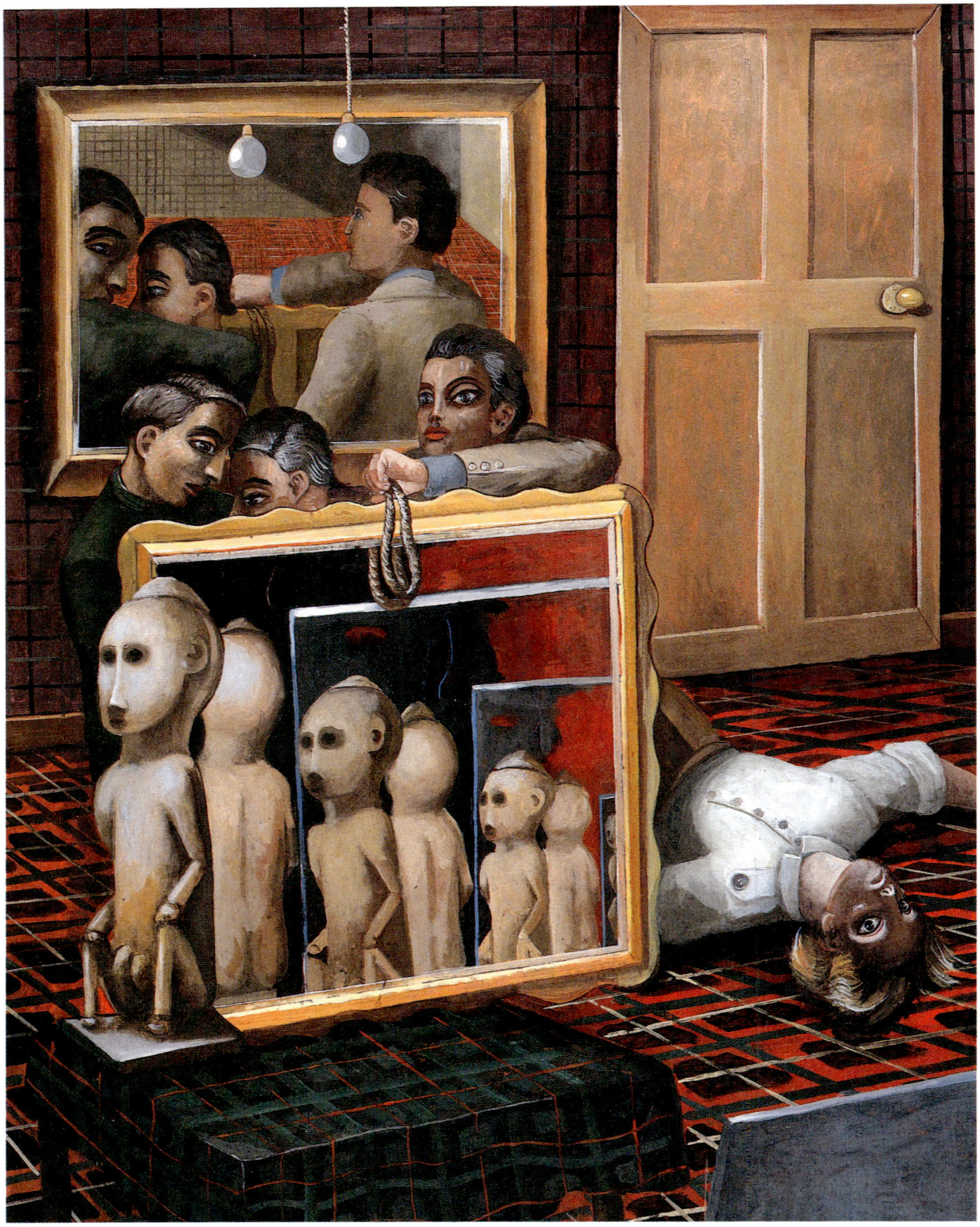

(PLATE 84) *Ethnic Event*, acrylic on paper, 188 × 144.5 cm, 1992 (CAT. 19)

THE ARTIST IN CONVERSATION

Steven Campbell describes his recent paintings in conversation with Duncan Macmillan, Ballochleam, Wednesday 10 March 1993

I started these paintings a year last December, so they are about fifteen months' work. It was just a crazy sort of run. *The Dream of St Sebastian* was the first thing I began after the collages. I think I became less interested in art, conceptual versus figurative, that kind of thing, and I became more interested in thinking about why things are the way they are. There were quite a lot of painful memories about how I felt about what was happening to me. I was just working blind over all this period with the collages and the paintings. I just wanted to give myself time to try to work out something a bit more real maybe than some kind of facile look at art. I think everything I did just came from how I was feeling.

Among the first were the family pictures. There are three of them. They started when I went down to the local school to pick up my daughter and they were throwing away some children's books, books from the sixties. I picked up a couple of them. They were about a stereotype family, a girl, a boy, the mother and the father. They all looked exactly the same. So I did a group of works based on the family, the family as this, the family as that. There were actually five of them, but two were destroyed.

There is *The Family as a Motorbike Road Sign*, which is self-explanatory. There is *The Family as Memory* and *The Family as Memory II*, with an angel. The picket-fence that appears in all of them comes from Indonesian funerary art, the art of the dead. They make puppet-like imitations of the dead and slot them into the walls. They can see them, but they put a picket-fence in front of them. It separates the living and the dead. I thought this was comical compared to how we use picket-fences. I wanted the family to look like Barbie dolls. This painting, *The Family as Memory*, meant a lot to me. They are a Barbie family and I wanted the African and Indonesian sculptures to look like the real people mourning the dolls, a reversal of the normal situation. The little boy was between life and death, not mourning just hovering, just at that mid-point. For an artist, or for anyone, the mid-point between life and death is important.

Young Offenders is just a piece of perverse cruelty. I wanted to get the magic of African sculpture in with the children and the televison. I tried to imagine a children's prison. Nothing horrible happens there. It is just a place of cruelty. The script behind them says 'put the television off'.

Heroic Emblems is about abandonment. The motorbike is up a tree because something has happened, but years ago. No one has done anything about it and the tree has grown up round about the motorbike. This is what is left. It is like a memory.

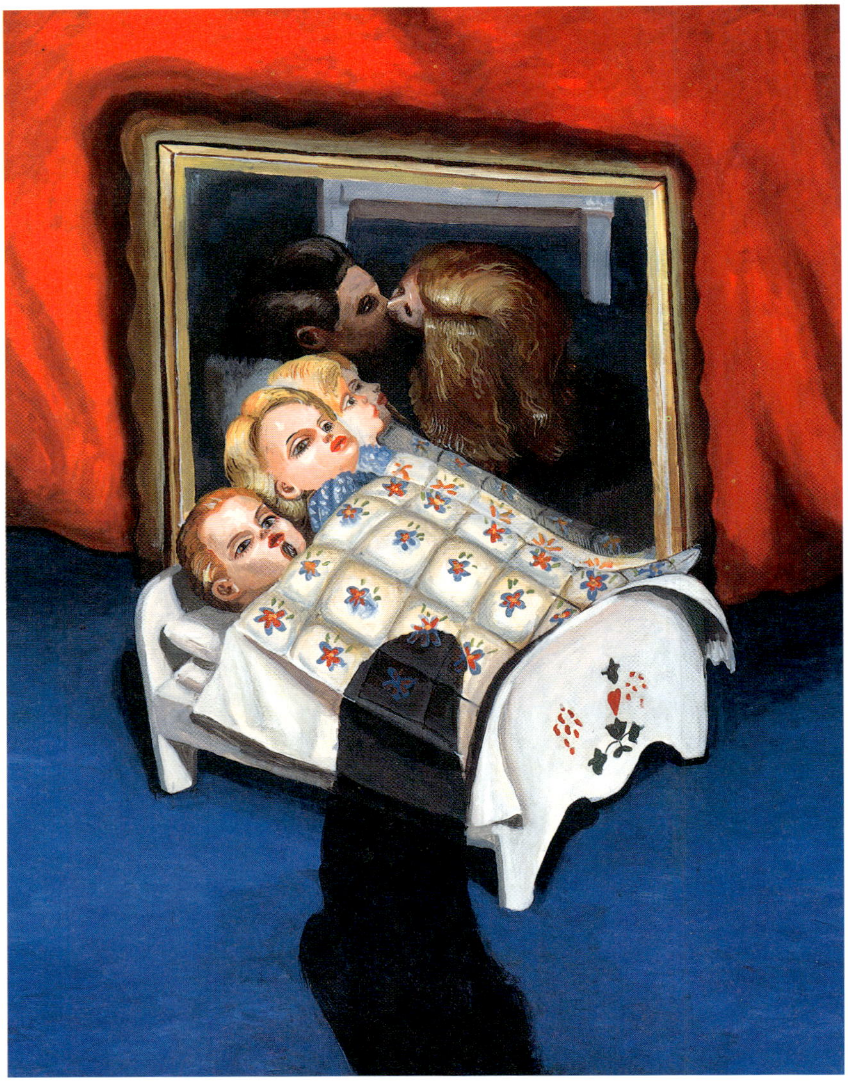

(PLATE 85) *Dolls 'R' Us*, acrylic on paper, 182.3 × 144.4cm, 1992 (CAT. 20)

The Croatian Blouse. In places of terror, there must also be places that are perfect and untouched. We live perverse lives. You think you are living a normal life like the people in the picture. It is clean and tidy, but round about everything is chaos. They think they are unaffected, but when you look at this unaffected place, it makes the cruelty even more apparent. They think they have not been touched by it, but something is dripping down on to her all the same. The man has not got a prick. That is my Joycean pun on Bosnia, no balls.

Painting in Defence of Migrants. This picture is a comment on how people are vulnerable. All the birds are migrants. Although we are cruel to nature and there are hunters in the sky and the clouds, I wanted to convey the idea that when people are in terrible circumstances, nature still has a sensitivity. Because we are part of nature, it will come to our defence when things are so bad. The people are migrants and they are exhausted, but the migrant birds come to help them. I think it is a defence of sensitivity.

The Dream of St Sebastian was the first thing I did after the collages. Sebastian seems to love violence, but he always seems to be untouched by it and never to be terribly involved in it. In this one, all the arms and legs are like a many-limbed animal. It is like an octopus or an Indian sculpture. At the point of sleep sometimes you feel your mind being pulled down, a terrible pulling under. This suggests the pulling under to death and all the limbs are like the beast that is pulling him under.

St Sebastian-Curtain represents the choice for Sebastian between physical love and his love of suffering. He wants to suffer and to die. He wants to be heroic, but he is being held back by physical love. The net curtain is like a waterfall.

Two Years of my Time is a picture of time going by. The waterfall is a symbol of time for me. I have been here three years. All I have done is work and as I have worked I have seen time going by. The Brylcreem brought this home to me. Every year my mother-in-law has given me a tub of Brylcreem and I never use it. It stacks up in the toilet. One day I went to the toilet and I noticed the three tubs and that they stood for three years, so I did this painting. I think the wheel and the waterfall and the two tubs of Brylcreem represent me standing there seeing time just tumbling by.

Pinocchio, the Habit of the Shrike. Ah Pinocchio! I am very keen on Pinocchio. When I first painted him, it was just after I had done the collages and I did not know what was the truth and what was lies in painting. It is a kind of play on what is honest art and what is untrue art. His nose is pretty big so basically his paintings are lies.

Pinocchio in Chains. There is a little park in Umbria where there is an actual figure of Pinocchio chained like that. I think what attracts me about Pinocchio is the idea of lying and truth. The idea was to have a couple of Pinocchio pictures alongside work that I liked, but I was insecure about it and in that way to show, as it were, that some are lies and some are truths.

Pinocchio in Exile, Alone. I like him when he is old and pissed off just standing there. He is by the sea, sad, with a glass, waiting to become a myth. People do not know he is made of wood.

Penelope. This is the only picture that I am worried about. This is the one you put Pinnochio beside. The woman is being tied up to a tree with handcuffs. I know she is being rescued, but there is just too much sex in it. She is lovely, but she is fake.

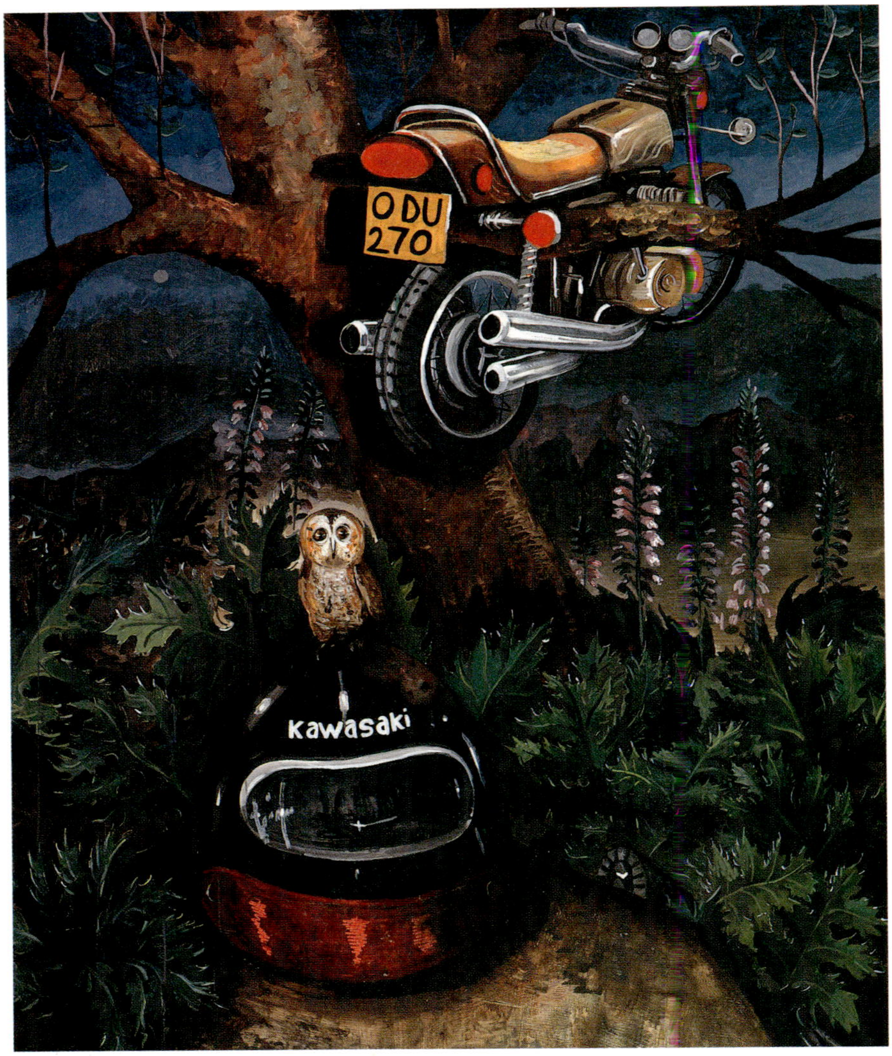

(PLATE 86) *Heroic Emblems*, acrylic on paper, 183.5 × 147 cm, 1992 (CAT. 22)

Alice. This is just the simple, beautiful world, the world of innocence. It happens to all of us doesn't it? But she herself is not destroyed. She is still holding a light and a candle. She is still very strong, but nothing about her world is turning out very well. She still believes, but the innocence and the goodness of the world do not seem to be matching up to her beliefs. She is still there though and it is optimistic because of that.

Spider on the Window. This is the second thing I did after the collages. It is an Edgar Allan Poe story. A man is in a room, looking though a window and he sees a monster on the hill far away. He looks at it in complete terror. He has never been so terrified, but he looks again and finds it is a spider on the window. In this painting there is a spider on the window and exactly where the spider is there are men running away in terror. The flatness of the window is like the flatness of the canvas and the flatness of the mirrors. I painted the chairs and the women in the foreground flat to play with this idea of distance and flatness and what a canvas is. There is a murder taking place here, too. A woman is murdering a man. She sees it, but he does not see it. Edgar Allan Poe must have been looking at pictures. There are a couple of poems by Rimbaud in which it seems to me he is looking at paintings and making up things about them. There is a painting that I did inspired by a poem by Rimbaud called *The Bridges*. The poem suggests to me that he was looking at a painting so I turned it back into a painting.

The Spider. This is the spider again. Quite a lot of the paintings use mythological things and the spider became my mythological beast. I turned it into a person, but a malevolent spirit. There seems to be a malevolent spirit in the world at the minute. It is like a sprite, a germ, or a rogue gene. This little guy, this spider was my idea of this rogue gene. It is as though there was one person sitting there with the power to disrupt everything. He does not have a prick or balls or anything. He does not have to indulge himself sexually. His reason for existence is pure malevolence and disruption.

Murder Running Through the Woods. There is calm and pleasantness around the table, but running through the pagan wood there are men about to change everything. It is the calm before the storm. It is the moment when the calm is about to give way to the storm, the point of revolution and a calm, classical world about to be destroyed.

Dead Man's Cocktail Party. I love this amalgam of memory. The whole memory of the world is looking down on them, either for the good or for the bad. It is probably chaos because they are having a drink up there and they do not really care what is happening down below. It is the force of history, the force of history acting in a way that only pleases itself. It does not seem to do any good for us. We do not learn from it, but it is the nature of human beings that we never learn a damn thing. Away back in Hieronymous Bosch's time, it would still be the same thing.

Poetess. This is partly autobiographical. There is a place we used to go last summer near Crieff on picnics. We went in June and there was a plastic sack there. We went again in September and the sack was still there, but it had changed. It looked quite different. First I thought it was an animal and then it changed into something else. So I took it away and I painted it lying on the floor. As I painted it, it seemed to become wave-like and so suggested the figure and the water. It became like

Cézanne's *Bathers*. She is a vulnerable young poetess thinking about drowning. There is a film about Casanova with Donald Sutherland in it where the water is black plastic. The sacks remind me of water. The black plastic because of Casanova and the mirrors because mirrors are like water too. In a way it is just her thinking of water in a basement. There are men there, but it is not sexual. They are her imaginings. It is a painting as if she had painted it herself, not as if I had painted it.

The Devil's Eye. I am quite keen on the devil's eye. The devil is supposed to have a second eye, one up here and one down there. It is only when he pulls down his cheek that you can see it. The scene has the appearance of suburban normality, but this is how he sees it. Nobody else sees it like that. He pulls the eye down and he sees the world like this, but other people just see it as a normality. I wanted the devil to show how he feels. I suppose he is pained.

Born under a Cloud. This is very obvious. Everyone else is in the sun and you are in the darkness. The child is the same. If you have got it, you just cannot get rid of it.

Dolls 'R' Us. It is about trying to have sex in a house full of children. It is nearly impossible. You become like them.

The Drowned. This is just romantic. It imagines how at the end of a day all the drowned come together to play on the beach.

Before I was looking for innovation stylistically. In these I have tried to drop some of the irony and go for something a bit more emotional. Living here, it is as though you are alone on a hill. There is nothing round about you. It is like listening to the world service at two o'clock in the morning. You think you are the only one listening.

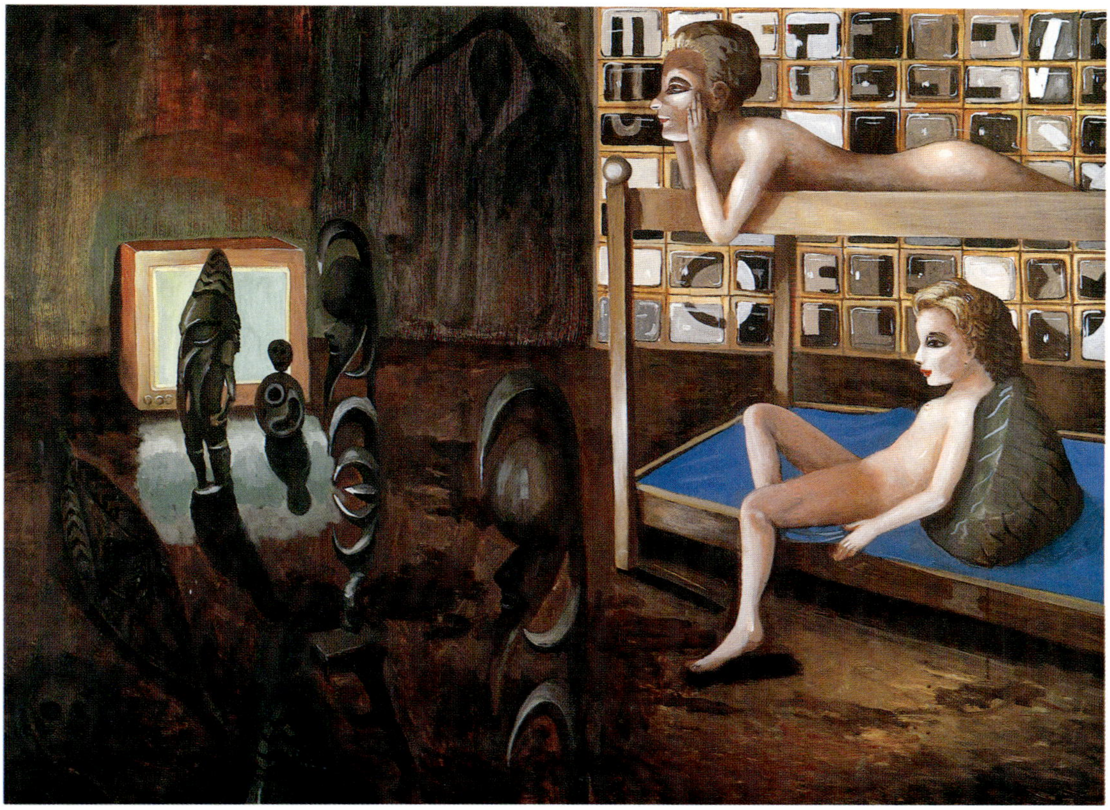

(PLATE 87) *Young Offenders*, acrylic on paper, 144.5 × 194.6 cm, 1992 (CAT. 23)

NOTES

1. John Ruskin, The Lamp of Power, *The Seven Lamps of Architecture* (London 1890), p.153

2. Thomas Reid, *An Inquiry into the Human Mind* (1764), *Works of Thomas Reid* (London 1863) I, pp.135-7, see Duncan Macmillan, *Scottish Art 1460-1990* (Edinburgh 1990), p.157

3. James Collins, 'Interview with Steven Campbell', *Flash Art*, Feb-Mar 1987

4. Stuart Morgan, 'Soup's On: An Audience with Steven Campbell', *Artscribe*, Sept-Oct 1984

5. John Bayley, 'Mrs G', *London Review of Books*, 11 March 1993

6. Stuart Morgan, *Artscribe*, Sept-Oct 1984

7. James Collins, *Flash Art*, Feb-Mar 1987

8. Ibid.

9. *Narrative Paintings: Figurative Art of Two Generations*, selected by Timothy Hyman, Arnolfini Gallery, Bristol, Sept-Oct 1979 and later Fruitmarket Gallery, Edinburgh

10. Barry Yourgrau, 'Steven Campbell', *Arts Magazine*, Jan 1984

11. Stuart Morgan, *Artscribe*, Sept-Oct 1984

12. Andrew Wilson's essay in the catalogue of Campbell's exhibition in New York in 1988 takes its title, 'The Frozen Gesture', from his discussion of this feature of his art. *Steven Campbell*, Marlborough Fine Art, New York, 1988

13. I discussed this painting in an article in *The Scotsman*, 5 March 1977

14. James Collins, *Flash Art*, Feb-Mar 1987

15. John Russell, 'Art in Summertime: Discoveries at the Galleries', *New York Times*, 24 June 1983

16. Todd McEwen, 'Through the Ceiling, Through the Floor and Through the Streets of Glasgow', *Modern Painters*, Mar 1990

17. Campbell refers to Landseer in his interview with Stuart Morgan, *Artscribe* Sept-Oct 1984

18. Todd McEwen, *Modern Painters*, Mar 1990

19. Stuart Morgan, *Artscribe*, Sept-Oct 1984

20. Stuart Morgan, 'Steven Campbell: Between Oxford and Salisbury', *Steven Campbell, New Paintings*, Edinburgh and London, winter, 1984-5

21. Ibid.

22. *The Independent*, 22 September 1992

23. Stuart Morgan, *Artscribe*, Sept-Oct 1984

24. Writing about Campbell in 1988, Andrew Wilson parallels this notion of the mistake with the aesthetics of Jacques Lacan. Andrew Wilson, 'The Frozen Gesture', Marlborough Fine Art Catalogue, New York, 1988

25. James Collins, *Flash Art*, Feb-Mar 1987

26. Richard Francis, 'Bonjour M. Foucault', exhibition catalogue, Tate Gallery, Liverpool, Summer 1986

27. Michel Foucault, *Madness and Civilisation* (London 1971), pp.94-5, quoted by Andrew Wilson, Marlborough Fine Art, New York, 1988. See also Tony Godfrey, *Steven Campbell*, Marlborough Fine Art, London, 1987

28. This is used as the cover of the Penguin edition of *The Foucault Reader*, edited by Paul Rabinow (London 1991)

29. Andrew Wilson, Marlborough Fine Art, New York, 1988

30. Steven Campbell, 'Pre-Ramble', *Steven Campbell* Marlborough Fine Art, April 1987

31. Andrew Wilson, Marlborough Fine Art, New York 1988

32. Clive Bell, *Art*, first published 1914 (London 1961), p.97

33. Ibid., p.40

34. James Collins, *Flash Art*, Feb-Mar 1987

35. See note 1

36. It was actually Charles Collins's contemporary painting, *Convent Thoughts*, which Ruskin praised for its botanical accuracy, but Millais's son, J. G. Millais, quotes as the greatest compliment ever paid the picture, the story of a professor of botany taking his class to see Millais's *Ophelia* when he was unable to take them to the country. *Life and Letters of J. E. Millais* (London 1899) I, p.145

BIOGRAPHY OF THE ARTIST

1953 Born in Glasgow
1970-77 Steel Works Maintenance Engineer
1978-82 Glasgow School of Art
1979 John D. Kelly Memorial Medal, Glasgow School of Art
1982 Bram Stoker Gold Medal, Glasgow School of Art
Awarded Fulbright Scholarship, stayed in New York until 1986
1986-88 Lives and works in Glasgow
1989 Moves to Kippen in Stirlingshire, Scotland
1990 Artist in Residence, Art Gallery of New South Wales, Sydney

SELECTED ONE-PERSON EXHIBITIONS

1983 Barbara Toll Fine Art, New York
John Weber Gallery, New York
1984 Dart Gallery, Chicago
Rhona Hoffman Gallery, Chicago
Galerie Six Friedrich, Munich
Riverside Studios, London
1985 The Fruitmarket Gallery, Edinburgh
Barbara Toll Fine Art, New York
Walker Arts Center, Minneapolis
Middendorf Gallery, Washington D.C.
1986 Galerie Pierre Huiber, Geneva
John Berggruen Gallery, San Francisco
1987 Marlborough Fine Art, London
1988 Marlborough Gallery Inc., New York
1989 Riva Yares Gallery, Scottsdale, Arizona
1990-91 'Steven Campbell: On Form and Fiction', Third Eye Centre, Glasgow and tour to Oriel Mostyn, Llandudno; Marlborough Fine Art, London; Aberdeen Art Gallery; Whitworth Art Gallery, Manchester; Southampton Art Gallery
1990 Rex Irwin, Sydney, Australia
Marlborough Fine Art Ltd, Tokyo

SELECTED GROUP EXHIBITIONS

1981 *Group Show*, New 57 Gallery, Glasgow
1982 *Group Show*, Compass Gallery, Glasgow
Expressive Images, New 57 Gallery, Edinburgh
1983 *Four Figurative Artists*, Barbara Toll Fine Art, New York
New Works-New York, Carol Taylor Art, Dallas
The Figurative Mode: Recent Drawings from New York City Galleries, Dowd Fine Arts Center Gallery, State University of New York at Cortland, New York
Contemporary Works on Paper, Frumkin & Struve Gallery, Chicago
1984 *The New Landscape*, Brooklyn Arts and Culture Association at the Downtown Cultural Center Gallery, Brooklyn, New York
Swimming and Other Pools, Getler/Pall, Saper Gallery, New York
Contemporary Woodcuts, Middendorf Gallery, Washington, D.C.
The Human Condition: Biennial III, San Francisco Museum of Modern Art, California
Contemporary Cuts, Summit Art Center, Summit, New Jersey
Images on Paper, Art and Architecture Gallery, University of Knoxville, Tennessee
Contemporary Woodcuts, Sonja Henies Og Niels Onstads Foundation, Hovikodden, Norway
Works on Paper, Barbara Krakow Gallery, Boston
La Narrativa Internacional de Hoy, Museo Rufino Tamayo, Mexico City
1984-85 *The British Art Show*, Arts Council Exhibition, Ikon Gallery, Birmingham; Royal Scottish Academy, Edinburgh; Mappin Art Gallery, Sheffield; City Art Gallery, Southampton
1985 *Contemporary Issues III*, Holman Art Gallery, Trenton, State College, New Jersey
Large Figurative Drawings, Virginia Museum, Richmond, Virginia
Hayward Annual, Hayward Gallery, London
New Image Glasgow, Third Eye Centre, Glasgow; Air Gallery, London
Selection Two, Metropolitan Museum of Art, New York
1986 *Neo-Figure*, Yares Gallery, Scottsdale, Arizona
Forty Years of Modern Art 1945-85, Tate Gallery, London

Britain in Vienna, Künstlerhaus, Vienna
New Visions in Contemporary Art, The RSM Company Collection, Cincinnati Art Museum, Ohio
Artificial Paradise, Asher/Faure, Los Angeles
Metropolitan Museum Travelling Exhibition, Phoenix Art Museum, Arizona
Events Summer 1986, Tate Gallery, London

1987 *Current Affairs: British Painting and Sculpture in the 1980s*, British Council Exhibition, Museum of Modern Art, Oxford; Mucsarnok, Budapest; National Gallery, Prague; Zacheta, Warsaw
British Art of the 1980s, British Council Exhibition, Liljevalchs Konsthall, Stockholm; Sara Hilden Museum, Tampere, Finland
The Vigorous Imagination – New Scottish Art, Scottish National Gallery of Modern Art, Edinburgh

1988 *Mother and Child*, The Lefevre Gallery
Cries and Whispers, British Council Touring Exhibition, Queen Victoria Museum and Art Gallery, Launceston; Australian Centre for Contemporary Art, Melbourne
Columner, Hudson River Museum, New York

1989 *Scottish Art Since 1900*, Scottish National Gallery of Modern Art, Edinburgh; Barbican Art Gallery, London
The New British Painting, Contemporary Arts Center, Cincinnati and tour

1990 *Now For the Future: Purchases for the Arts Council Collection since 1984*, Hayward Gallery, London
Glasgow's Great British Art Exhibition, McLellan Galleries, Glasgow
The Compass Contribution: 21 Years of Contemporary Art, 1969-1990, Tramway Gallery, Glasgow
New North: New Art from the North of Britain, Tate Gallery, Liverpool; Laing Art Gallery, Newcastle-upon-Tyne; Tramway Gallery, Glasgow; Orchard Gallery, Derry; Mappin Art Gallery, Sheffield
British Art Now: A Subjective View, British Council Exhibition, Setagaya Art Museum, Tokyo; Fukuoka Art Museum; Nagoya City Art Museum; Tochigi Prefectural Museum of Fine Arts, Utsunomiya; Hyogo Prefectural Museum of Modern Art, Kobe; Hiroshima City Museum of Contemporary Art

1991 *Kunst Europe – British Art Today*, Kunstvereine in Baden;
Contemporary Scottish Painters and Sculptors, Royal West of England Academy, Bristol

1992-93 *The Figure in the City – Urban Themes in New Scottish Painting*, Talbot Rice Touring Exhibition; Mia Joosten Gallery, Amsterdam; Muziekatelier Kunstactiviteiten Theatre Aan Het Vrythof Maastricth; Y'art and P Gallery, Utrecht; BP Gallery, Brussels; Welsh Arts Council Gallery, Oriel, Cardiff; Arts Gallery, Aberdeen

BIBLIOGRAPHY

Peter Hill: 'Scottish Art Now', *Artscribe*, October 1982

John Russell: 'Reviews-Art: Summertime Discoveries at the Galleries', *New York Times*, June 24, 1983

John Russell: 'Reviews: Steven Campbell', *New York Times*, 9 December 1983

Kim Levin: 'Reviews: Steven Campbell', *Village Voice*, 20 December 1983

Guy Trevay: 'Voice Centerfold-Art: Steven Campbell', *Village Voice*, 27 December 1983

Barry Yourgrau: 'Review: Steven Campbell', *Arts Magazine*, January 1984

Jacqueline Brody: 'New Editions: Steven Campbell', *The Print Collector's Newsletter*, Vol. XIV, No. 6, January-February, 1984

Theodore Wolff: 'Art as a Warning', *The Christian Science Monitor*, 26 January 1984

Nicholas Moufarrege: 'The Mutant International; VII: Time and Timing, Shelter and Storm'; *Art Magazine*, March 1984

Peter Hill: 'Review: Steven Campbell', *Artscribe*, February-April 1984

Lisa Liebmann: 'Review: Steven Campbell', *Artforum*, April 1984

Brooks Adams: 'Review: Steven Campbell', *Art in America*, May 1984

Harold Haydon: 'Galleries: Campbell Makes Tales Come Alive on Canvas', *Chicago Sun-Times*, 27 April 1984

Alan Artner: 'Galleries: Curious Mix of Odd Style, Grotesquerie', *Chicago Tribune*, 27 April 1984

Michael Brenson: 'Art: Swimming and Other Pools', *New York Times*, 29 June 1984

Marian Pallister: 'Painting the Big Apple Red', *Glasgow Evening Times*, 5 July 1984

Stuart Morgan: 'Soup's on: An Audience with Steven Campbell', *Artscribe*, September-October 1984

Stuart Morgan: 'Steven Campbell: Between Oxford and Salisbury', Riverside Studios, London and The Fruitmarket Gallery, Edinburgh, *Exhibition Catalogue*, November 1984

Ronny Cohen: 'Jumbo Prints', *Artnews*, October 1984

William Packer: 'The Great British Show Hits the Road', *Financial Times*, 6 November 1984

Richard Cork: 'Second City First', *The Listener*, 8 November 1984

Marina Vaizey: 'Painting Takes to the Stage', *Sunday Times*, 2 December 1984

Waldemar Januszczak: 'Galleries Briefing: Steven Campbell', *The Guardian*, 4 December 1984

William Packer: 'A Scot Comes to Artistic Judgement', *Financial Times*, 4 December 1984

Stuart Morgan: 'The Case of the Waggling Leg', *Artforum*, December 1984

Sandra Miller: 'Putting Flesh on to Oil Painting: Steven Campbell New Paintings', *The Times*, 4 December 1984

Waldemar Januszczak: 'When Christ Came to Cookham', *The Guardian*, 12 December 1984

Nigel Pollitt: 'New Reviews: Steven Campbell', *City Limits*, 14-20 December 1984

William Feaver: 'Quirky Charades', *The Observer*, 16 December 1984

Sarah Kent: 'Steven Campbell', *Time Out*, 20 December 1984-January 2, 1985

William Feaver: 'Reviews', *Vogue*, January 1985

Waldemar Januszczak: 'The Church of the New Art', *Flash Art*, January 1985

Patrick Bishop: 'Young, Scots and Expressionist', *Literary Review*, January 1985

Clare Henry: 'An International Hot Property with his Feet on the Ground', *Glasgow Herald*, January 1985

Allen Wright: 'Artistic Filling of Gap Site', *The Scotsman*, January 1985

Robert Merritt: 'Drawings Represent Several Approaches', *Richmond Times*, 27 January 1985

James Collins: 'A Travelogue: Love and Loathing in Europe', *Flash Art*, March 1985

Caroline Collier: 'Review: Steven Campbell', *Flash Art*, March 1985

John Russell: 'Reviews: Steven Campbell', *New York Times*, 12 April 1985

Lucinda Bredin: 'Campbell Finds His Kingdom', *Scottish Field*, February 1985

Michael Spens: 'On the Plight of any Artist', *Studio International*, March 1985

Eduardo de Benito: 'Steven Campbell, La Pintura como Genero Literario', *Lapiz*, May 1985

Joan Hugo: 'Pick of the Week', *Los Angeles Weekly*, August 1985

Waldemar Januszczak: 'The Glow that Came from Glasgow', *The Guardian*, 13 August 1985

Clare Henry: 'Glasgow Stealing the Show for Art', *Glasgow Herald*, 14 August 1985

William Feaver: 'Welcome to Prehistory', *The Observer*, 25 August 1985

Alexander Moffat: 'New Image Glasgow', Third Eye Centre, Glasgow, *Exhibition Catalogue*, August 1985

Marge Goldwater: 'Of Hikers and Humeans', Walker Art Center, Minneapolis, *Exhibition Catalogue*, Summer 1985

Peter Fuller: 'Review: The Hayward Annual', *Artscribe*, September 1985

Marjorie Allthorpe-Guyton: 'New Image Glasgow', *Artscribe*, October 1985

Andrew Graham-Dixon: 'Is It Miles Better in Glasgow?', *Sunday Times*, October 1985

Leslie Geddes-Brown: 'On the City Full of Northern Promise', *Sunday Times*, 6 October 1985

Waldemar Januszczak: 'New Image Glasgow', *The Guardian*, 17 October 1985

Marina Vaizey: 'Paintings Hot Off the Easel', *Sunday Times*, 19 October 1985

Mary Rose Beaumont: 'New Image Glasgow', *Arts Review*, 25 October 1985

John Russell Taylor: 'Galleries: New Image Glasgow', *The Times*, 29 October 1985

Clare Henry: 'Five Scottish Artists', *Glasgow Herald*, 27 November 1985

Mel Gooding: 'New Image Glasgow', *Art Monthly*, November 1985

Helen Kohen: 'Focus New York-Hails Latest In Art', *The Miami Herald*, 10 January 1986

Richard Francis: 'Steven Campbell: *Bonjour Monsieur Foucault'*, Tate Gallery Liverpool *Exhibition Catalogue*, summer 1986

Tony Godfrey: 'The New Image: Paintings in the 1980s', *Phaidon Press*, Oxford, 1986

James Collins: 'Interview with Steven Campbell', *Flash Art*, February-March 1986

Tony Godfrey: 'The Recent Paintings of Steven Campbell', Marlborough Fine Art, London, *Exhibition Catalogue*, April 1987

Tony Godfrey: 'Steven Campbell: The Dangerous Early and Late Life of Lytton Strachey', *Burlington Magazine*, April 1987

Clare Henry: 'Scottish Whimsy', *Studio International*, August 1987

Andrew Wilson: 'The Frozen Gesture: Recent Paintings by Steven Campbell', Marlborough Gallery Inc, New York, *Exhibition Catalogue*, September 1988

Hugh Cumming: 'New Figurative Art: A Survey', *Art & Design* vol. 4, no. 9/10, October 1988

Judith Higgins: 'Steven Campbell', *Artnews*, November 1988

Robin Nicholson: 'Scottish Neo-Romantics', *The Antique Collector*, August 1989

Martin Gayford: 'Art Now Belongs to Glasgow', *The Daily Telegraph*, 6 January 1990

Virginia Fraser: 'City Lights', *Vogue*, February 1990

Euan McArthur: 'Steven Campbell's Uncertainty Principle', and Stuart Morgan, 'Leaves from a Campbell Notebook', Third Eye Centre, Glasgow, *Exhibition Catalogue*, March 1990

Clare Henry: 'Campbell Third Eye-Catching', *Glasgow Herald*, 10 March 1990

Clare Flowers: 'Campbell on Form', *Scotland on Sunday*, 11 March 1990

Meg Milne: 'Painter's Transformation Scene', *Sunday Express*, 11 March 1990

Emilio Coia: 'A First for Golden Old Boy', *The Scotsman*, 12 March 1990

Cordelia Oliver: 'Steven Campbell', *The Guardian*, 17 March 1990

W. Gordon-Smith: 'Tongue in Chic from the Prodigal', *Observer Scotland*, 18 March 1990

Todd McEwan: 'Steven Campbell: Through the Ceiling, Through the Floor, and Through the Streets of Glasgow', *Modern Painters, Vol. 3 No. 1*, Spring 1990

Andrew Gibbon-Williams: 'Glasgow's Painter in Residence', *The Times*, 6 April 1990

Andrew Nairne: 'Steven Campbell', Tate Gallery, Liverpool, *'New North' Exhibition Catalogue*, May 1990

Clare Flowers: 'Scotland on Sunday', *City Limits*, 26 April 1990

Stuart Cosgrove, 'Born Again Scotland', *The Sunday Correspondent*, 13 May 1990

Rose Paterson, 'Painterly Games', *The Daily Telegraph*, 28 May 1990

Murdo Macdonald, 'Steven Campbell – Third Eye Centre', *Artscribe*, Summer 1990

Charles Hall, 'Steven Campbell', *Arts Review*, 27 July 1990

Takeshi Sakurai, 'Steven Campbell', Introduction to Marlborough Fine Art, Tokyo, *Exhibition Catalogue*, August 1990

Steven Campbell, 'What I Hate About . . . Painting for a Gallery of Rogues', *The Scotsman*, 17 November 1990

Lorna Waite, 'Northern Viewpoints', *The Scotsman*, 12 December 1990

Marina Vaizey, 'Flying International Colours', *Sunday Times*, 16 December 1990

Brian Hayes, 'The Information Age', *The Sciences Magazine*, September-October 1991

Iain Wilson, 'Artist Eyes the New Choice', *The Glasgow Herald*, 20 December 1991

COLLABORATIONS

Barry Yourgrau: *A Man Jumps out of Airplane*, Collection of Poetry and Prose, SUN 1985, Cover illustration by Steven Campbell

Barry Yourgrau: 'Reading: I Keep my Father in a Bottle', Performing Garage 1985, Scenic Art by Steven Campbell

George Mackay Brown: *The Scottish Bestiary*, Collection of Poetry, Paragon Press 1985, illustrations by Scottish Artists including Steven Campbell

Bill Forsyth: 'Housekeeping', Film 1986-87, Scenic Art by Steven Campbell

Bob Clyde: 'Death of an Entomologist', Film for Scottish Television 1987

FILM INTERVIEW

Alistair Scott: 'Steven Campbell/Adrian Wiszniewski', Arena, BBC Television, February 1986

Interview with Professor Martin Kemp, The Third Ear Programme, BBC Radio 3, 23 March 1990

PUBLIC COLLECTIONS

Aberdeen Art Gallery and Museum
Arts Council of Great Britain, London
Art Institute of Chicago
British Council, London
Chase Manhattan Bank, New York
Contemporary Art Society, London
Dannheisser Foundation, New York
Glasgow Art Gallery and Museum
High Museum of Art, Atlanta
Hirshhorn Museum, Washington D.C.
Leeds City Art Gallery
Metropolitan Museum of Art, New York
Phoenix Art Museum, Arizona
Scottish Arts Council, Edinburgh
Scottish National Gallery of Modern Art, Edinburgh
Setagaya Art Museum, Japan
Southampton Art Gallery
Tamayo Museum, Mexico City
Tate Gallery, Liverpool
Tate Gallery, London
Walker Art Center, Minneapolis, Minnesota

CATALOGUE OF WORKS IN THE EXHIBITION

The following is a list of works shown at the Talbot Rice Gallery, Edinburgh, during the Edinburgh Festival, 16 August to 11 September 1993, and subsequently on show in London from 17 September until 29 October 1993 in two parts; the paintings (catalogue numbers 1–15) at the South London Art Gallery, 65 Peckham Road, London SE5 8UH, and the works on paper (catalogue numbers 16–28) and collages on canvas (catalogue numbers 29–38) at Marlborough Fine Art (London) Ltd, 6 Albemarle St, London W1X 4BY.

OILS ON CANVAS

1. *The Drowned*, 208.5 × 175.5 cm, 1992 (PLATE 75)
2. *The Croatian Blouse*, 210.8 × 226.7 cm, 1992 (PLATE 65)
3. *Two Women and Otter*, 216.2 × 199.4 cm, 1992 (PLATE 82)
4. *Spider on the Window, Monster in the Land – Edgar Allan Poe* , 220.4 × 232.7 cm, 1992–93 (PLATE 72)
5. *The Spider*, 221.5 × 234.3 cm, 1992–93 (PLATE 70)
6. *The Dream of St Sebastian*, 218.7 × 244.5 cm, 1992 (PLATE 76)
7. *St Sebastian – Curtain*, 220 × 193 cm, 1992 (PLATE 77)
8. *Penelope Rescued from her Suitors*, 218.7 × 194.6 cm, 1992–93 (PLATE 78)
9. *The Devil's Eye*, 218.7 × 211.4 cm, 1992–93 (PLATE 71)
10. *Dead Man's Cocktail Party*, 283.5 × 269.2 cm, 1992–93 (PLATE 68)
11. *Alice in Ruins*, 269.9 × 263.7 cm, 1992–93 (PLATE 67)
12. *The Poetess*, 211.1 × 199.7 cm, 1992–93 (PLATE 74)
13. *Murder Running Through the Woods*, 249.2 × 243.9 cm, 1993 (PLATE 66)
14. *Painting in Defence of Migrants*, 272.4 × 256.5 cm, 1993 (PLATE 69)
15. *Born Under a Cloud*, 215 × 181.6 cm, 1993 (PLATE 83)

ACRYLICS ON PAPER

16. *Pinocchio, The Habit of the Shrike*, 178 × 149.2 cm, 1992 (PLATE 79)
17. *Pinocchio in Chains*, 175.2 × 106 cm, 1992 (PLATE 80)
18. *Pinocchio in Exile, Alone*, 162.5 × 66.3 cm, 1992 (PLATE 81)
19. *Ethnic Event*, 188 × 144.5 cm, 1992 (PLATE 84)
20. *Dolls 'R' Us*, 182.3 × 144.4 cm, 1992 (PLATE 85)
21. *Two Years of My Time*, 185.5 × 144.2 cm, 1992 (PLATE 73)
22. *Heroic Emblems*, 183.5 × 147 cm, 1992 (PLATE 86)
23. *Young Offenders*, 144.5 × 194.6 cm, 1992 (PLATE 87)
24. *The Family as Memory*, 193 × 147.3 cm, 1992 (PLATE 62)
25. *The Family as Memory II*, 91.4 × 195 cm, 1992 (PLATE 63)
26. *The Family as Motorbike Road Sign*, 179.4 × 138.8 cm, 1992–93 (PLATE 64)
27. *Young Boy Imagines his Mother's Hair Like a River in a Storm*, 182.9 × 121.9 cm, 1992
28. *Composed Painting with Emotional Elements*, 182.9 × 121.9 cm, 1993

COLLAGES ON CANVAS

29. *The Artist's Chair*, 152.4 × 109.2 cm, 1990–91 (PLATE 53)
30. *I Dreamt I Shot Mussolini at Cowes Week*, 144 × 115.5 cm, 1991 (PLATE 56)
31. *Portrait of Two Cousins with the Same Mother who Left Them Alone when she was Seventeen*, 149 × 121 cm, 1991 (PLATE 57)
32. *Birth of Eurithia with Drowned Family*, 150 × 120 cm, 1991 (PLATE 55)
33. *The Family of the Accidental Angel*, 174 × 121.5 cm, 1991 (PLATE 61)
34. *Fake Ophelia*, 173.5 × 119.5 cm, 1991 (PLATE 59)
35. *A Small Death in the Family*, 152 × 115 cm, 1991 (PLATE 60)
36. *Penelope at Home Waiting for Dad's Return*, 114 × 158 cm, 1991 (PLATE 52)
37. *Love*, 177 × 121 cm, 1991 (PLATE 54)
38. *Dream of the Hunter's Muse*, 146.5 × 111 cm, 1991 (PLATE 58)